ANDREA PISTOLESI

INTRAMERICAS
CENTRAL AMERICA ON THE ROAD

15TH ANNIVERSARY EDITION

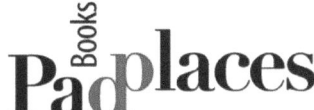

I needed big changes. A new start. Maybe a jump start. Definitely an evolution if not a revolution.
This was a personal, professional, and even philosophical decision: a turning point of my life.

Oh yes, the peak of a career as travel photographer, the end of a love relationship, the uncertainties of a changing world (in a few months 9/11 would happen and my presentiments would unfortunately find confirmation), all played a part in my decision. But mostly was the attraction to go back "on the road" which was, and still is, my ideal living condition, that encouraged me in that direction.

In the spring of 2001 I started my small, short Odyssey, not in space, but in the countries of Central America. This represented a combination of ideas: to explore the heart of the Pan-American path, the passage from the Latin world to the borders of the English-speaking one, the trail of million migrants.

The magazine Gulliver backed my proposal, and a journalist friend, Paolo Galliani, joined me, at least for a while (I was spending longer then he needed in order to assimilate the local stories).

We landed in Panama and from there we went north using only local and long distance buses; occasionally collective and private taxis.

I had only a Leica camera, two lenses and a backpack half full of film.
What that journey meant to me is evident in the work that came afterwards.
It conveyed a much more photo-journalistic approach to my travel photography.
The perfection of framing, using tripods and comprehensive thinking, gave space and precedence to capturing moments and situations.
The accuracy of technique was not a priority any more.

The rest of the story is history, my personal history.
The nice people I met as well as the intensity of moments of fear (it was a hard and dangerous land when lived from the bottom up, as we did) provided color to the picture.
And it is not a land of smiles: very few people find the courage to smile in such a tough living situation.

This work can be dedicated only to them: the natives who willingly allowed us into their lives patiently, hardly understanding the reasons why, if caring at all.
In a society of hardships they represent the better side of humanity.

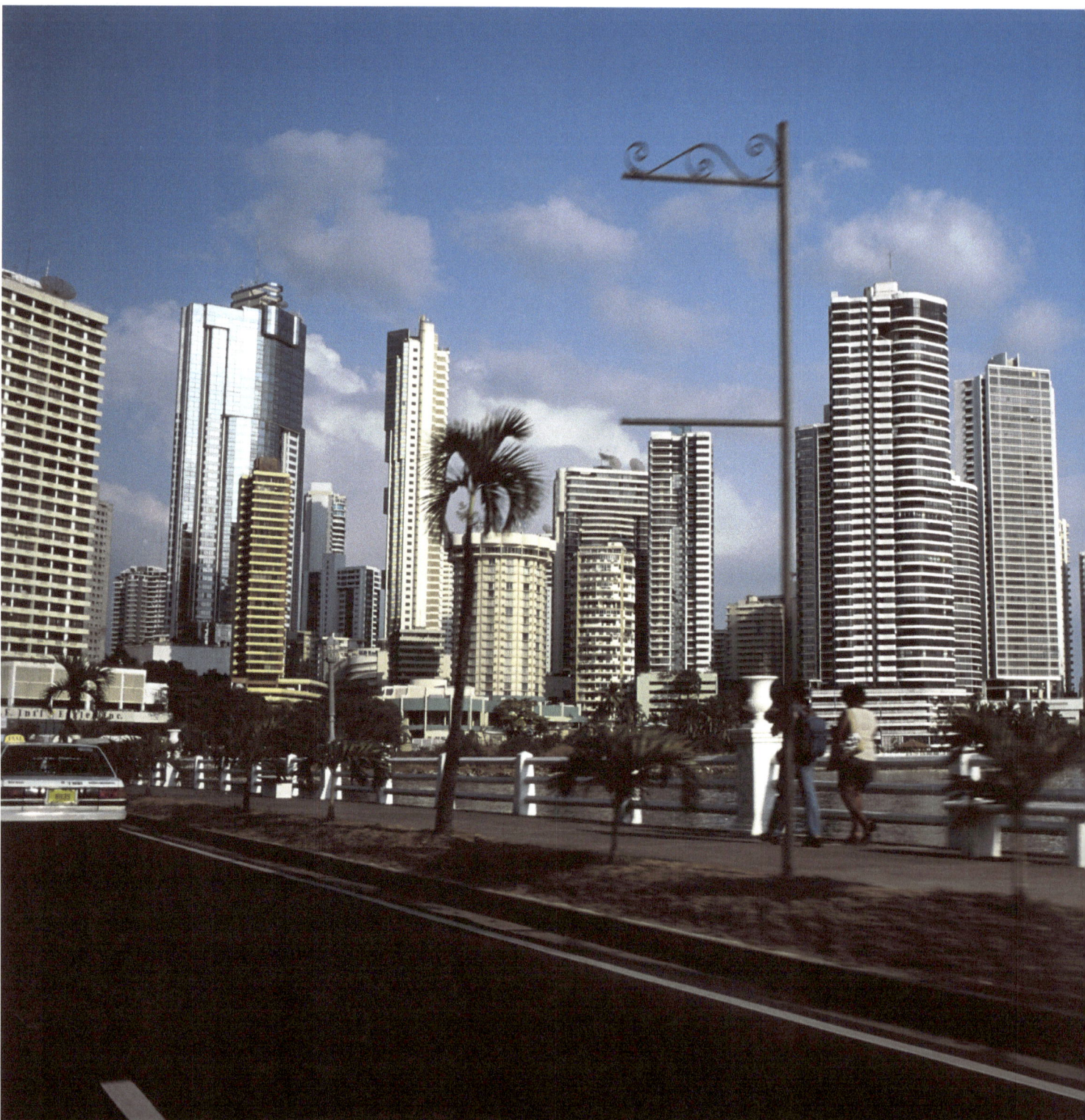

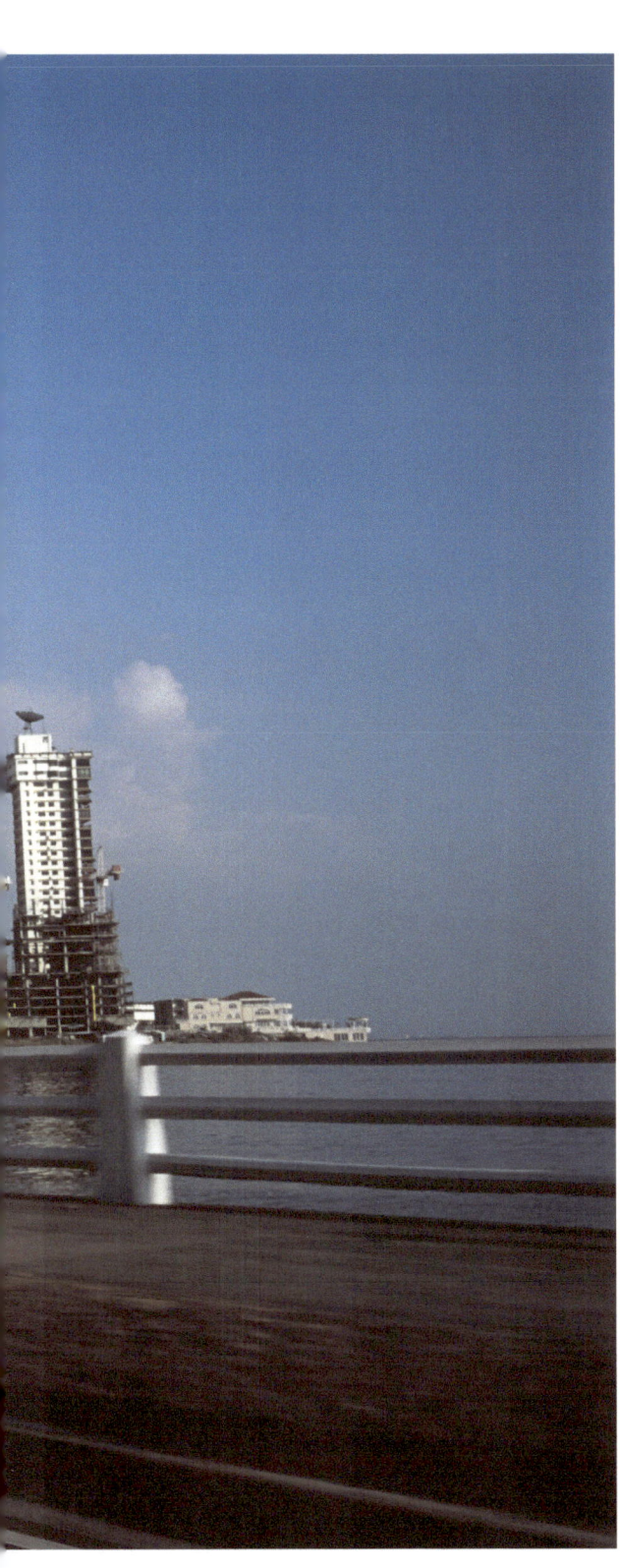

Panama

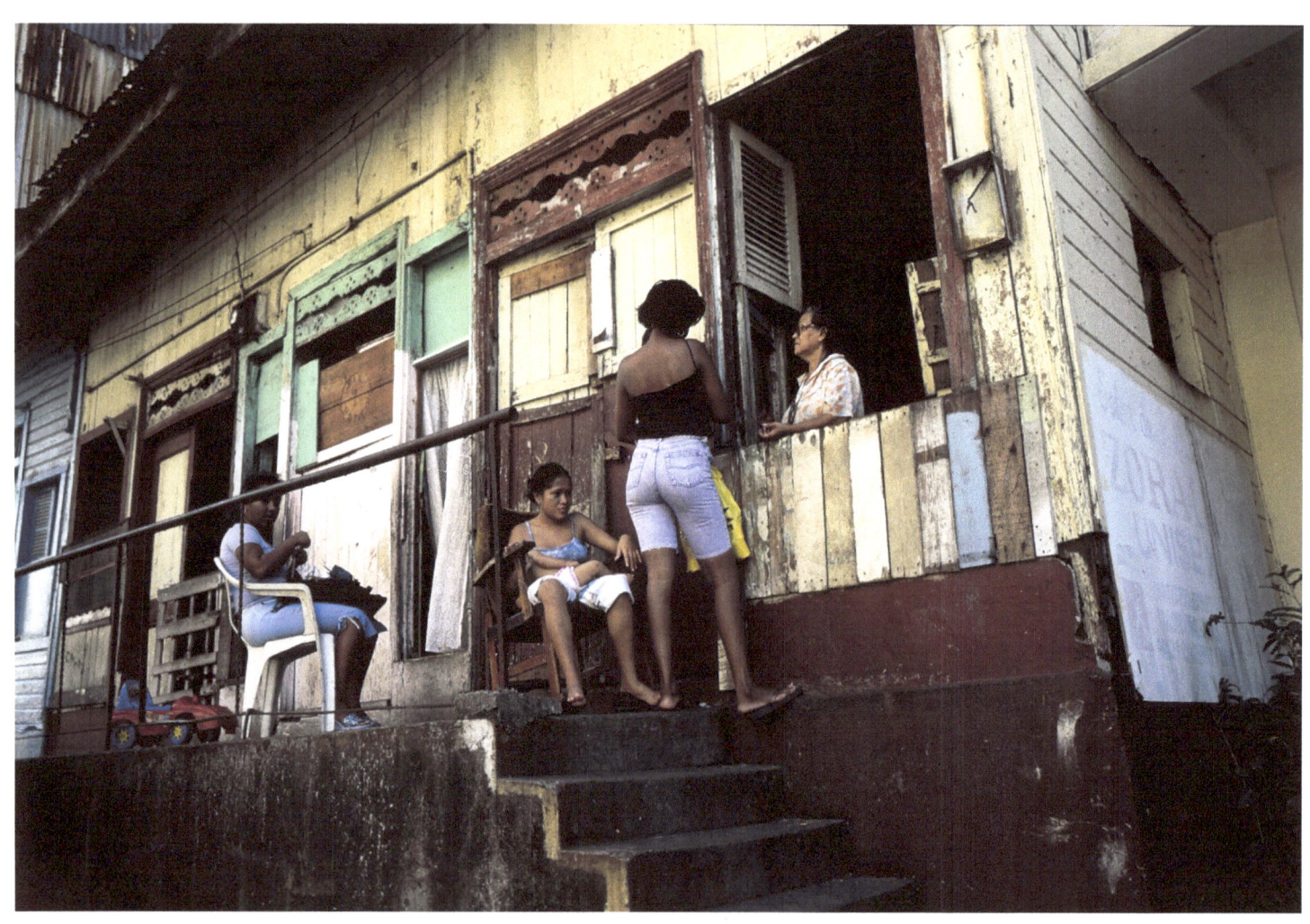

Once landed in Panama City we headed straight to the Old City, Panama Viejo, where the contrast of poor vs rich were more evident. It was a good start.

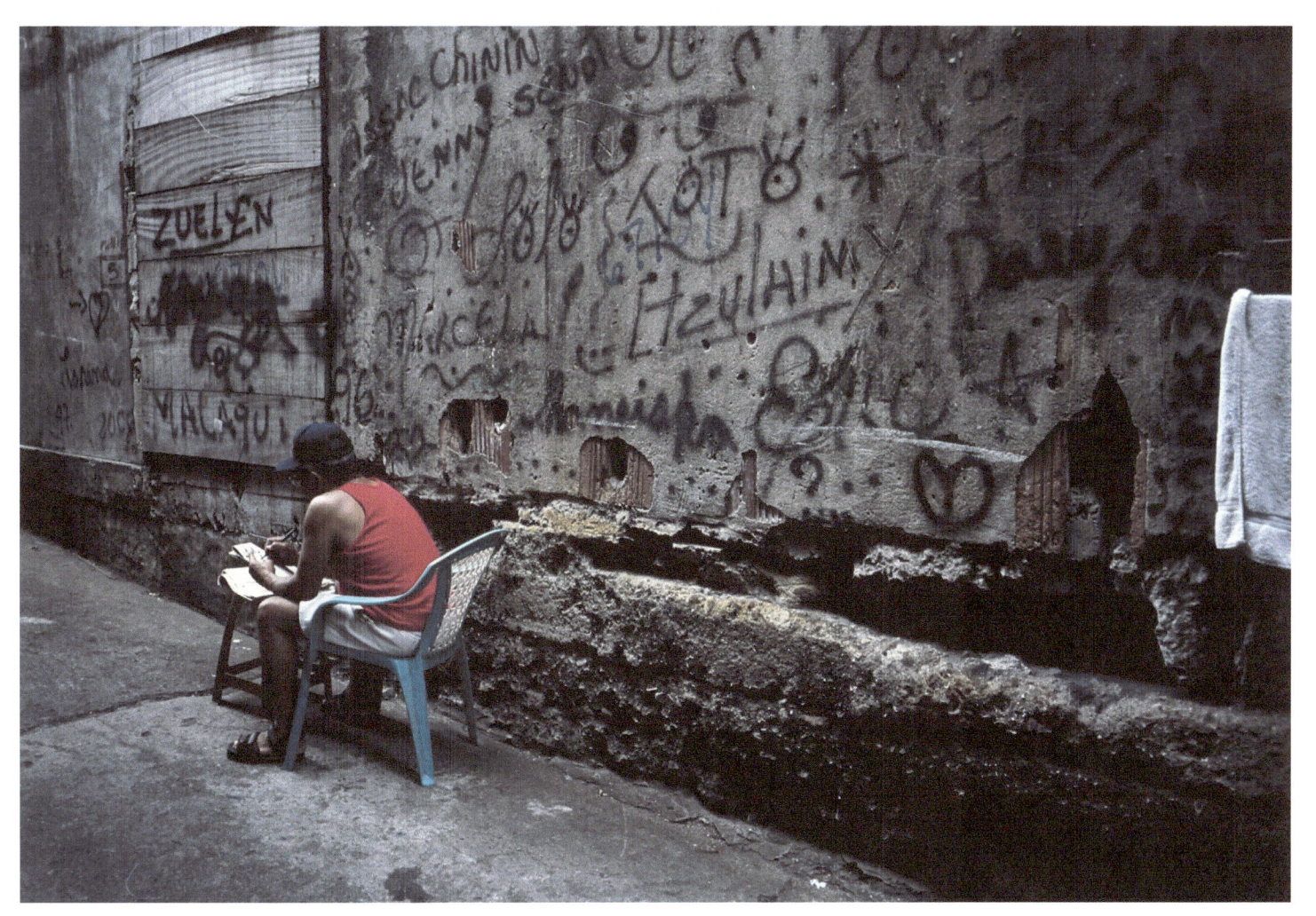
Panama Viejo street

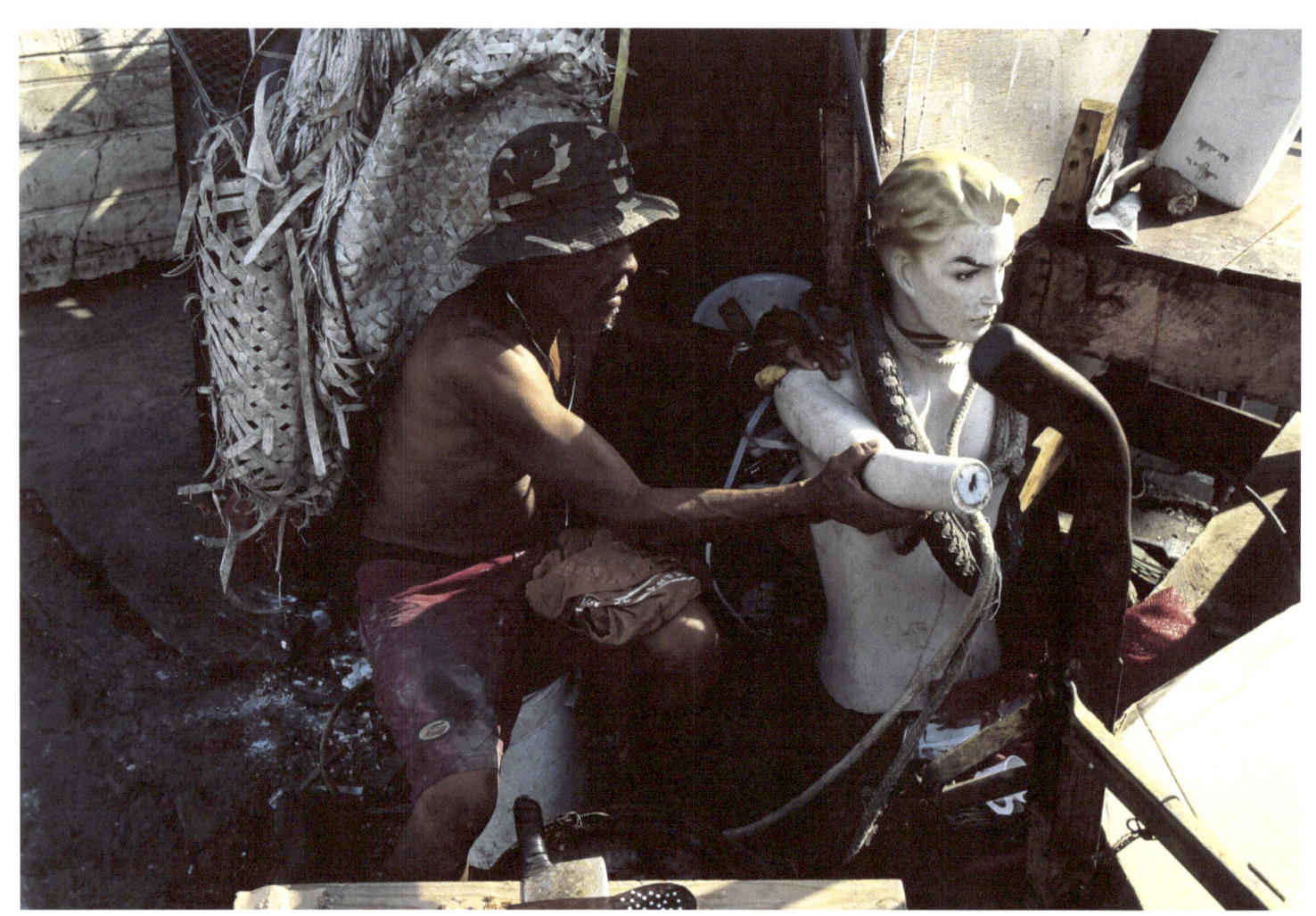

Living in Panama Viejo port

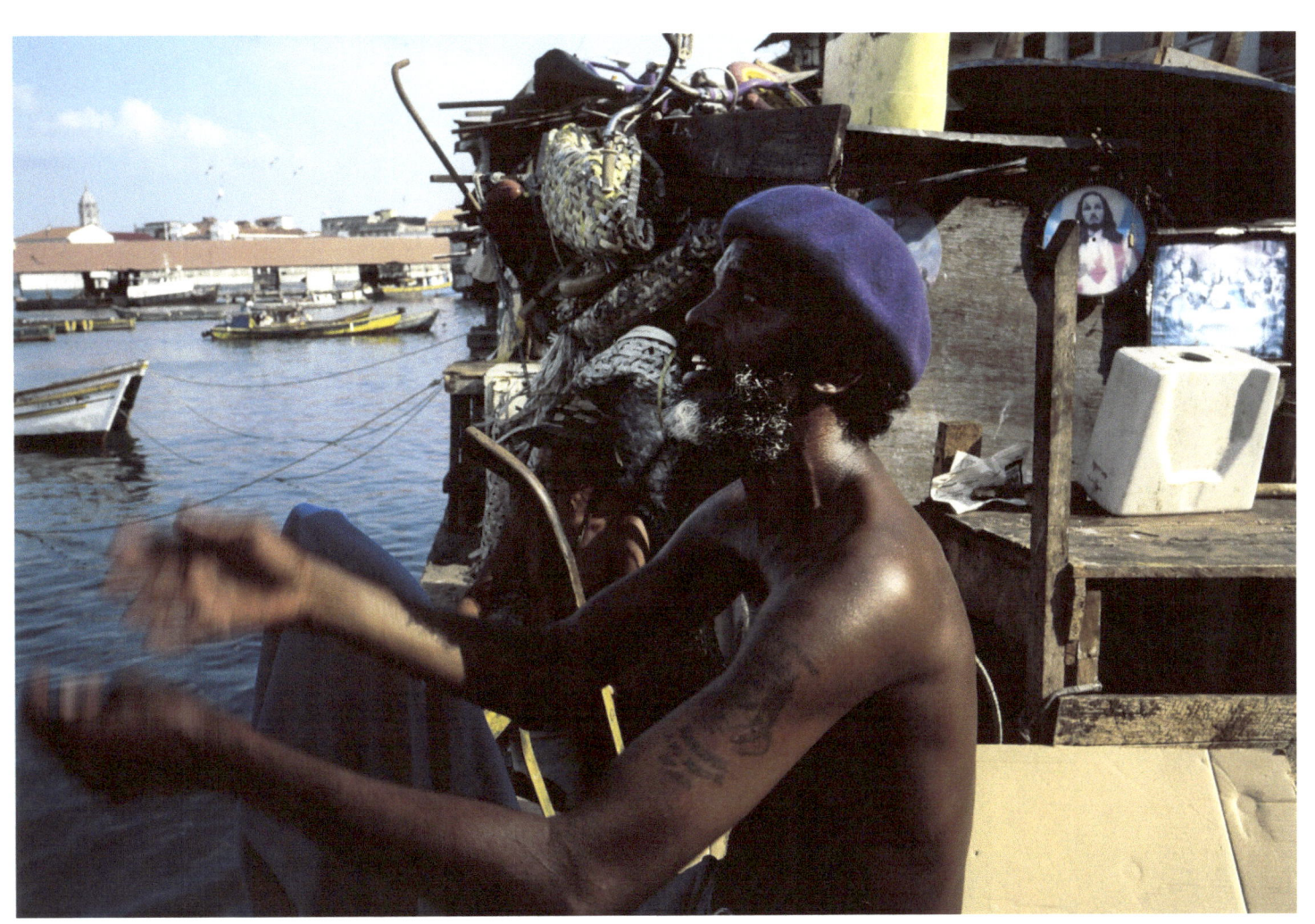

Living in Panama Viejo port

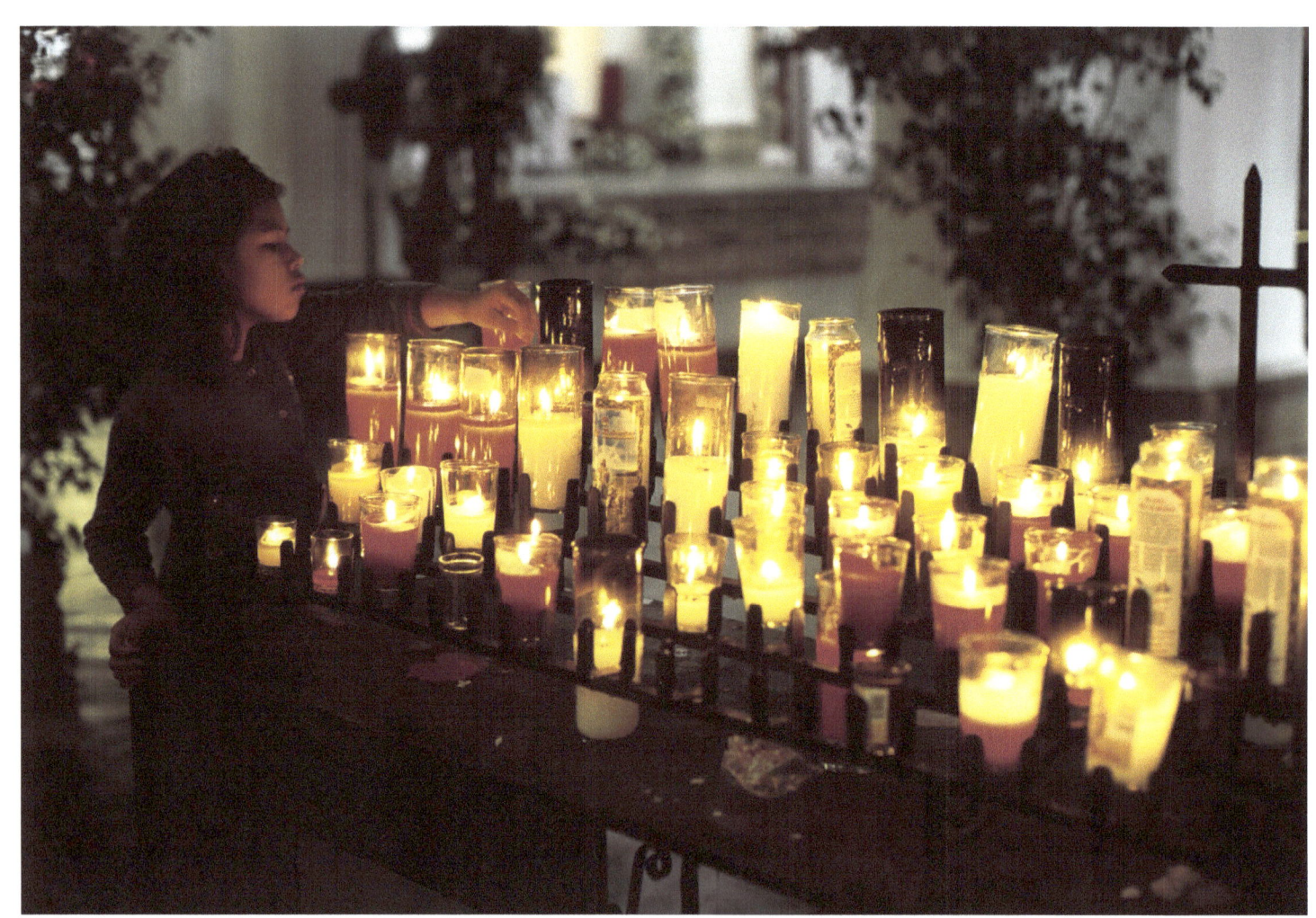

Panama Cathedral

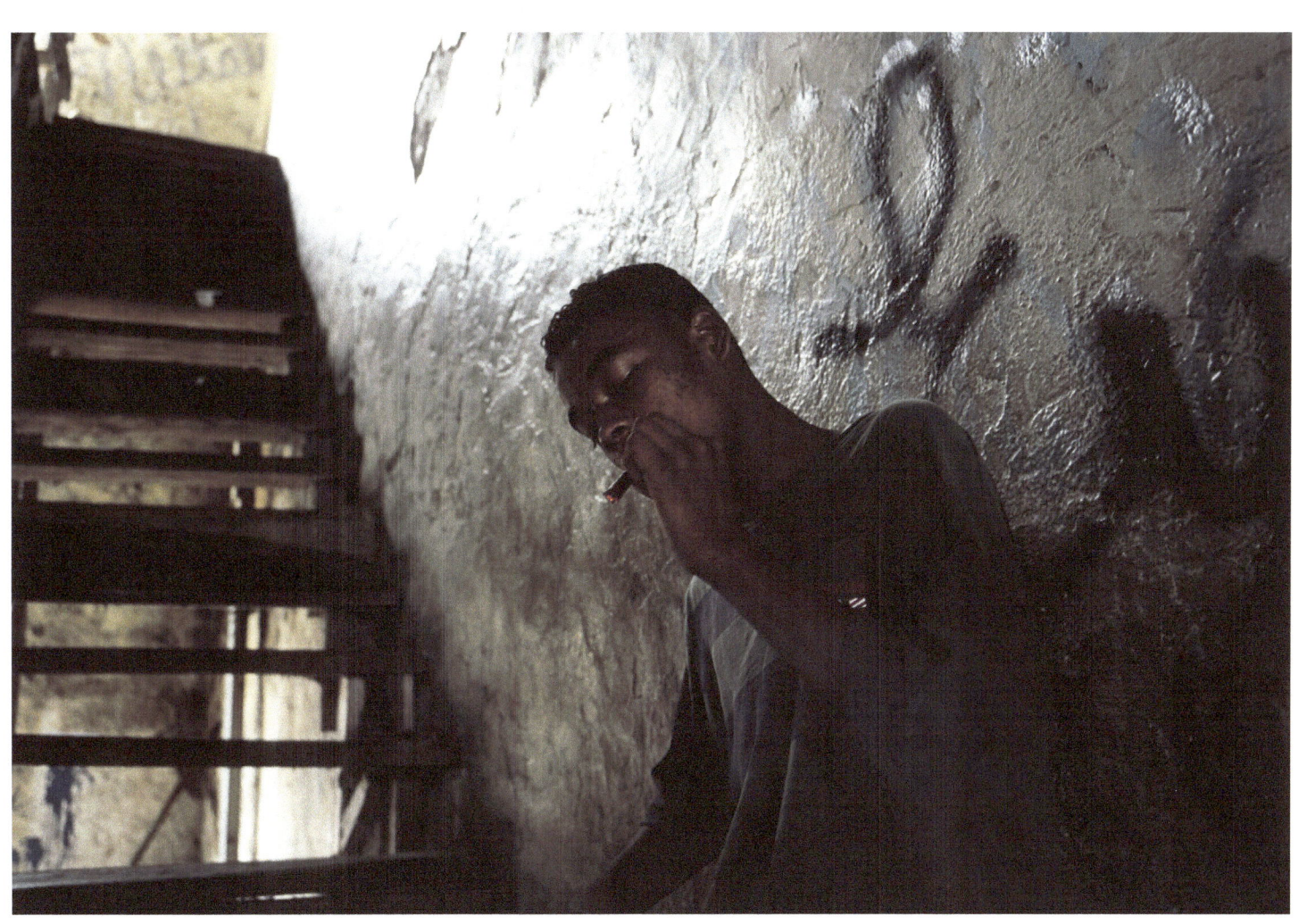
Young guy smoking one of my cigars in Panama Viejo

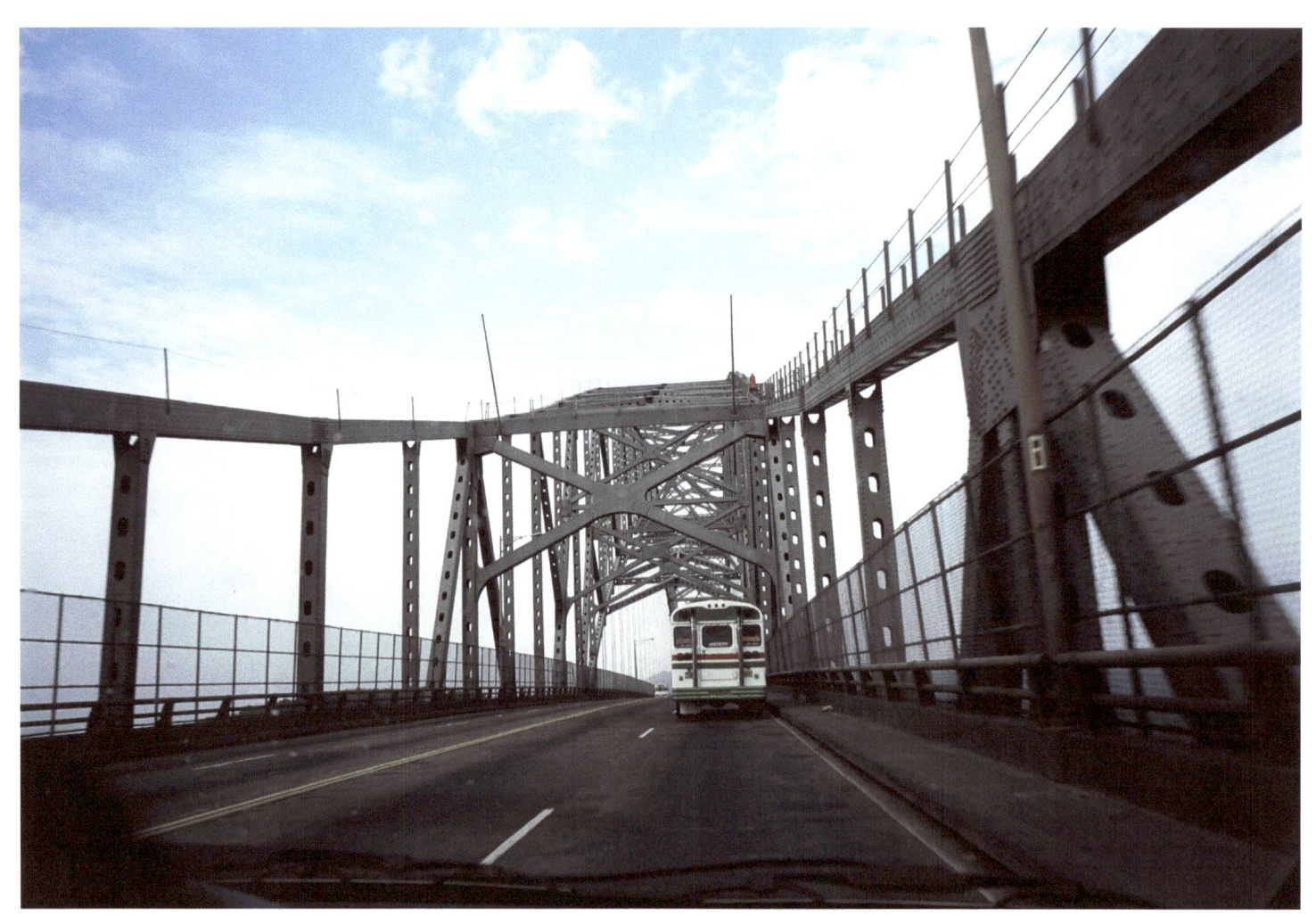

Bridge of the Americas, across the Panama Canal

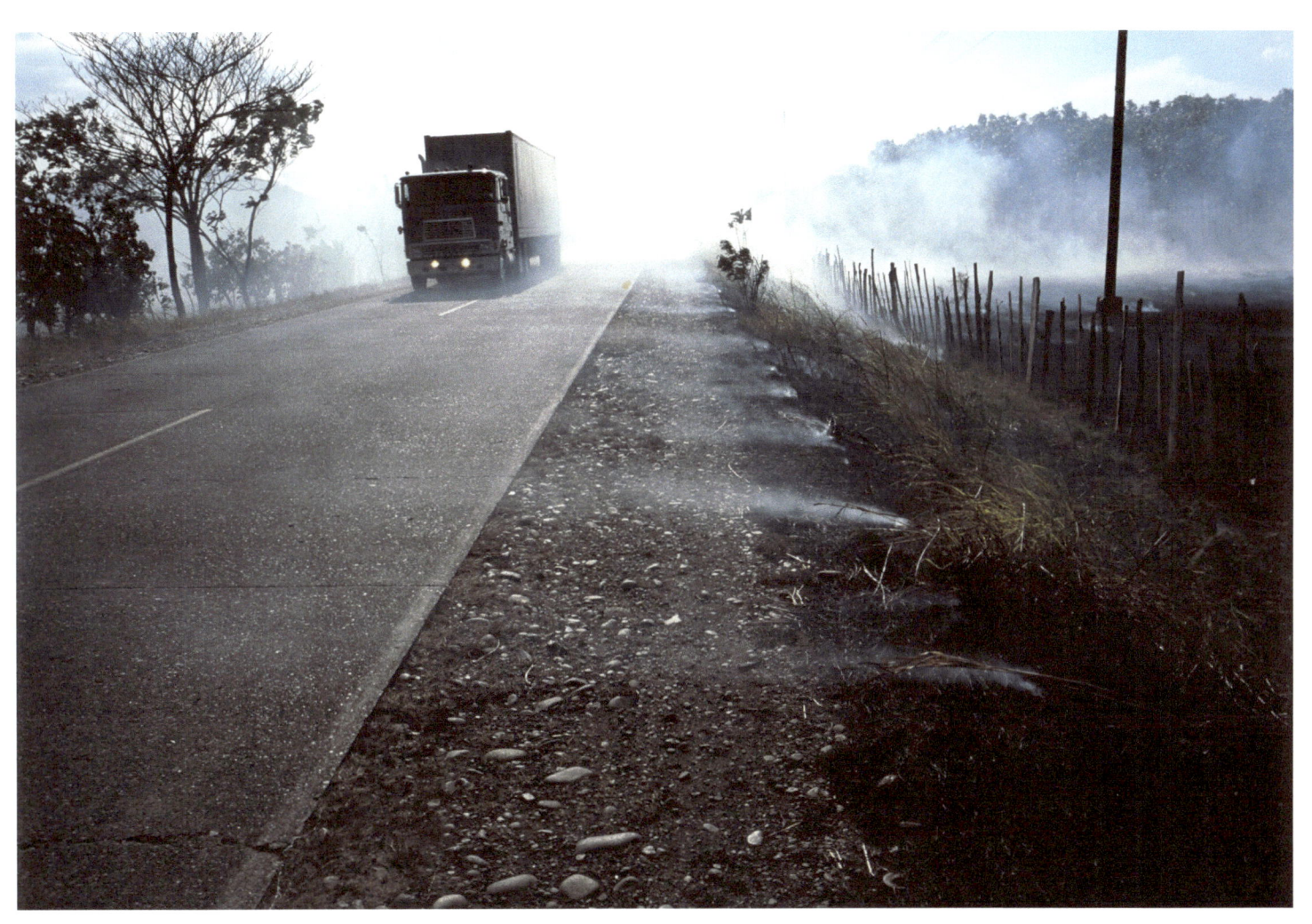

Pan-American Road between Panama City and David

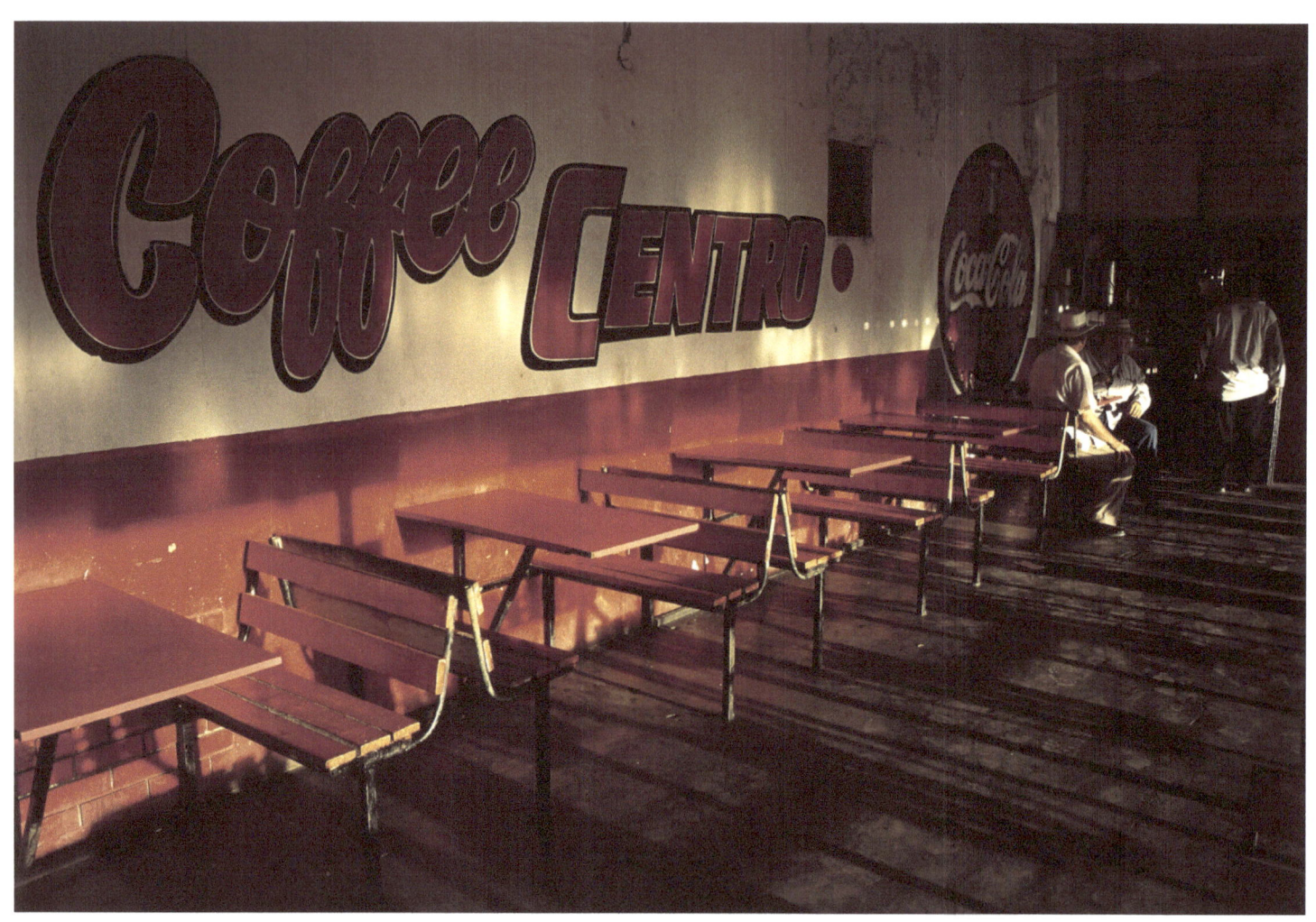

The bus station in the city of David was a good spot to see how life was for travelers headed across the country.

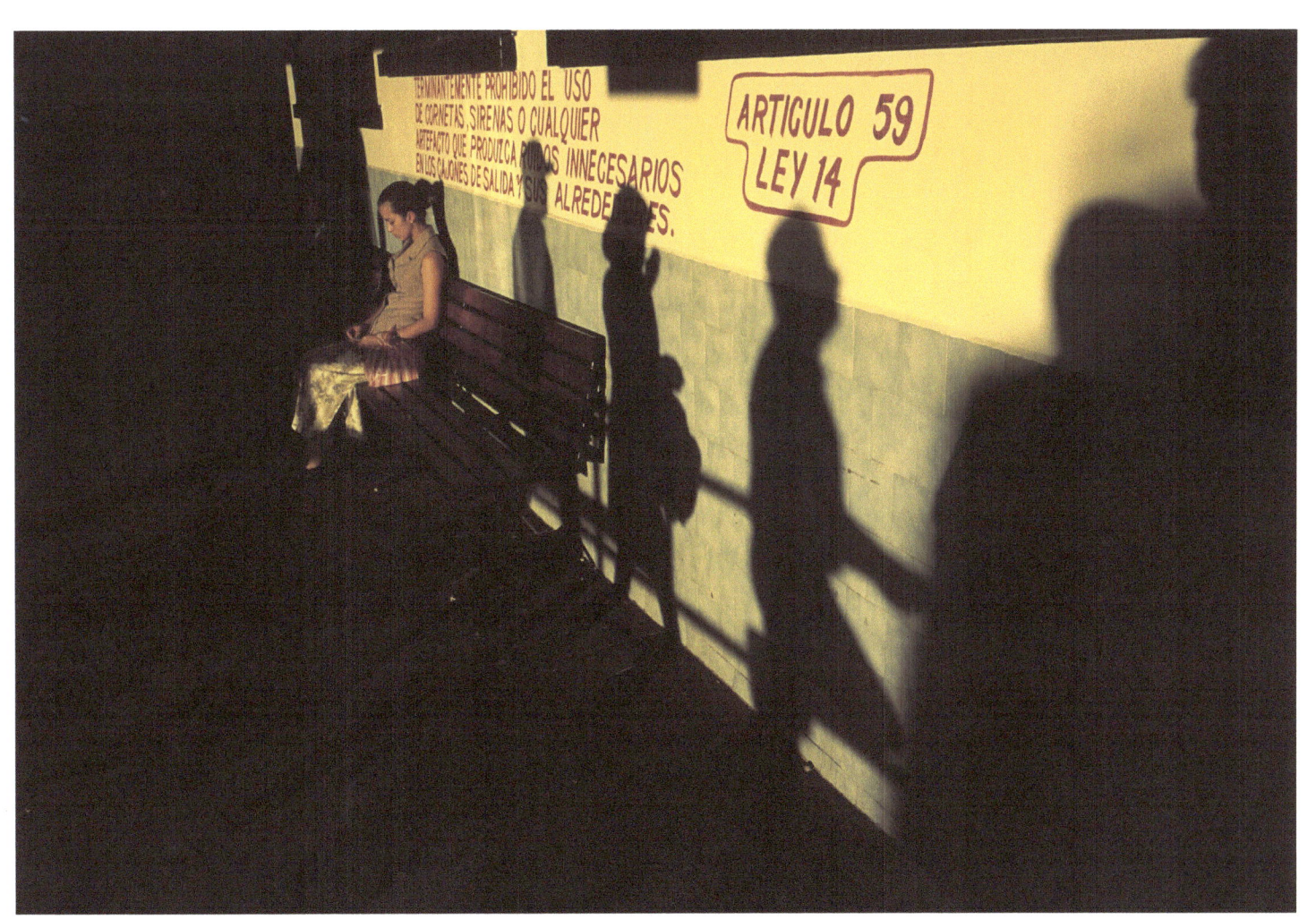

David City Bus Station

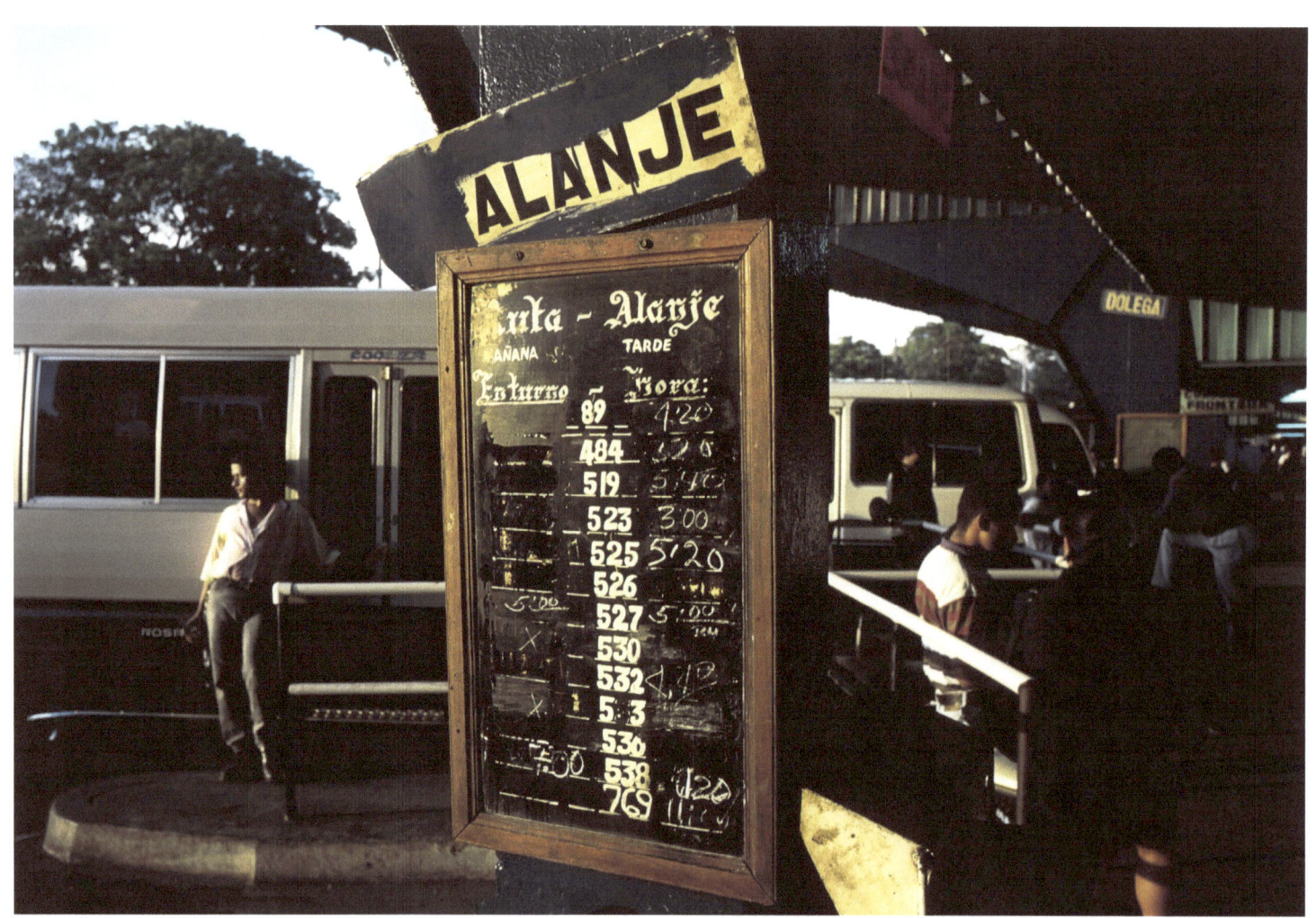

David City Bus Station

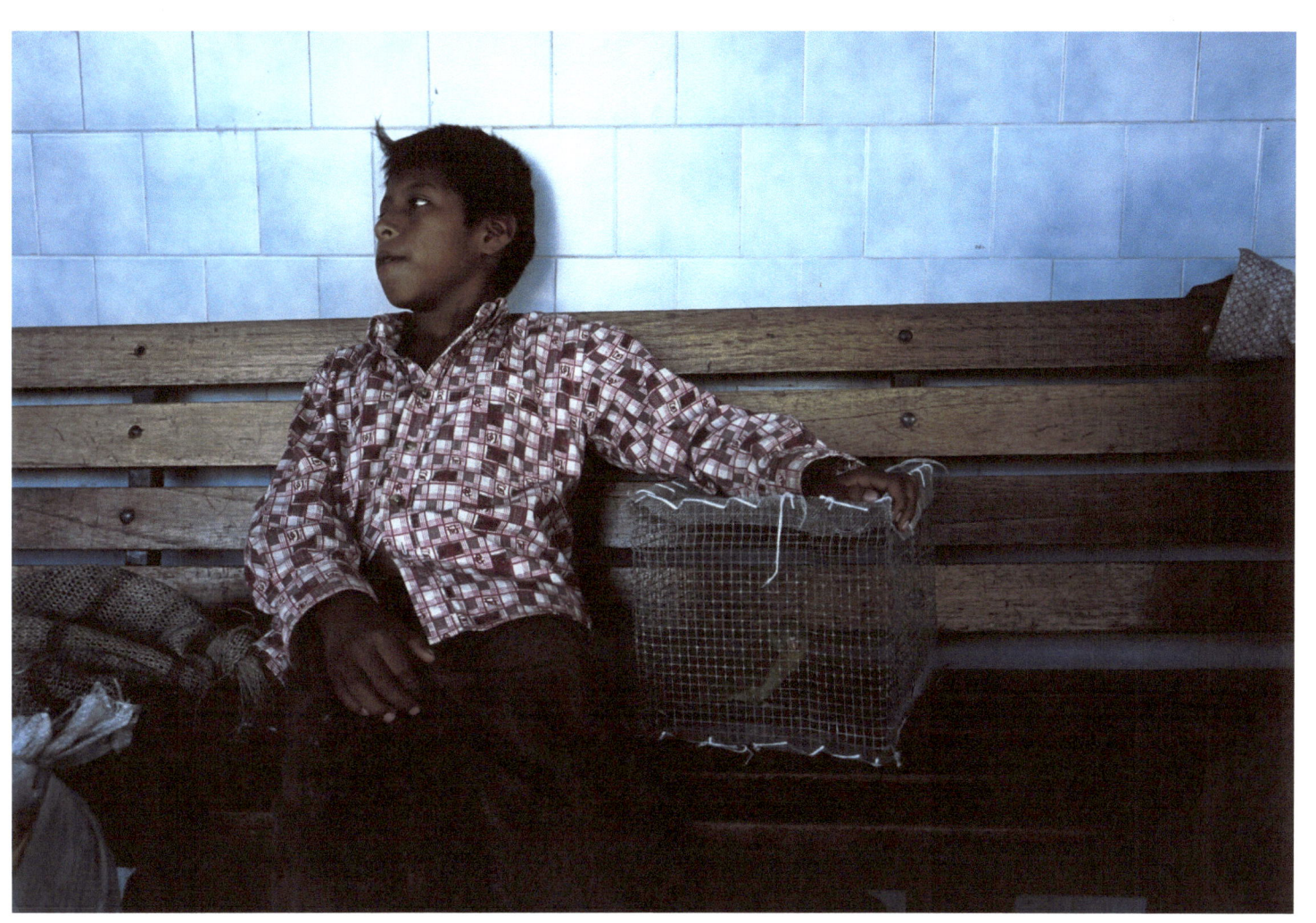

David City Bus Station

COSTA RICA

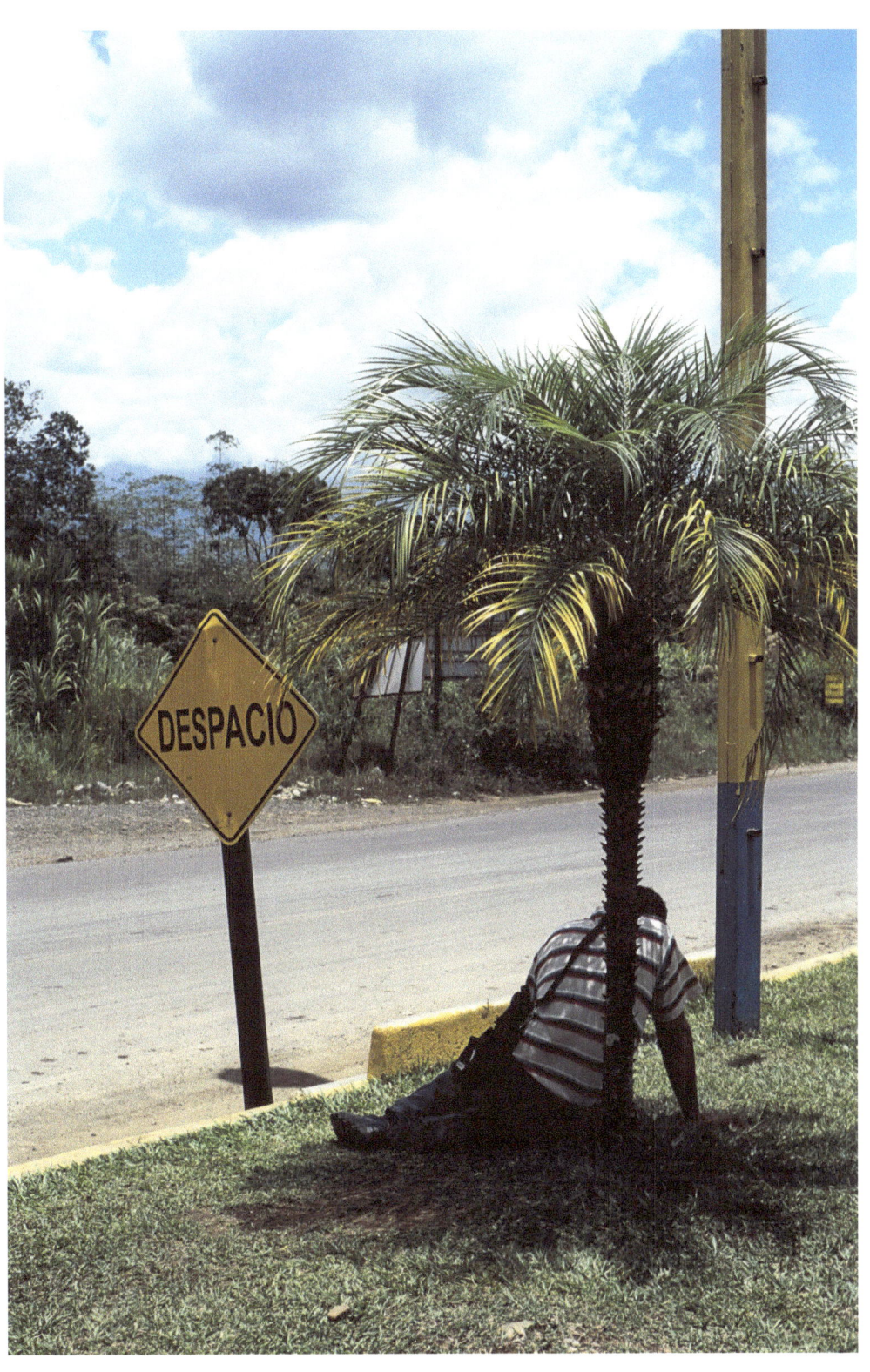

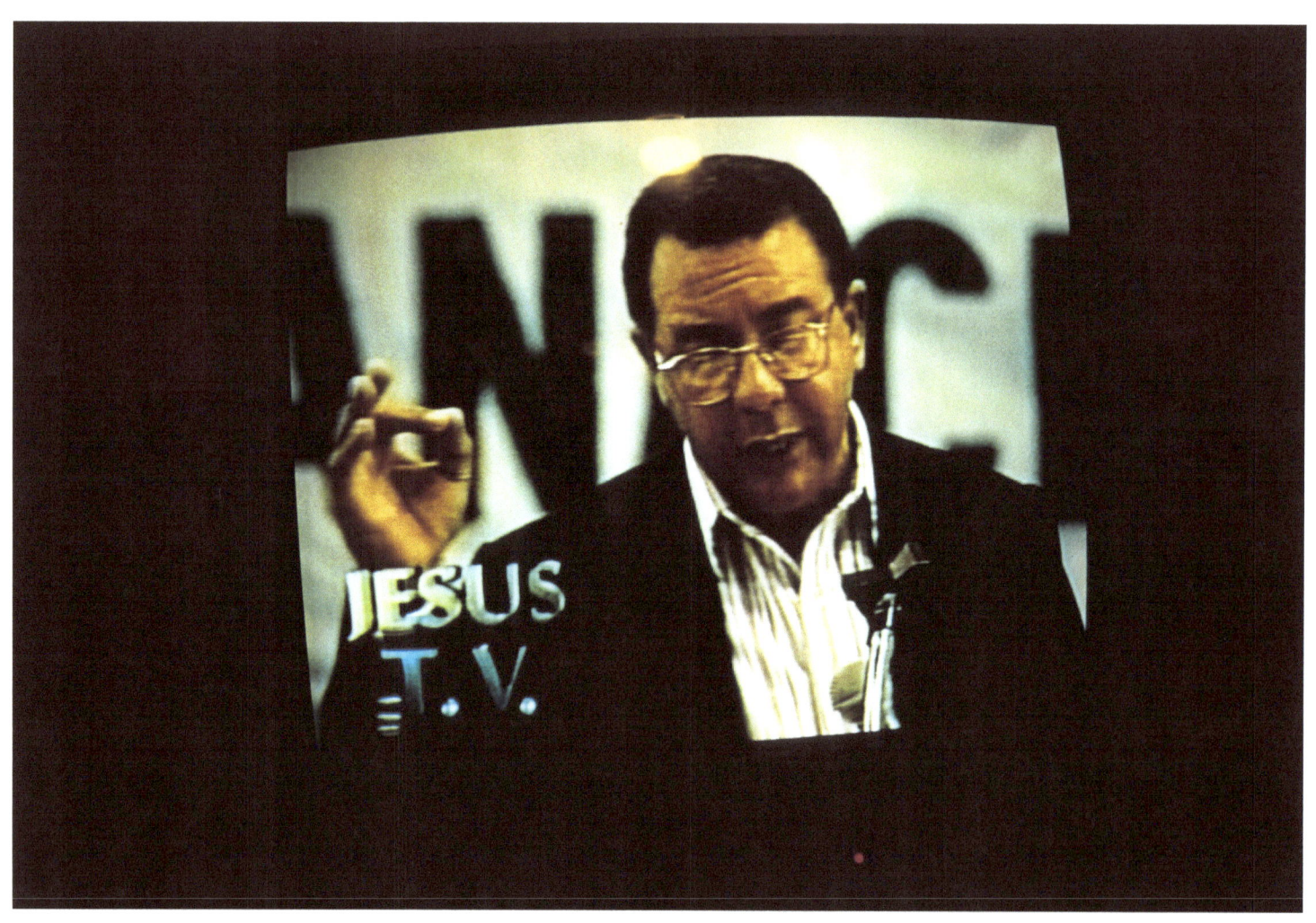

We spent a short time in Costa Rica: I had been there a couple of years before and I had a full coverage of the country. Still to find signs of contrasts and contradictions was far too easy.

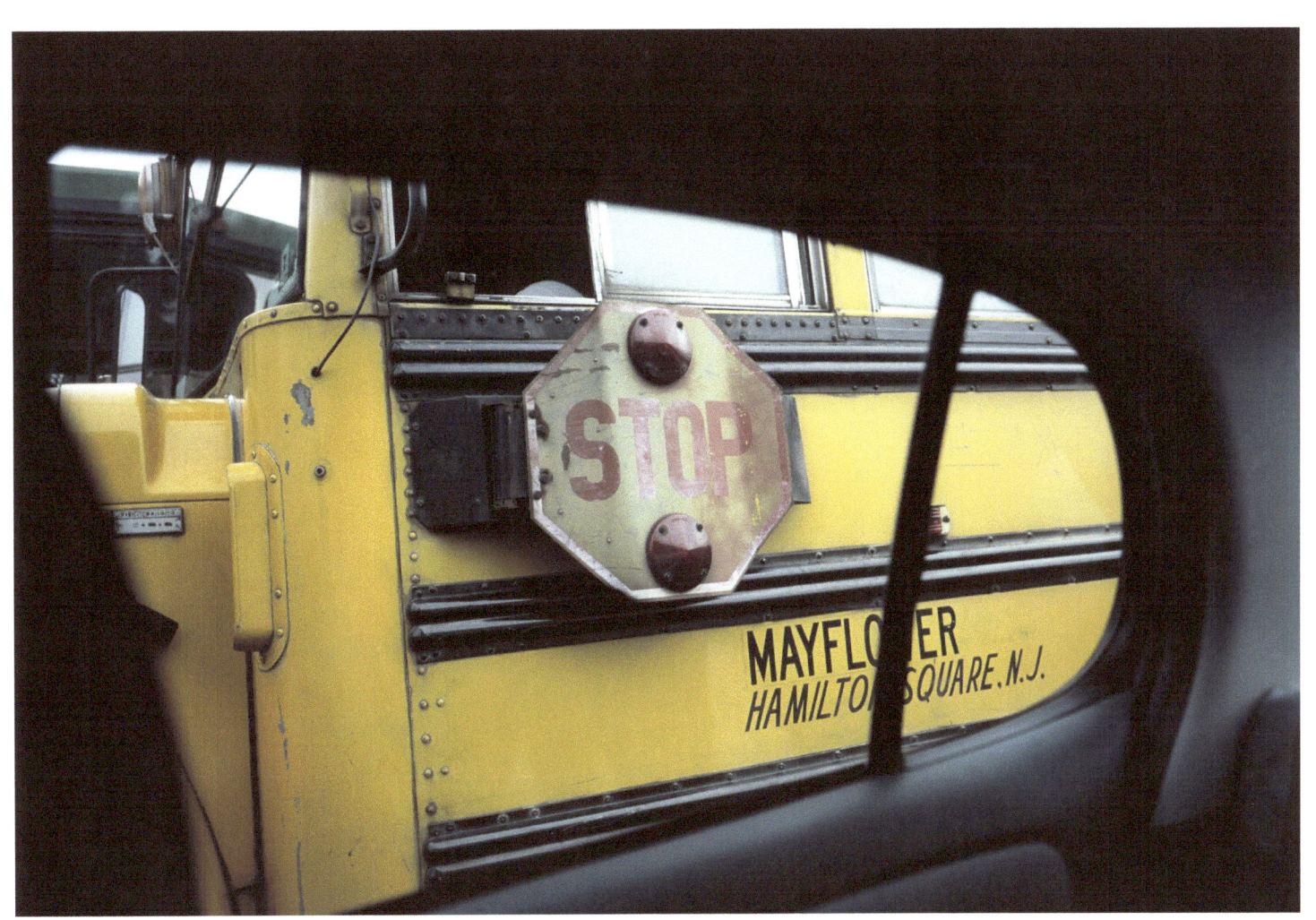

Jesus TV and New Jersey school bus used for local transport?

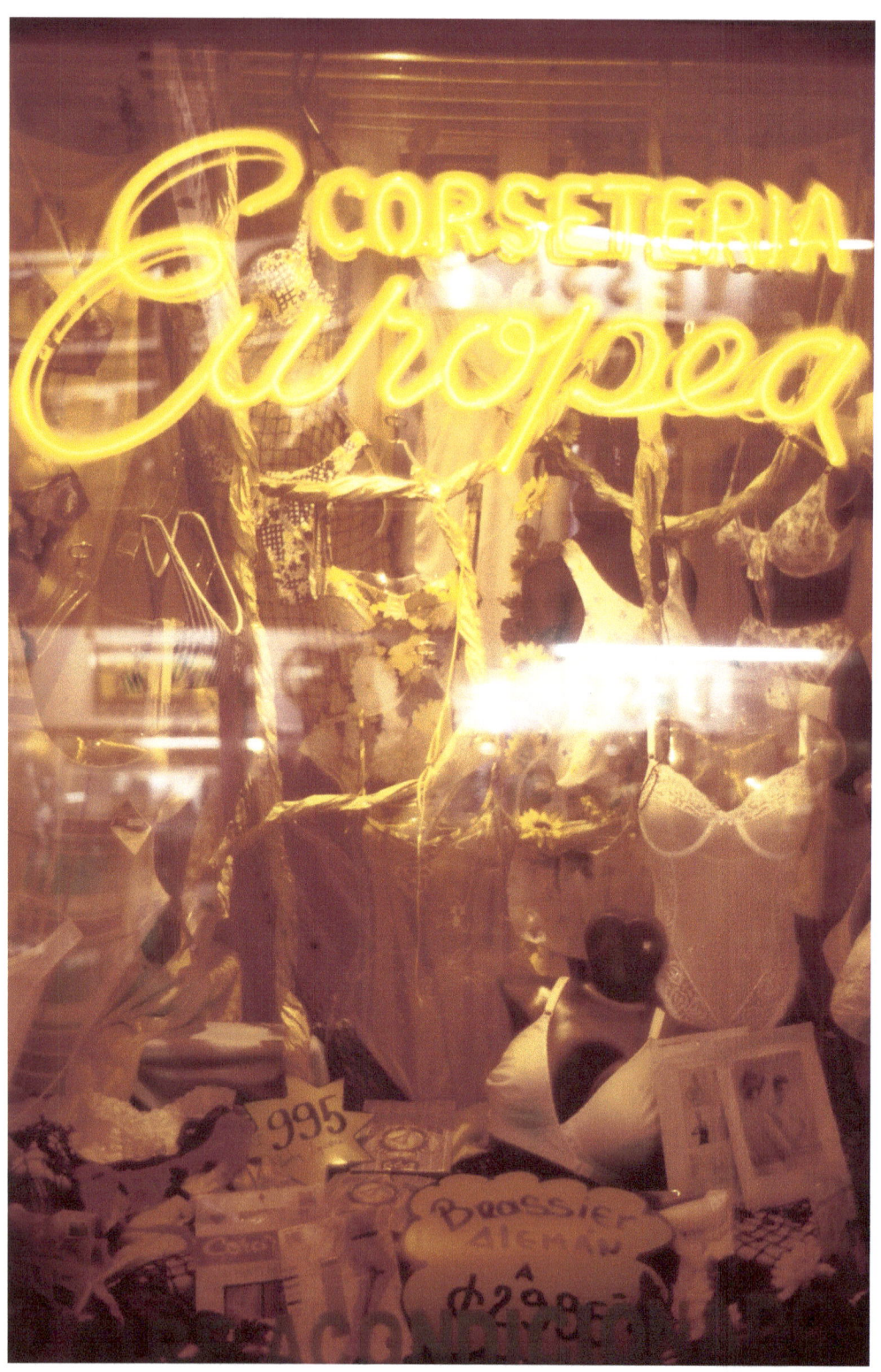

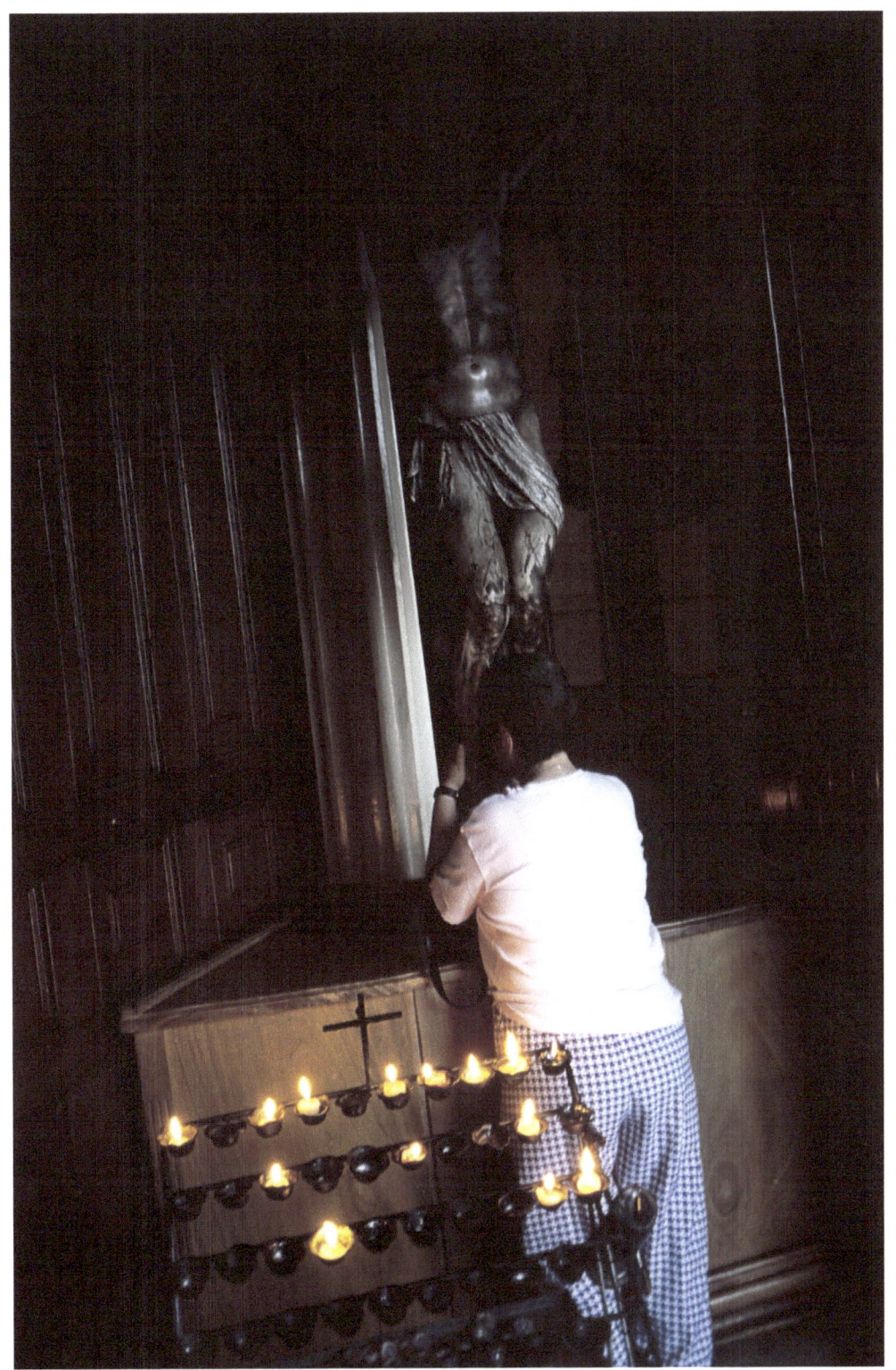

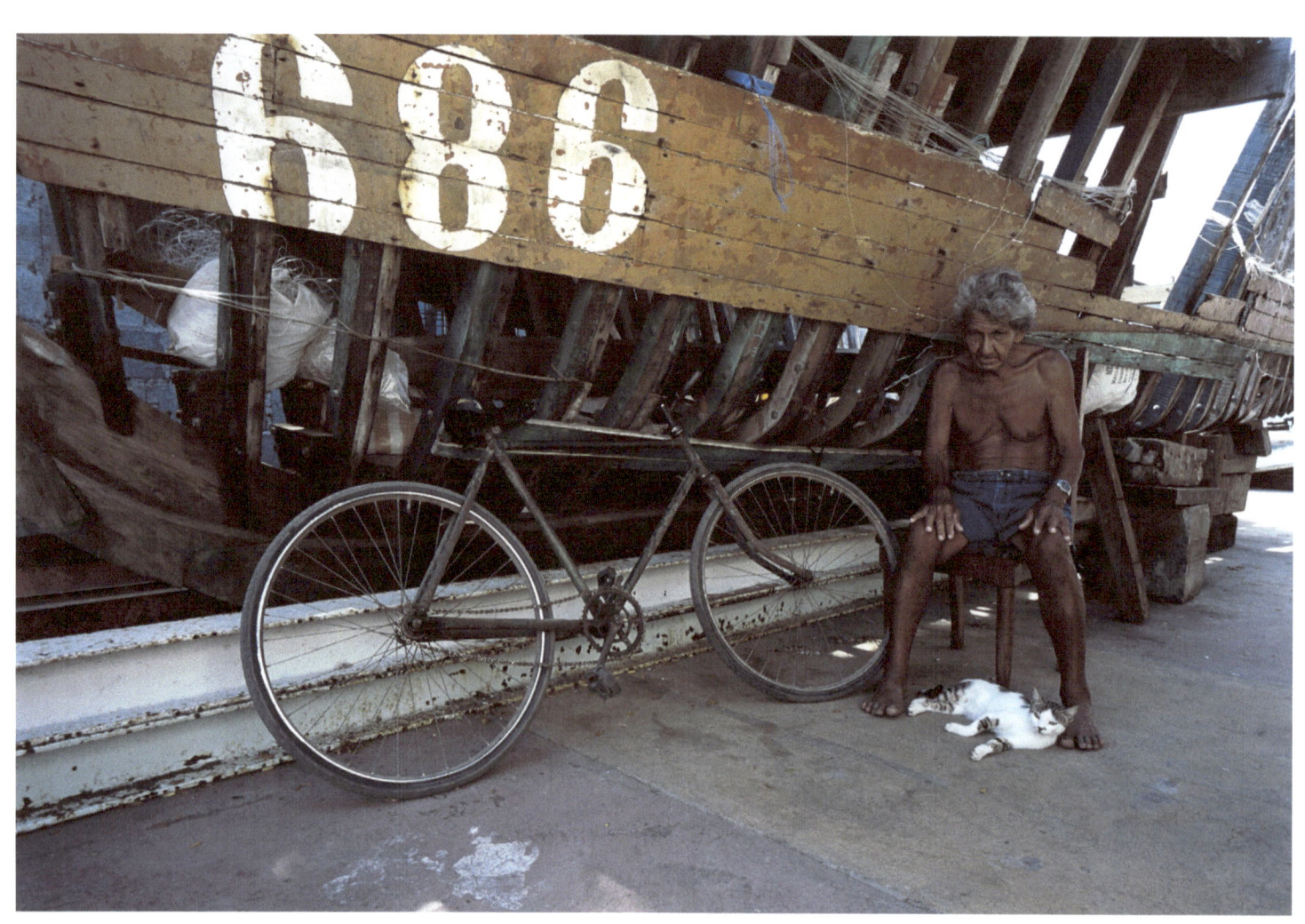

Puntarenas port

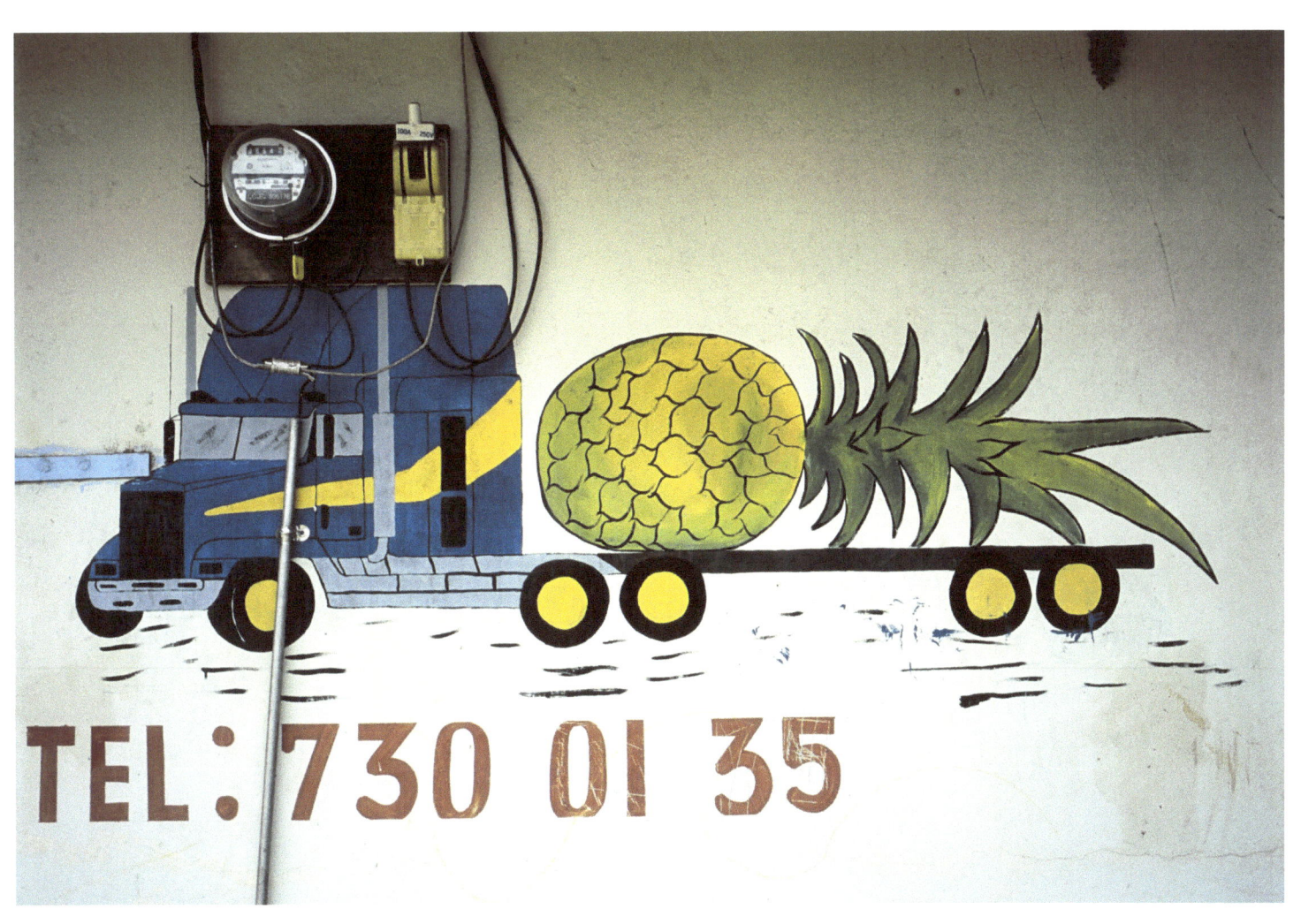

Well, appropriate Pan-American promo

Nicaragua

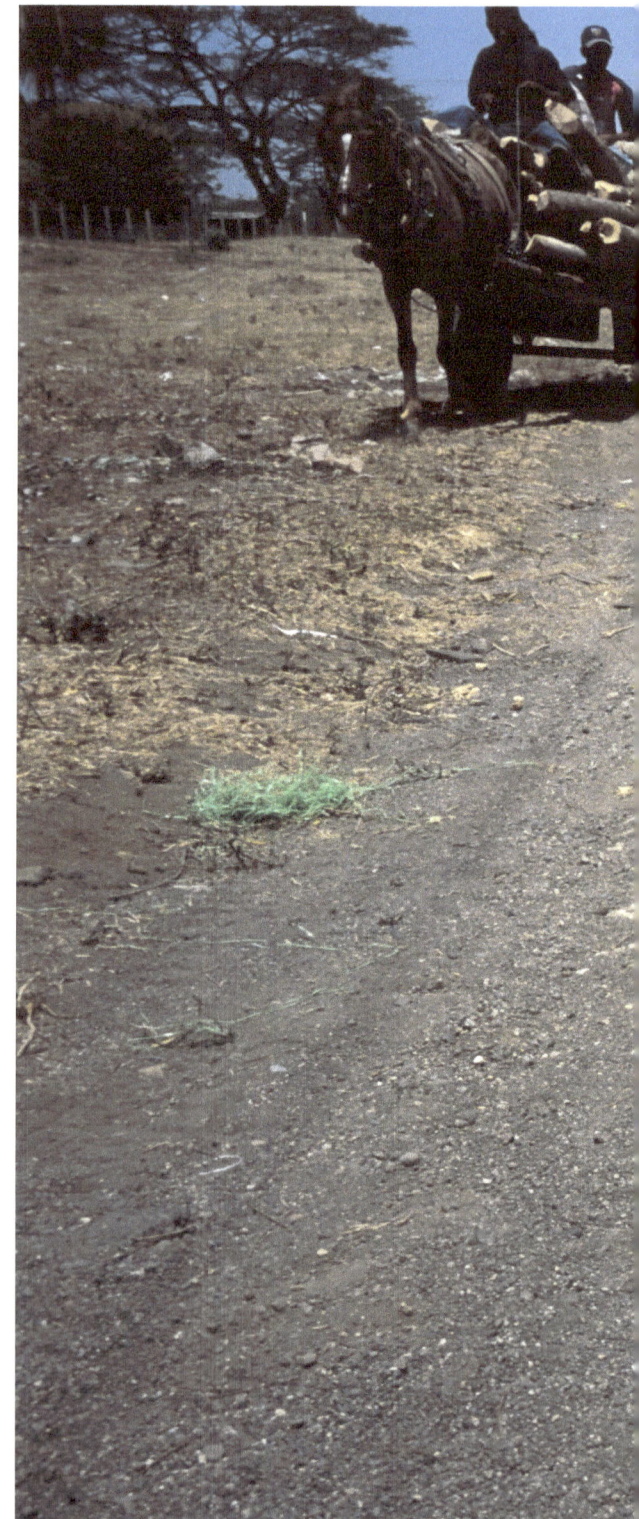

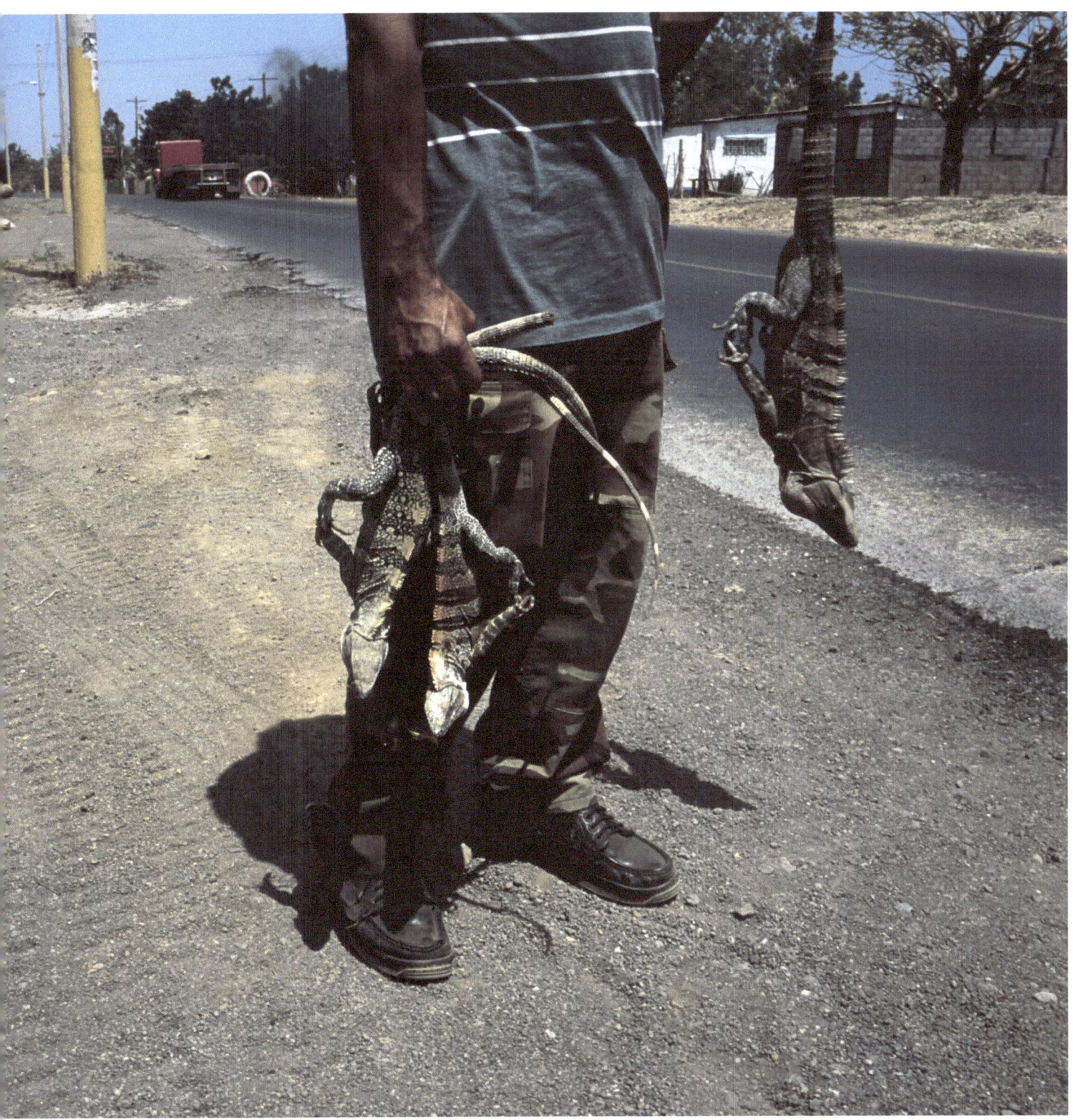

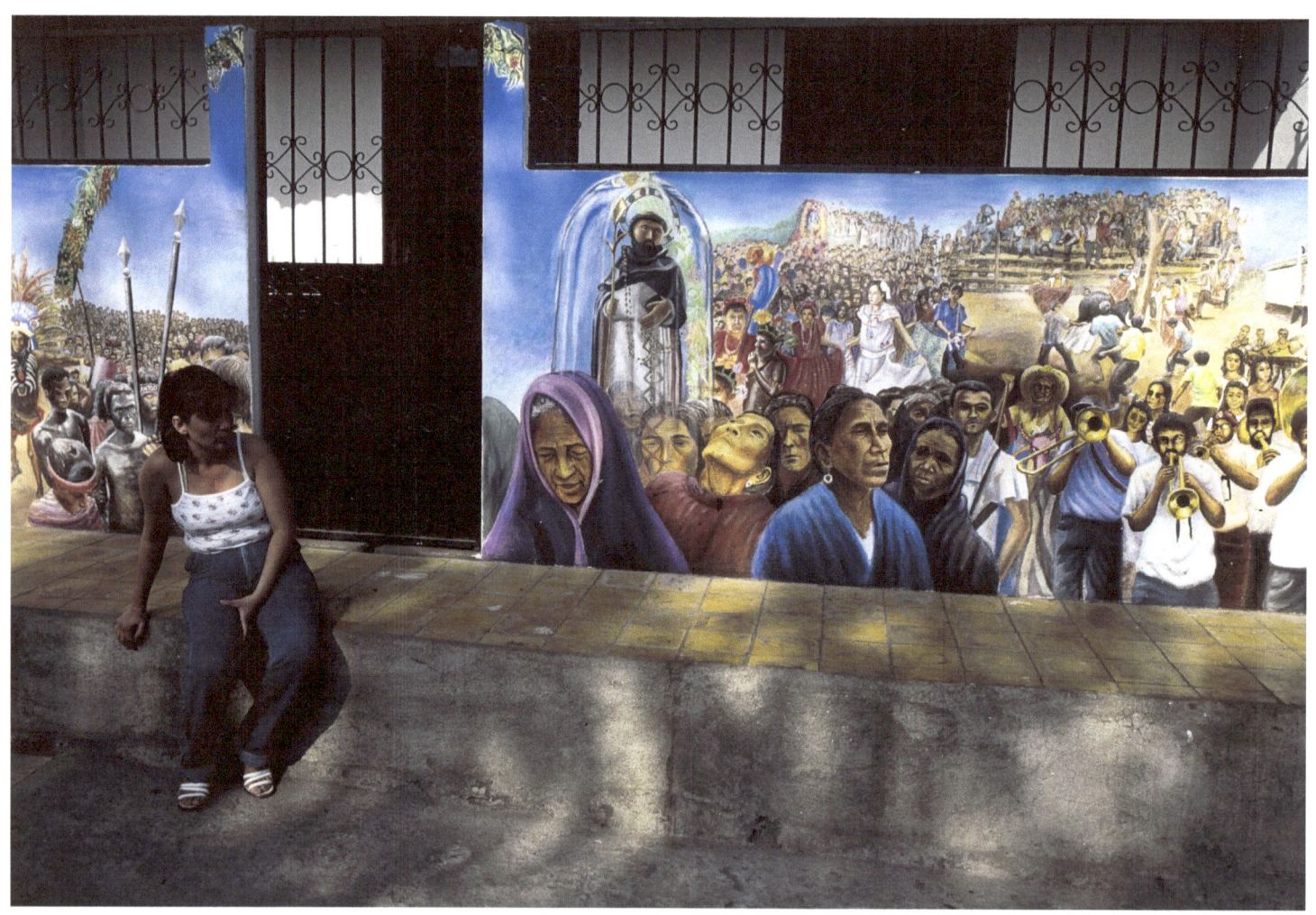

We had to crouch on the bottom of the taxi to get safely to the bus station at six in the morning: this is how bad the situation was in Managua. But Nicaragua was one of the most rewarding experiences of the whole trip thanks to the people that seemed to expect the wild and unpredictable event every step of their life.

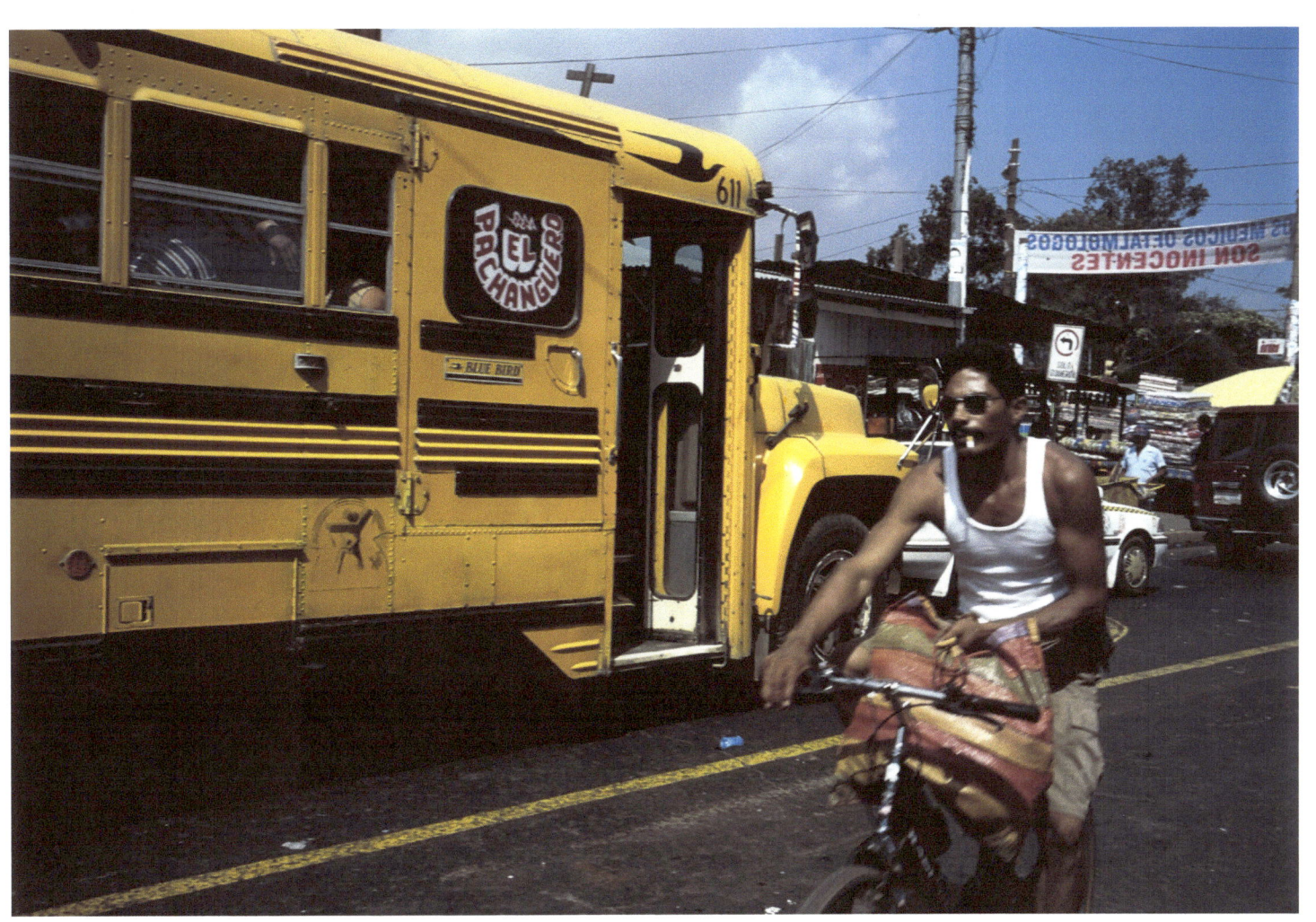

On the way to Managua

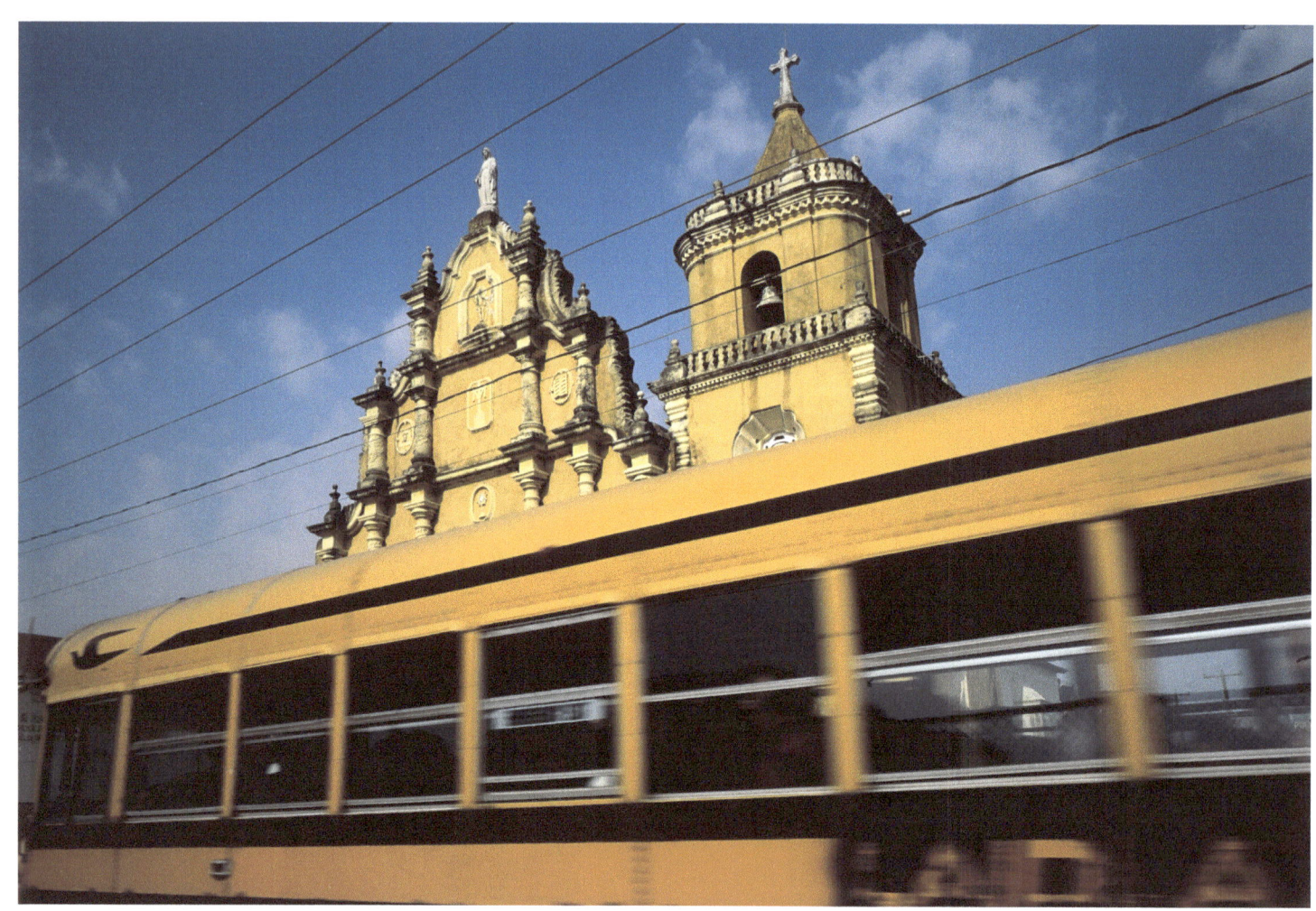

Managua Cathedral

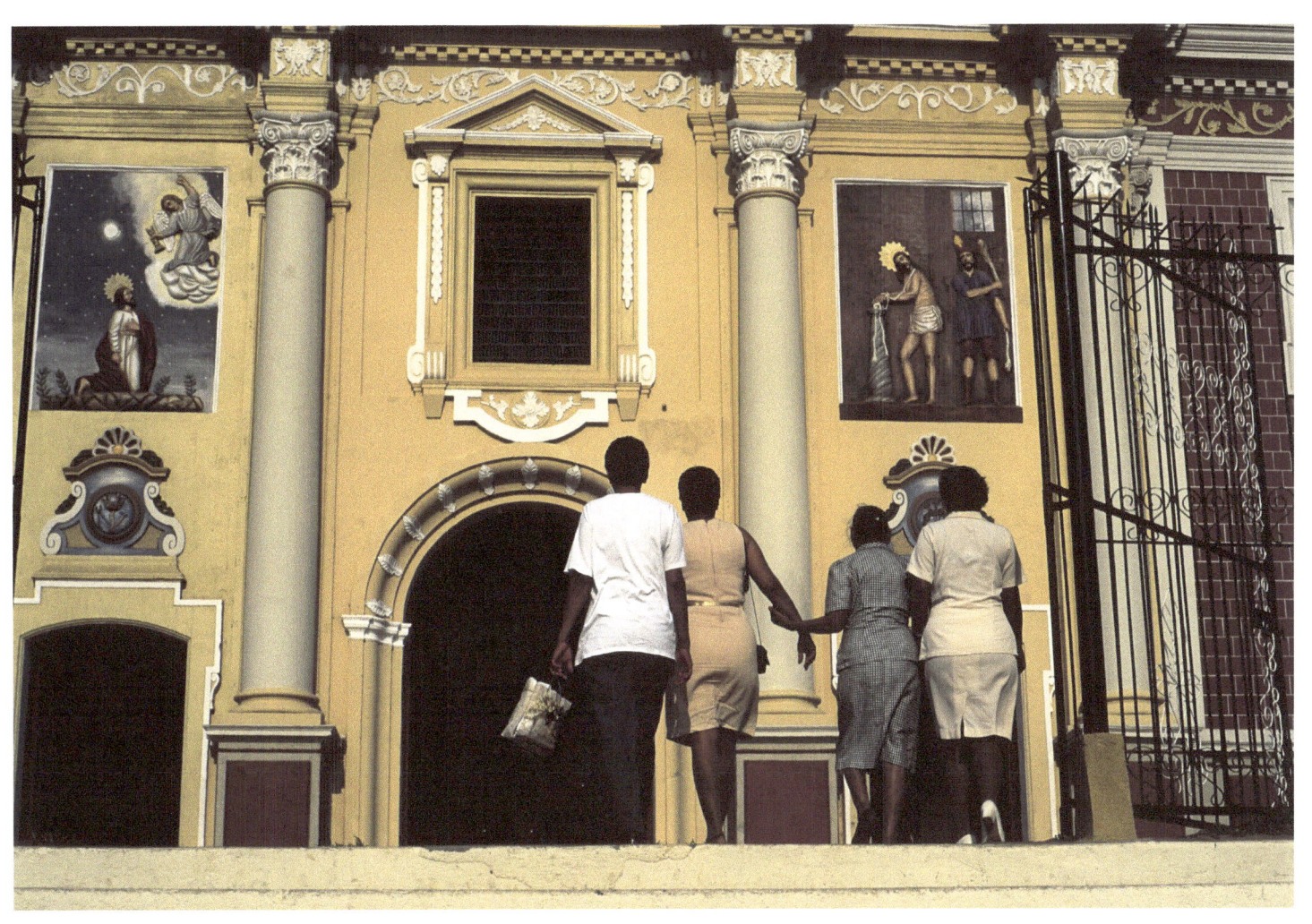

Managua Cathedral

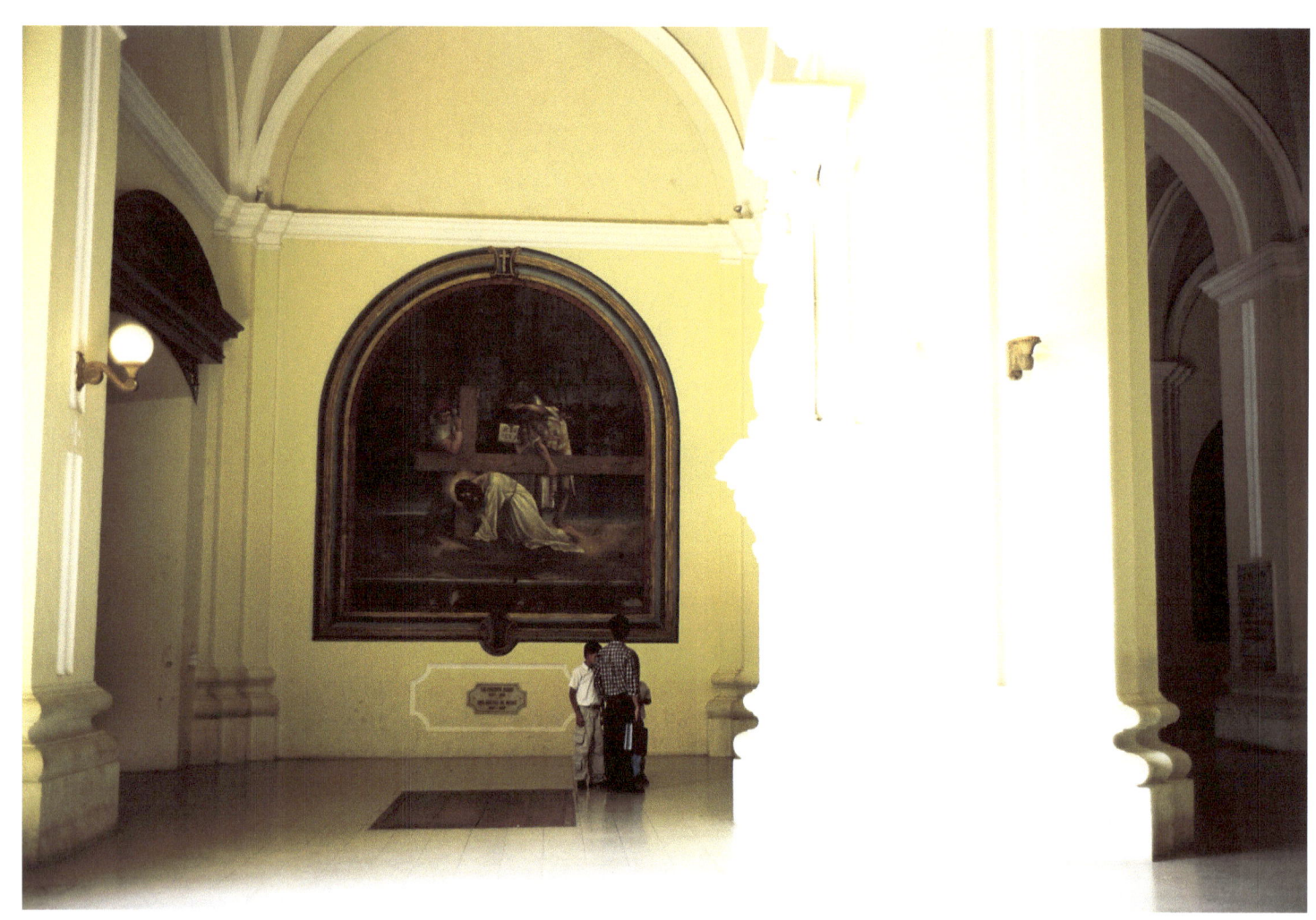

Managua Cathedral

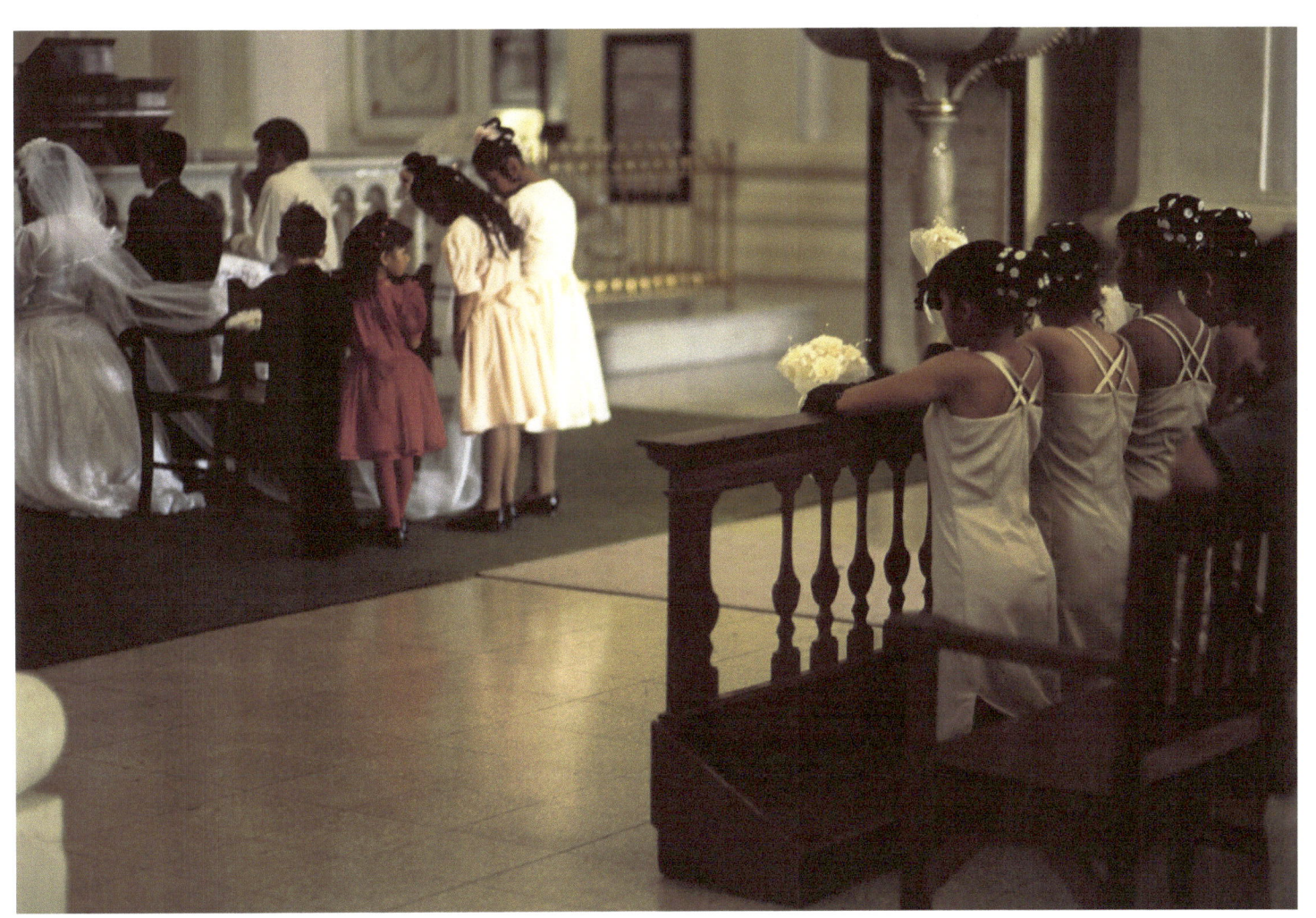

Wedding in the Managua Cathedral

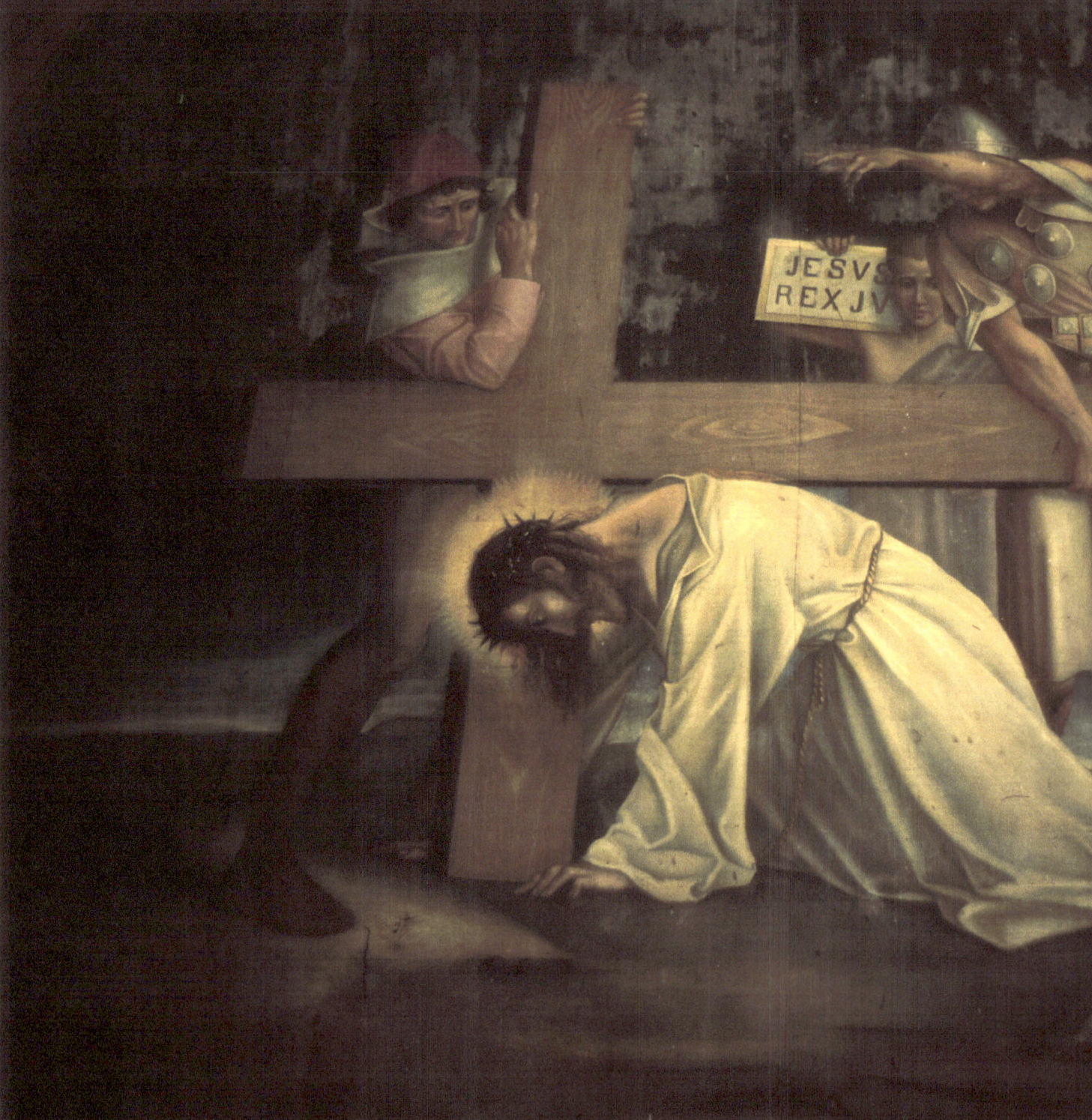

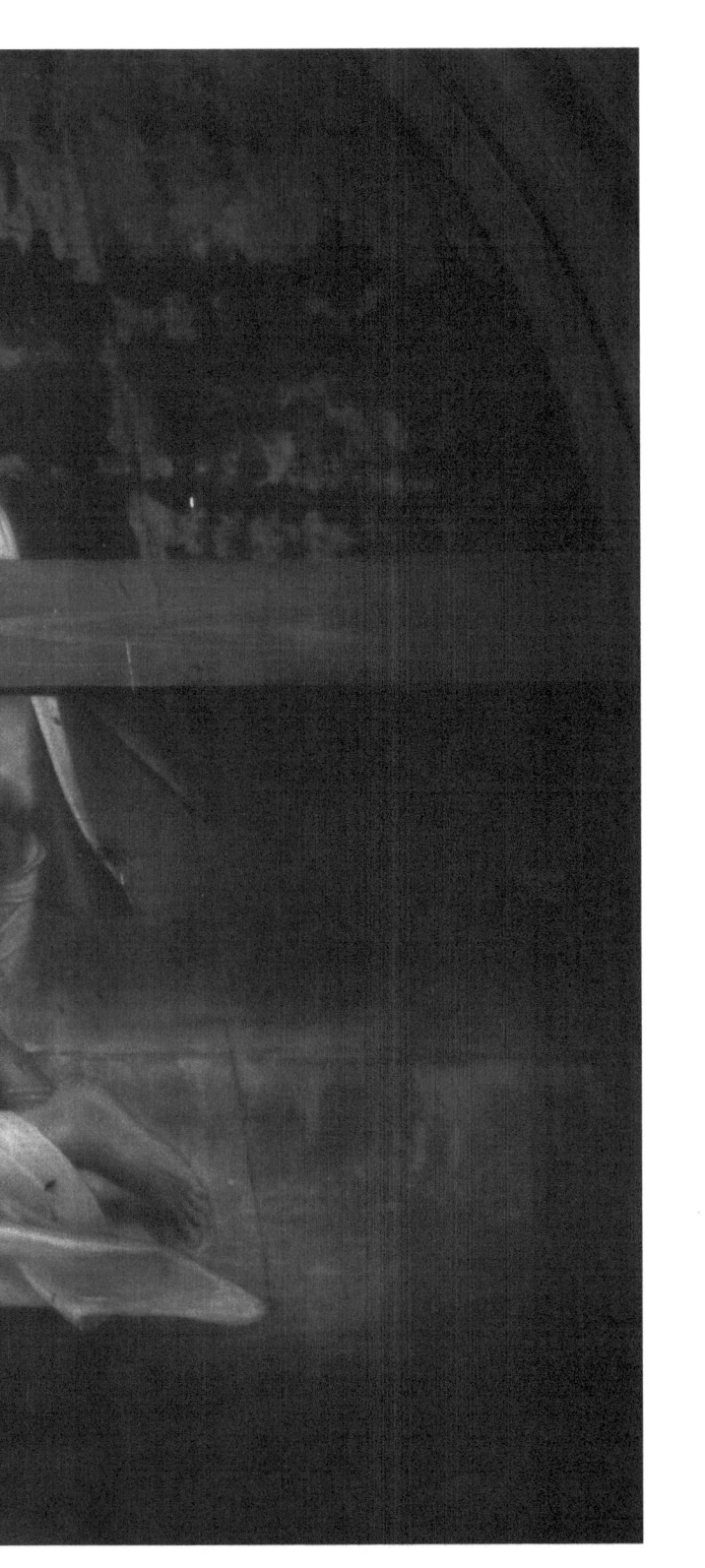

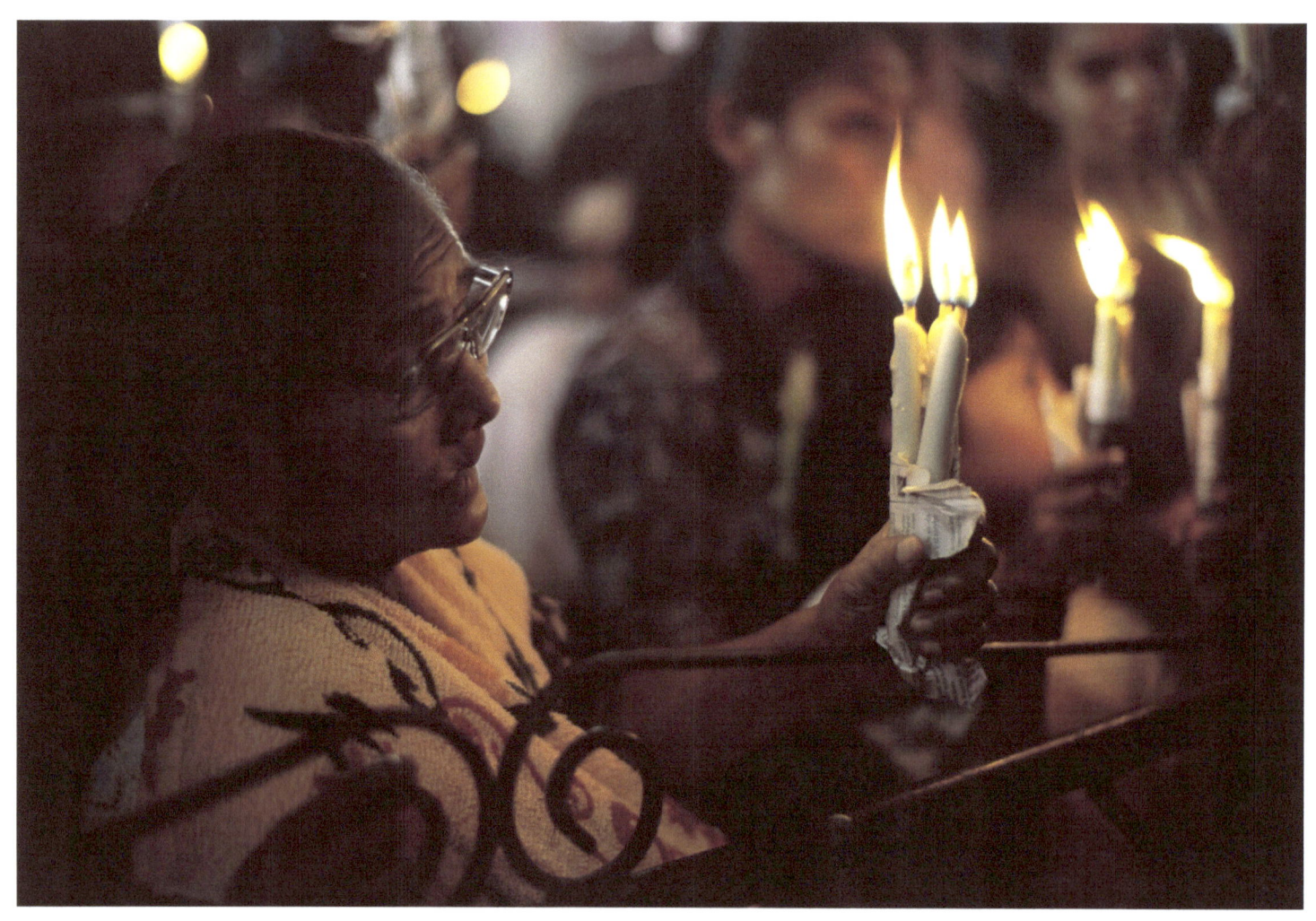

Managua: Catholic ceremony to bless the pets. The pets? Yes, the dogs actually..

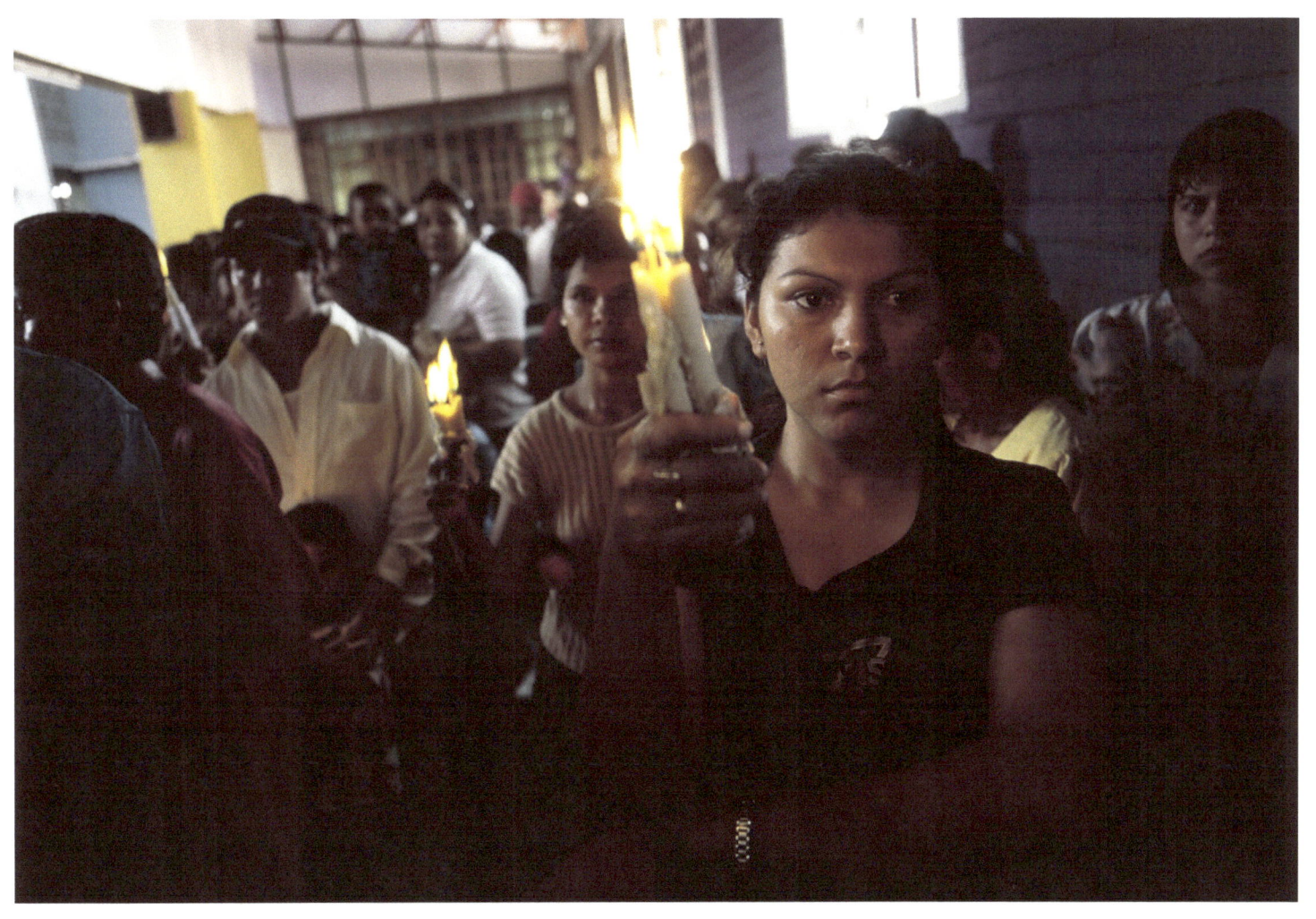
Managua: Catholic ceremony to bless the pets. The pets? Yes, the dogs actually..

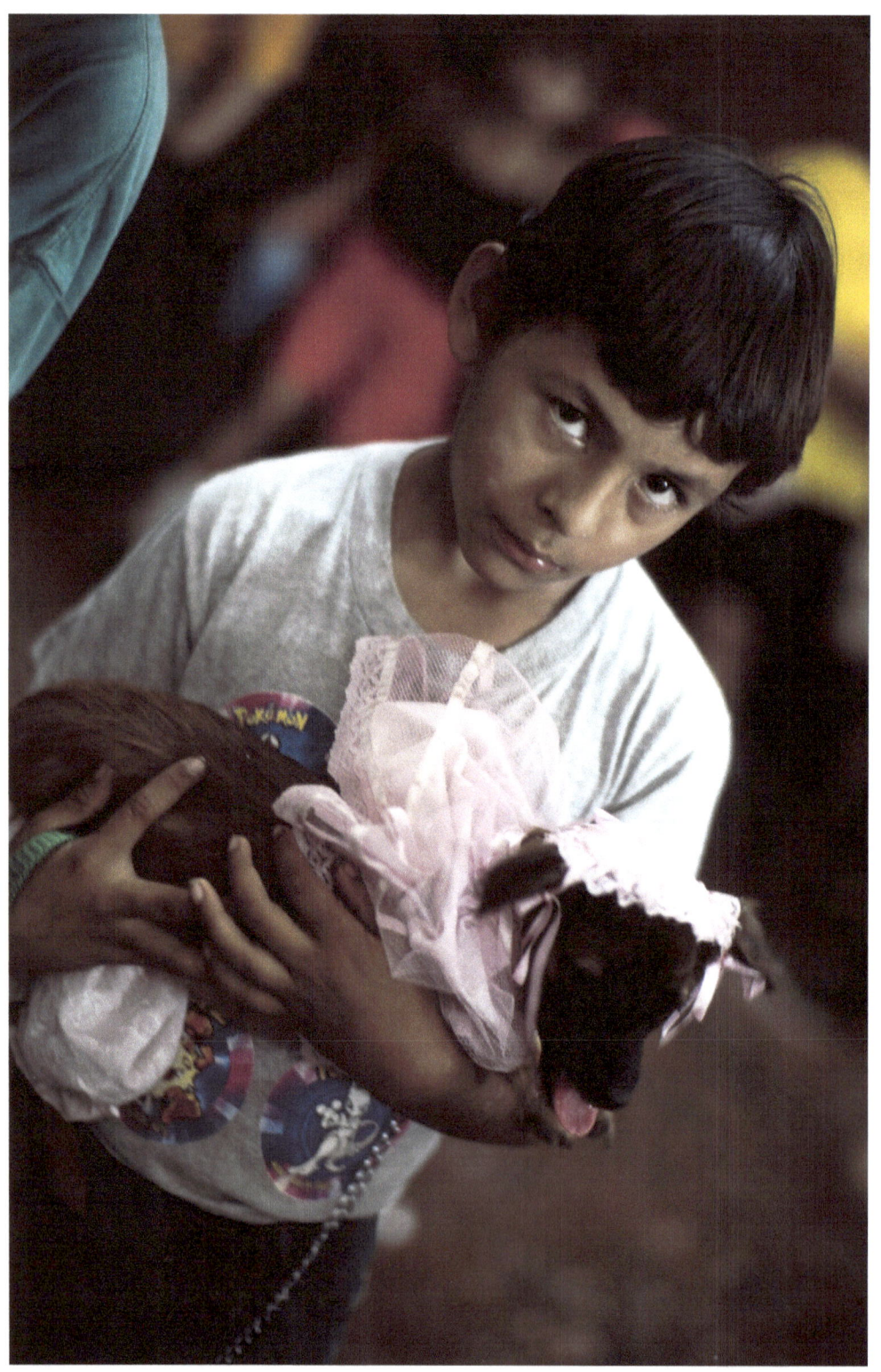

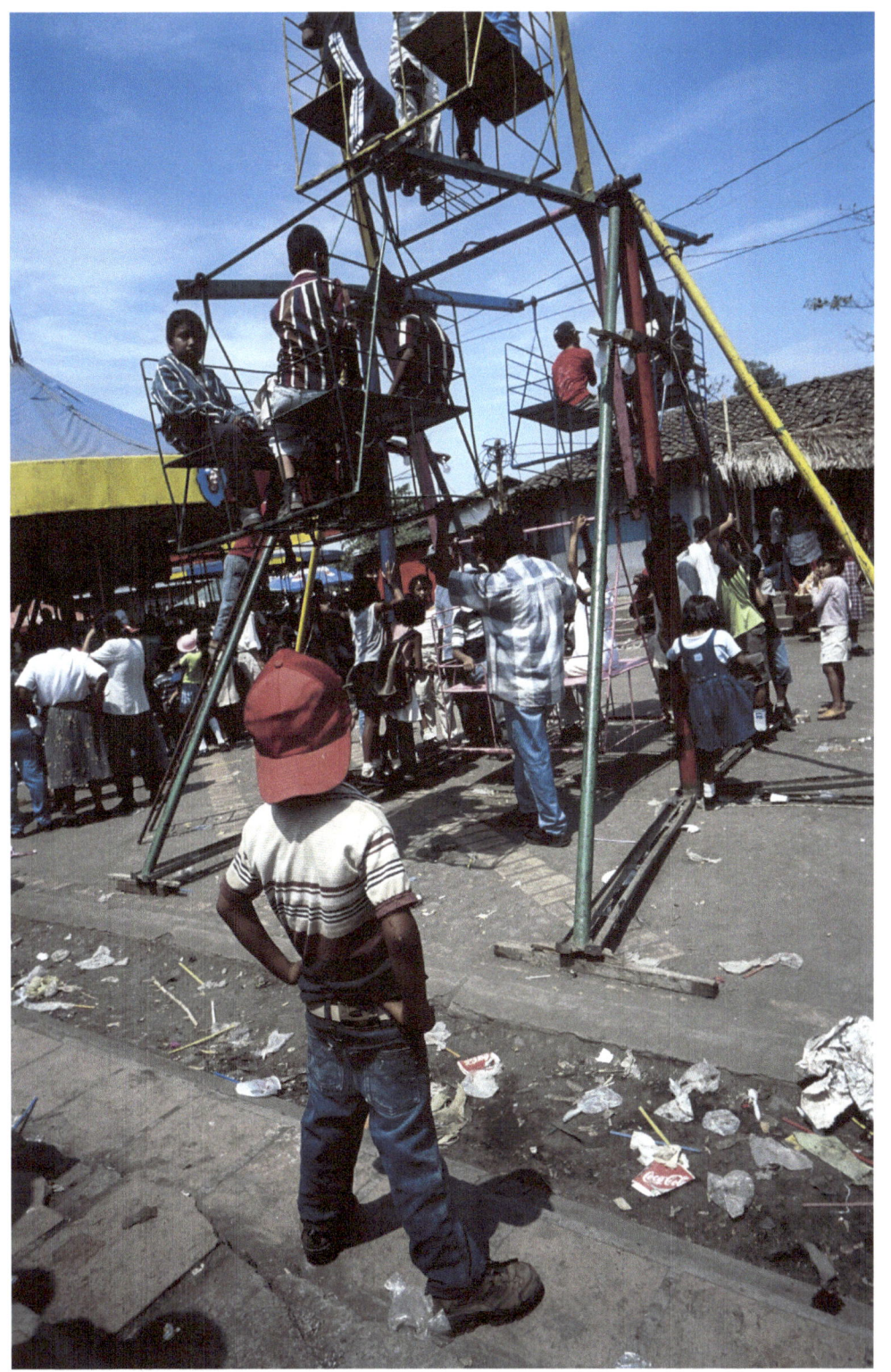

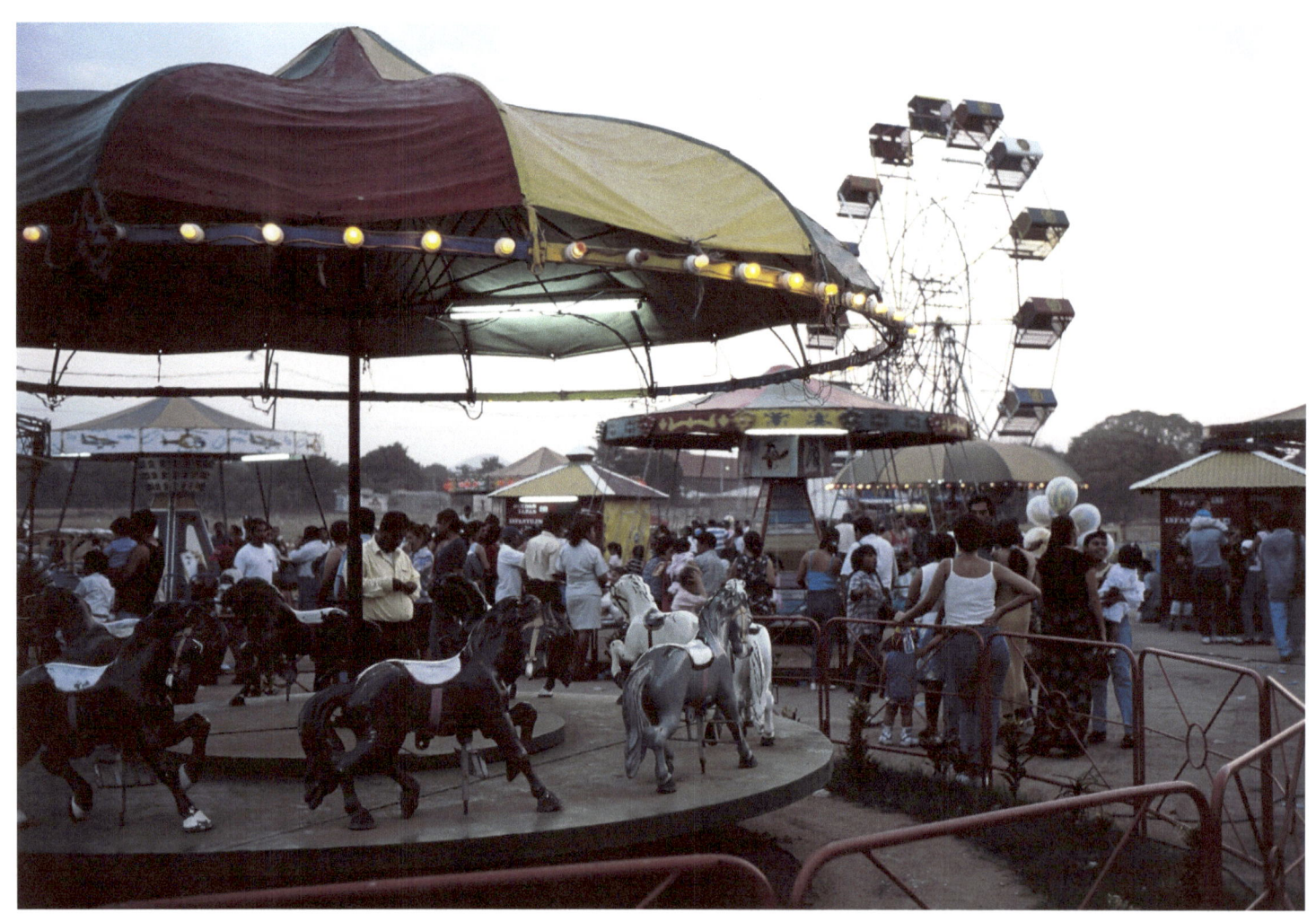

Managua: Sunday afternoon in the amusement park

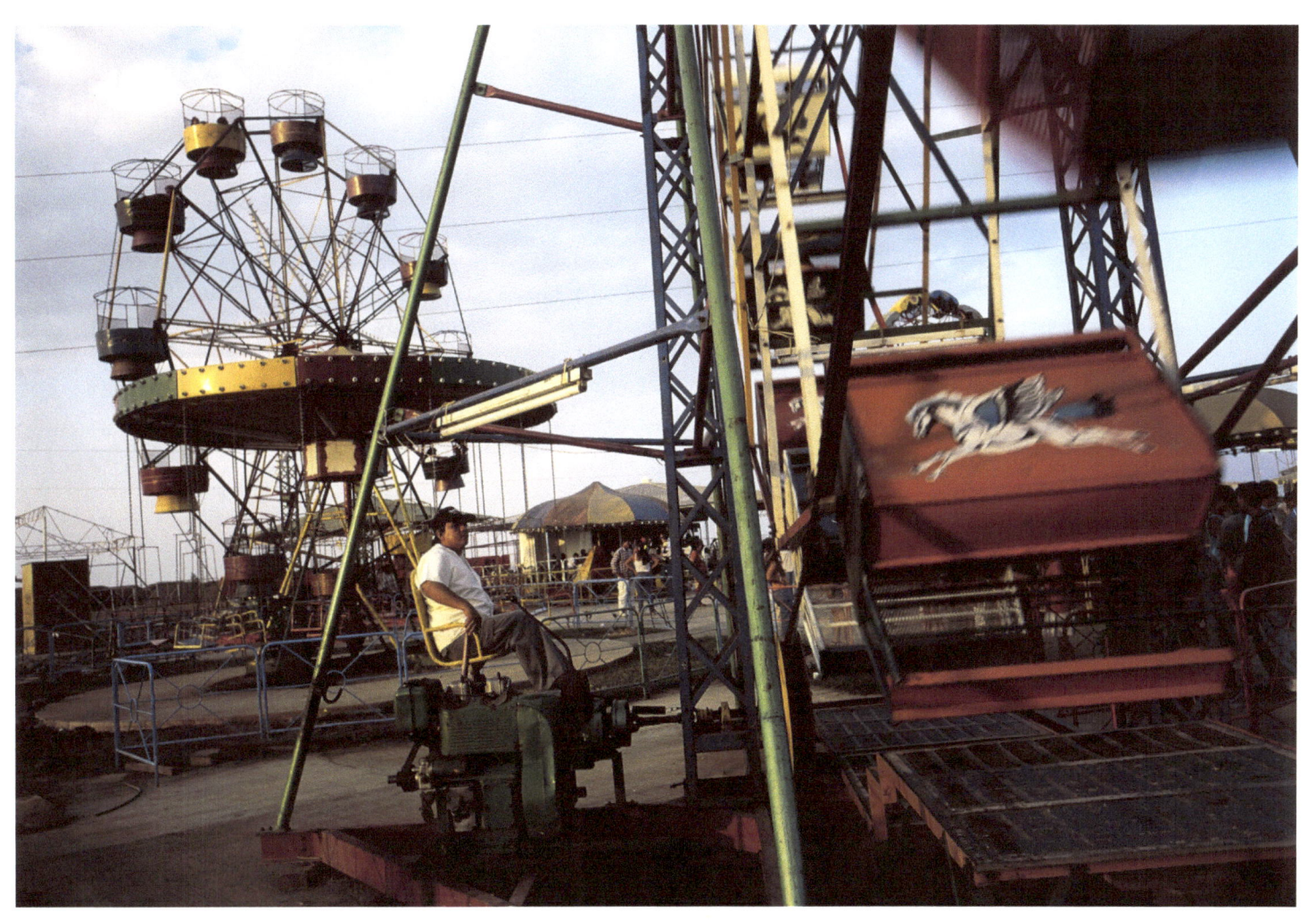

Managua: Sunday afternoon in the amusement park

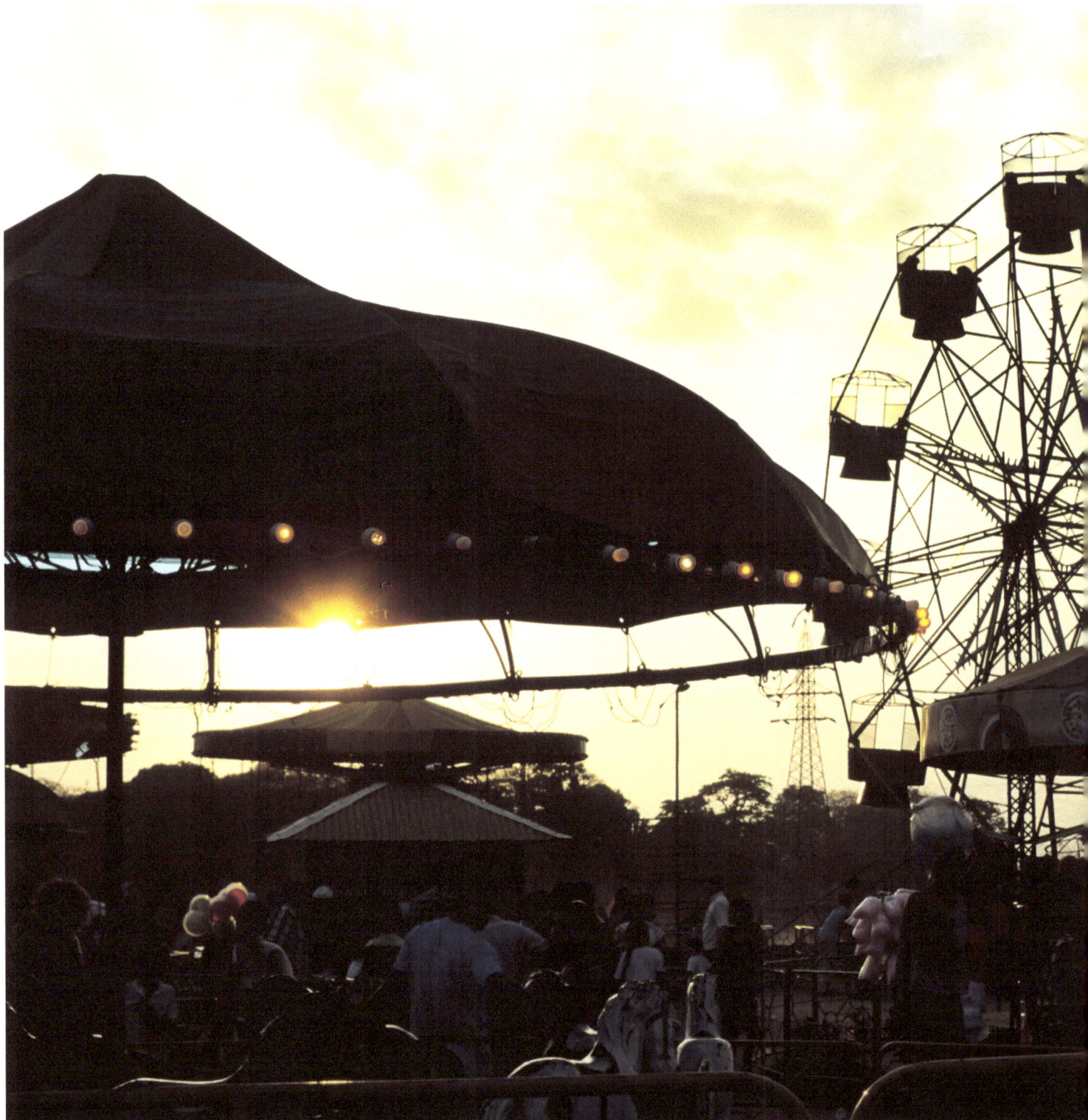

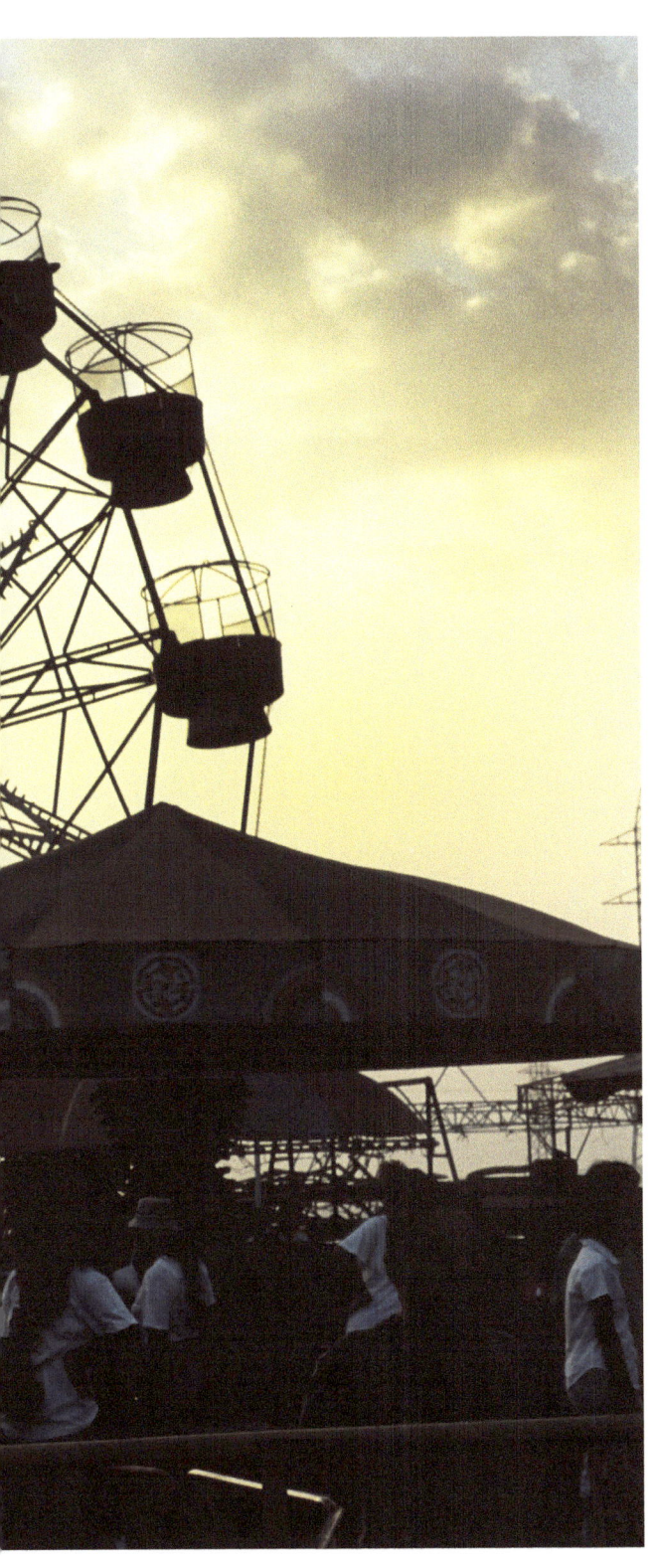

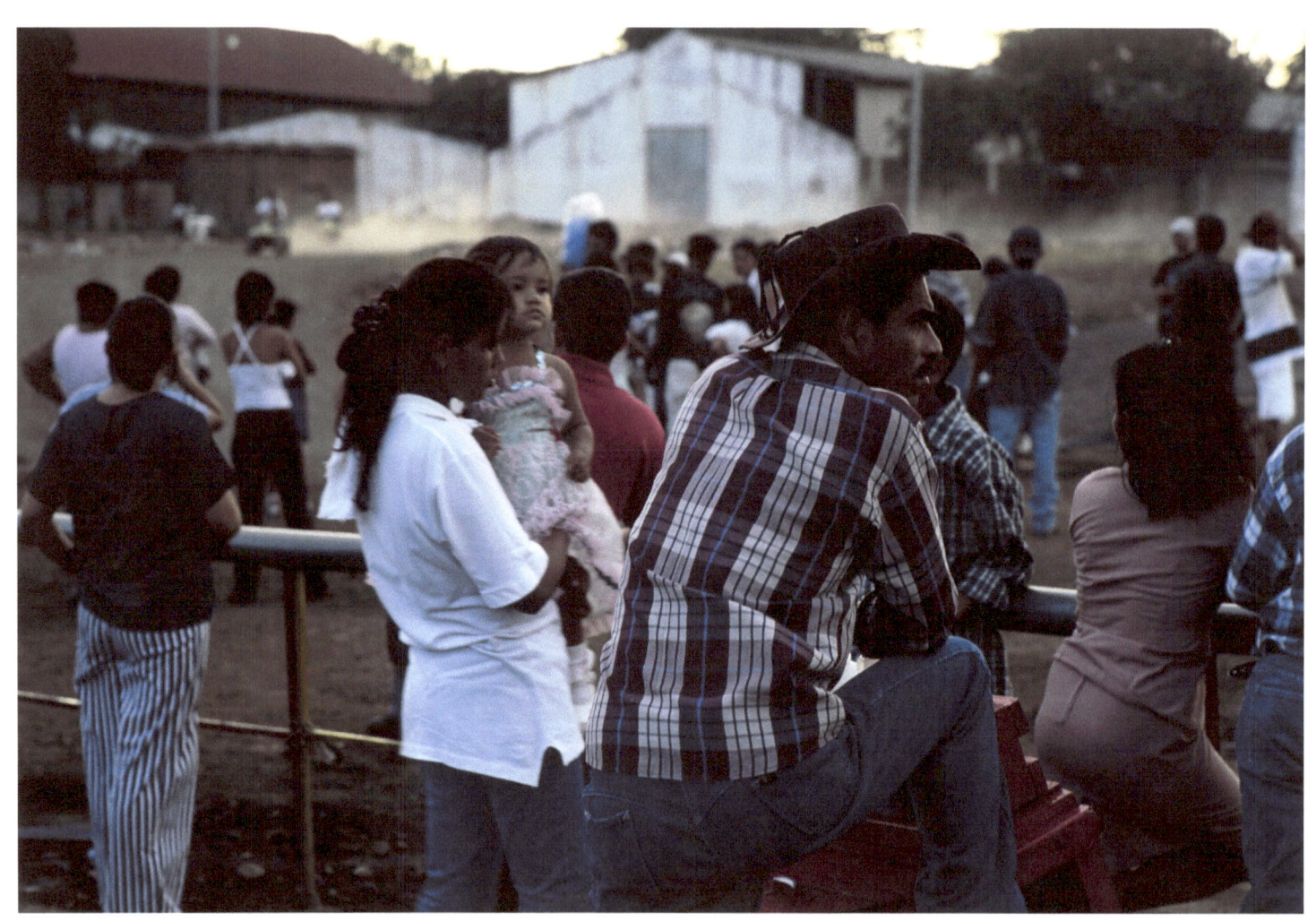

Managua: Sunday afternoon in the amusement park

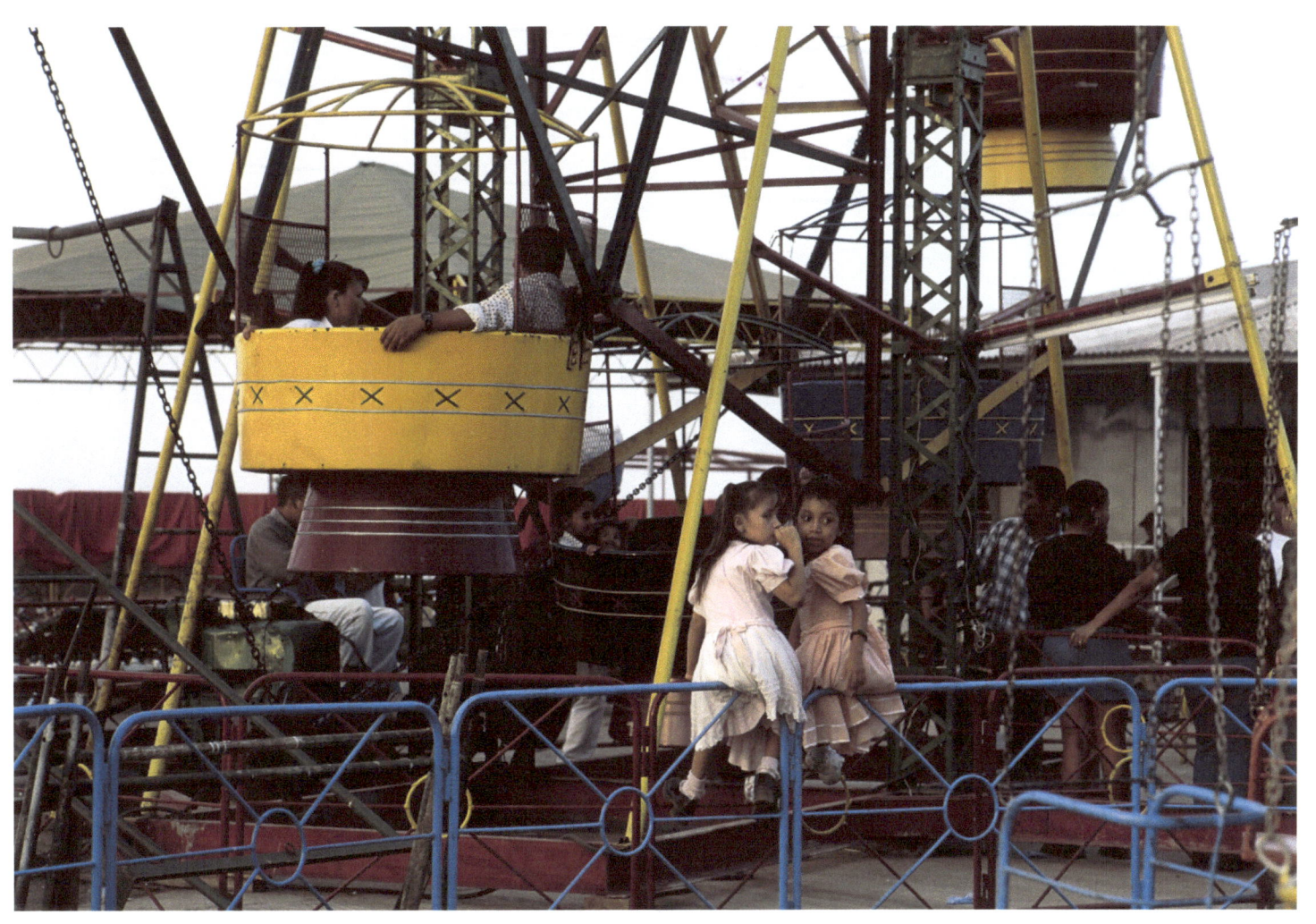

Managua: Sunday afternoon in the amusement park

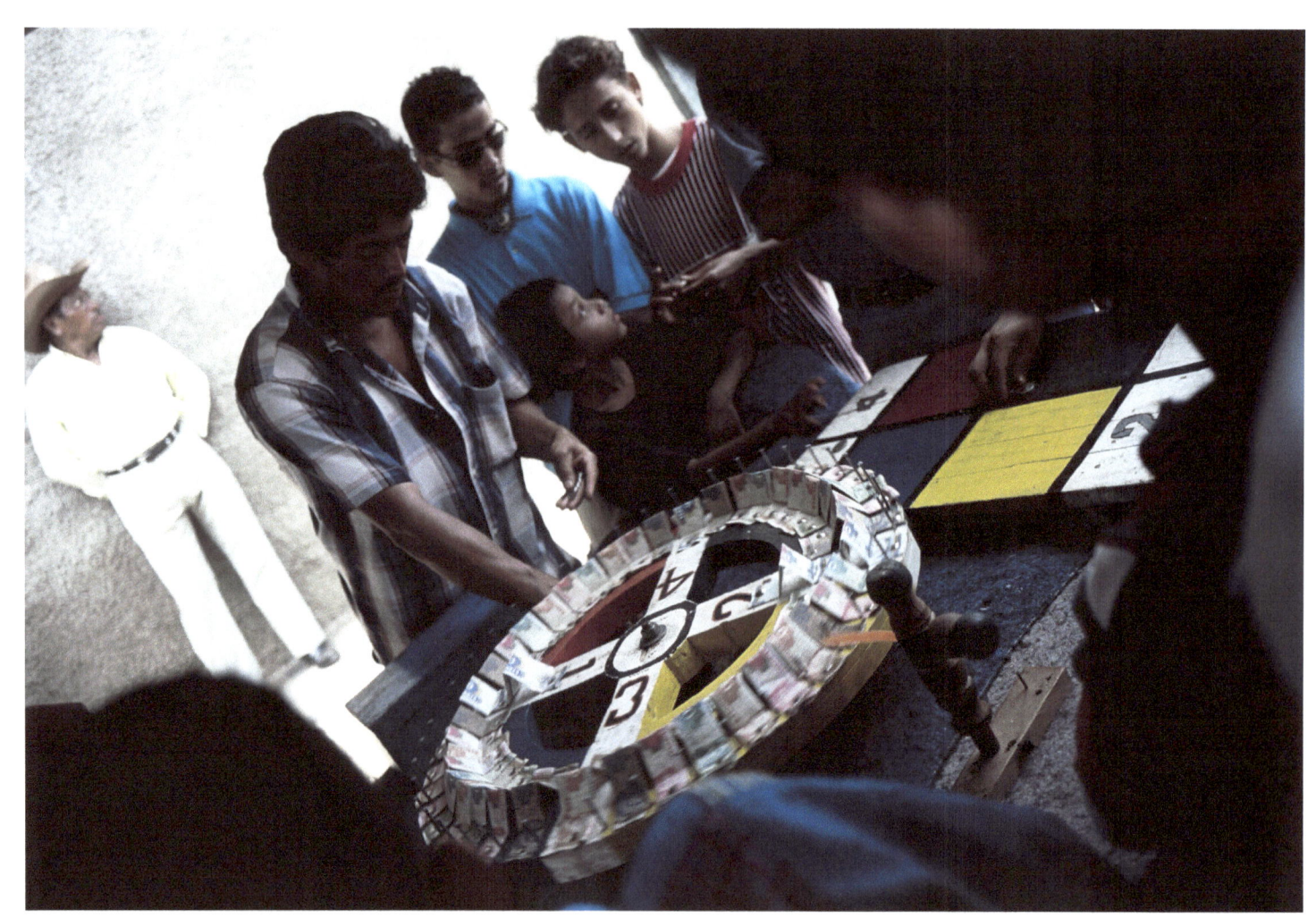
Leon: street roulette gambling

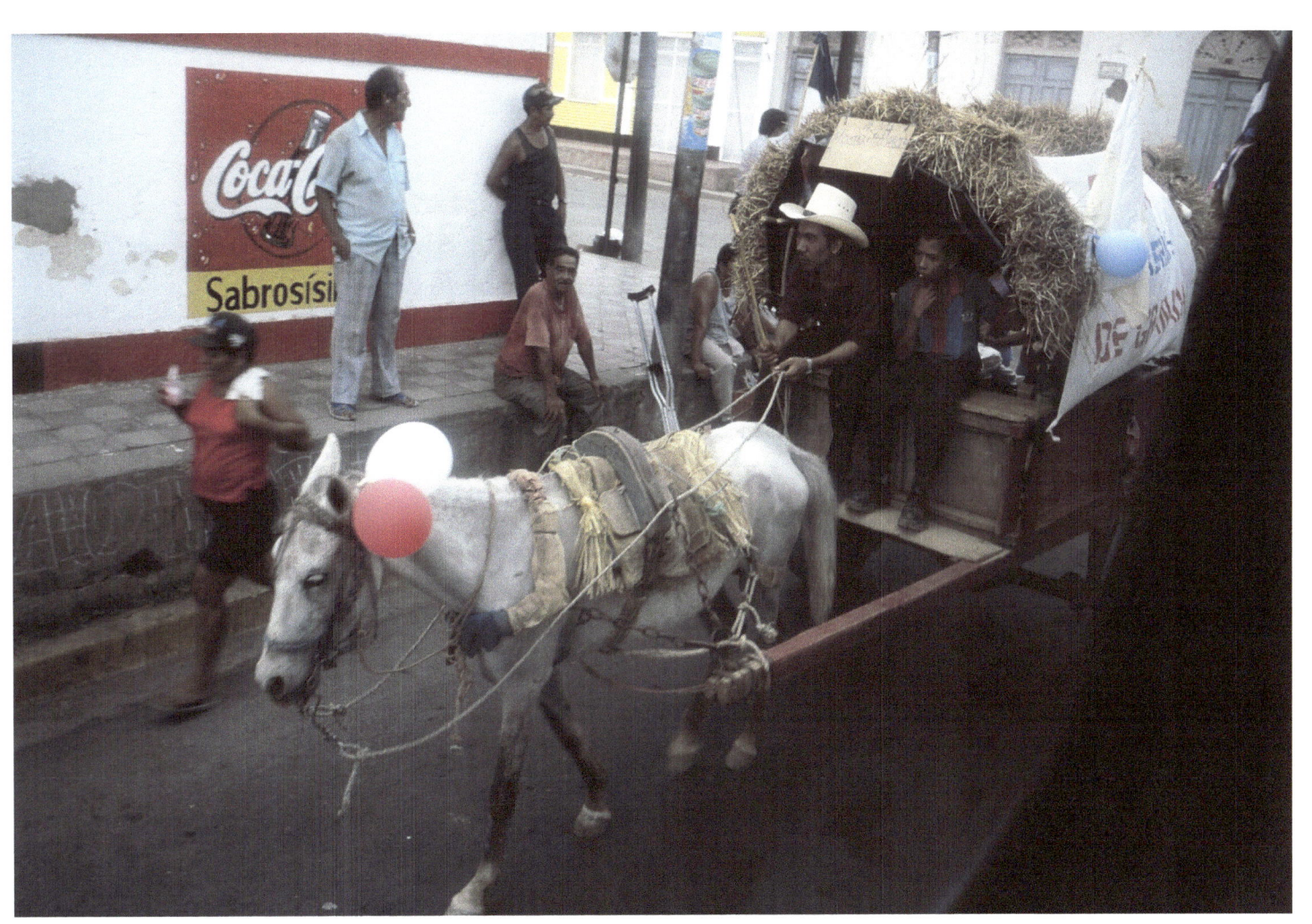
Street traffic in Leon

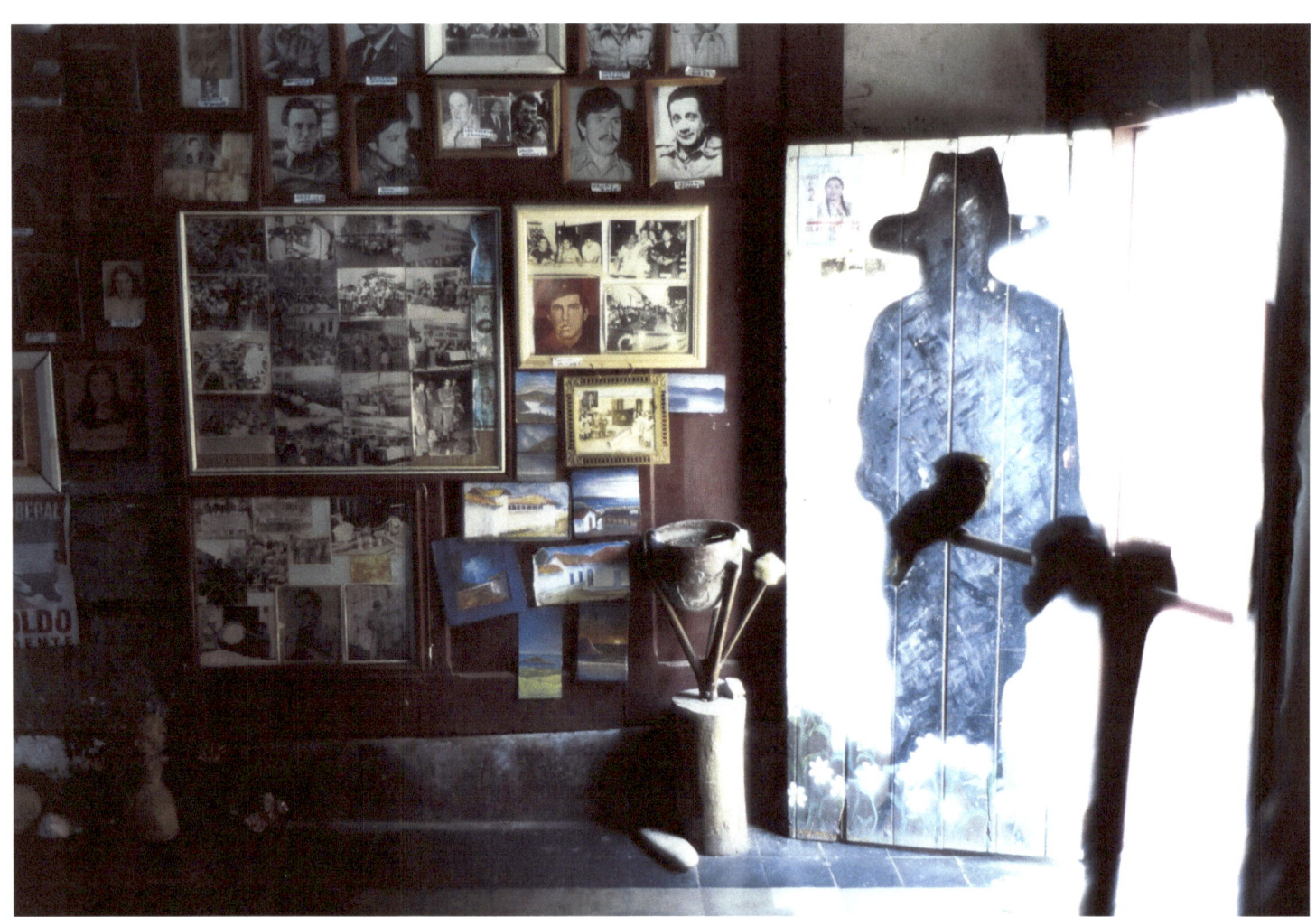

What is left of the Sandinista Revolution was clear in this shoemaker shop in Leon and in the decadent Sandinista Club. Pictures and statues of Sandino, Christ and Donna Summer were exposed side by side in a pantheon that, incredibly, made sense.

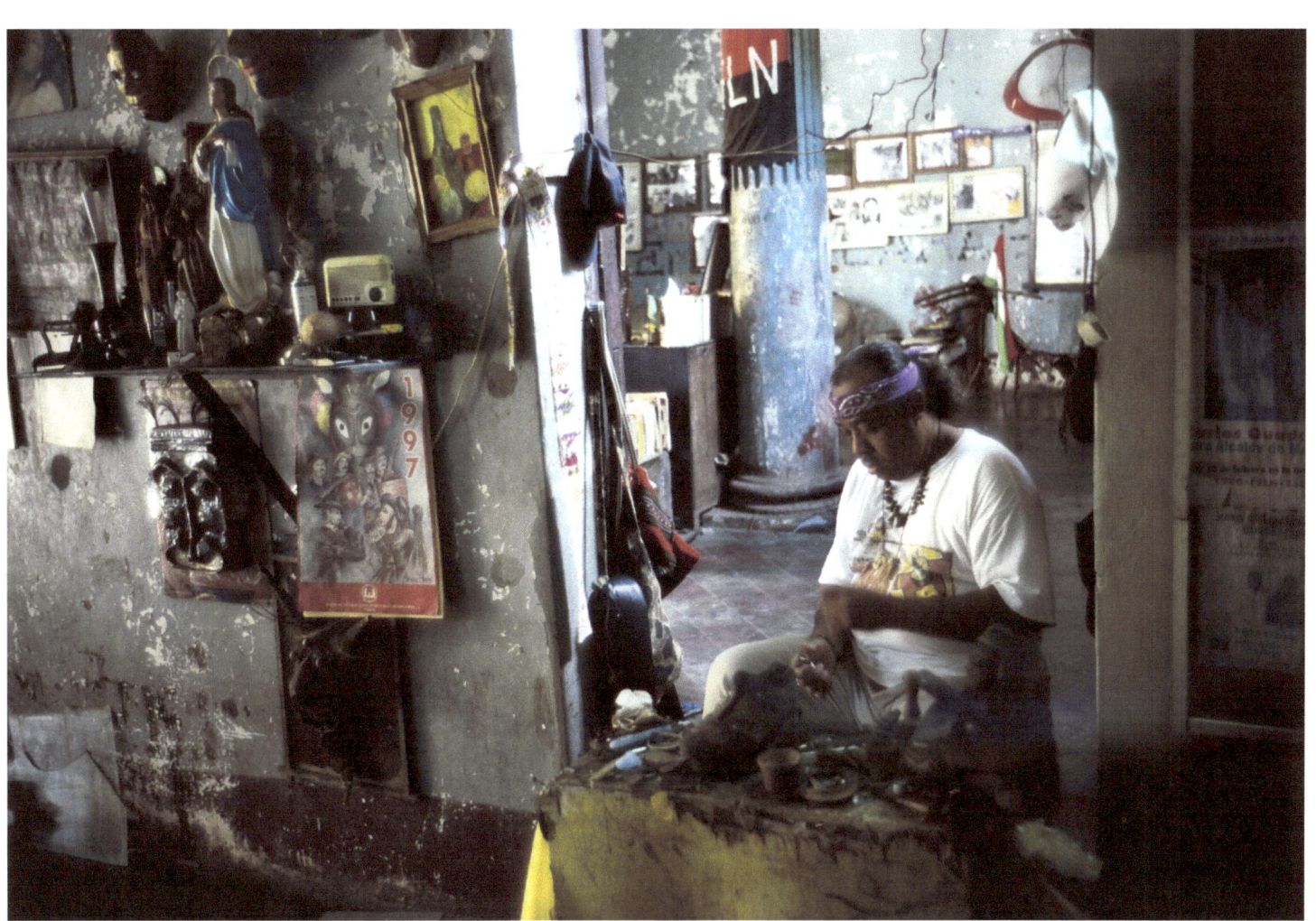

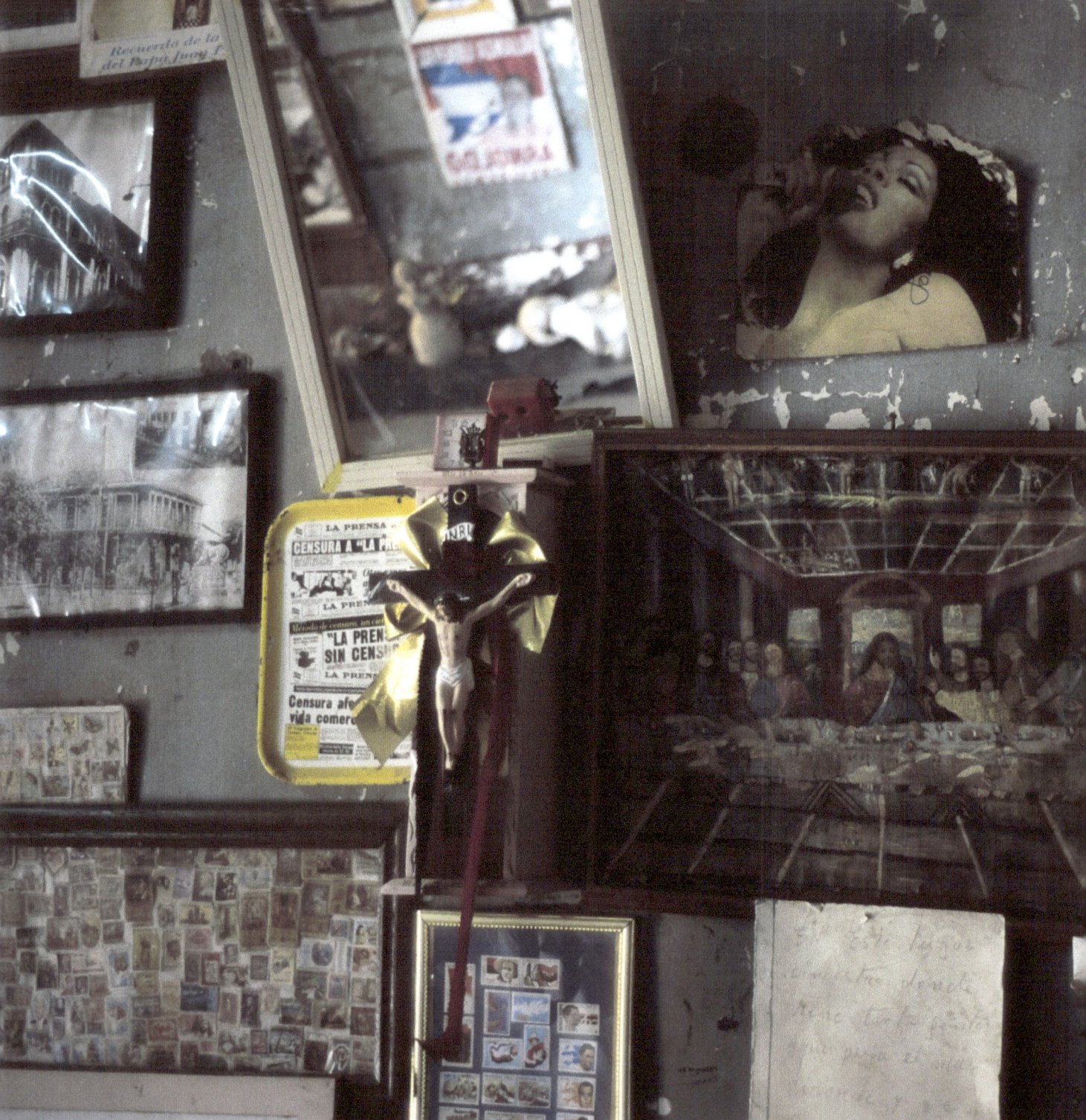

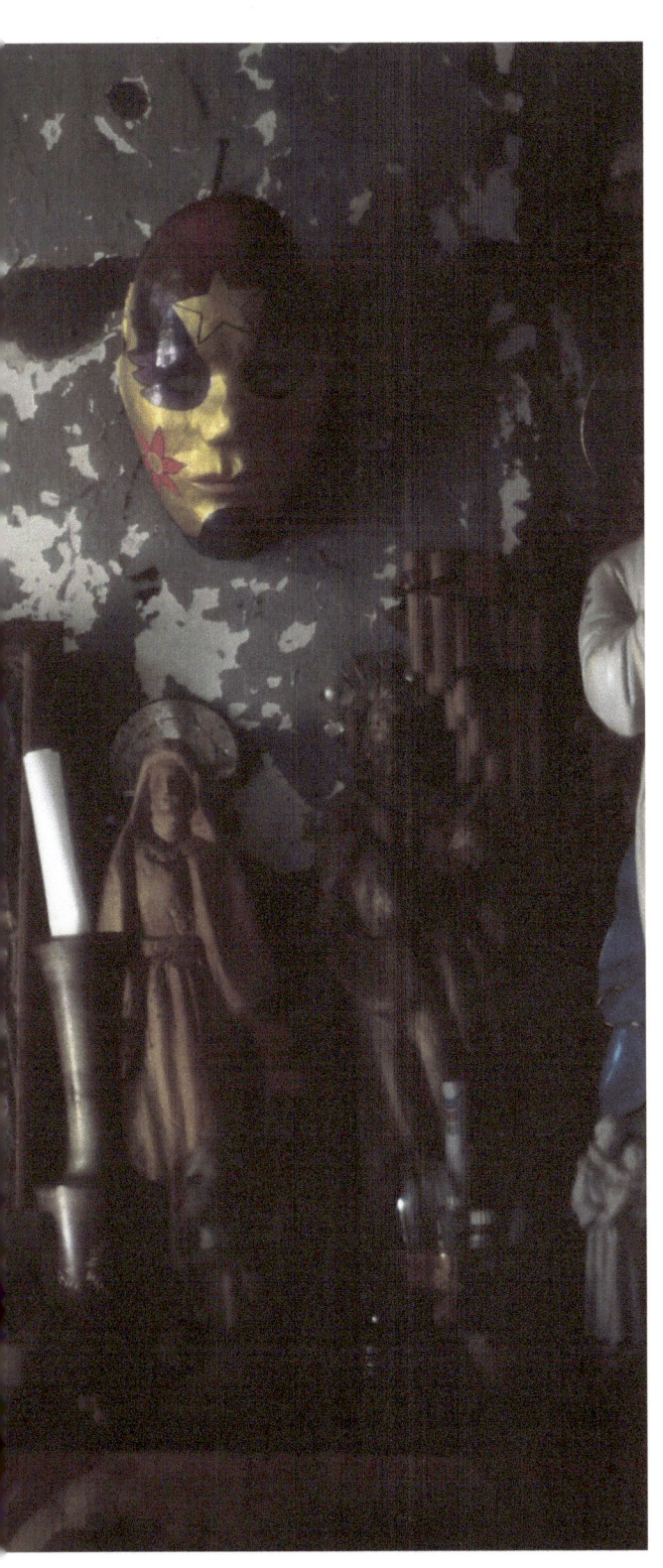

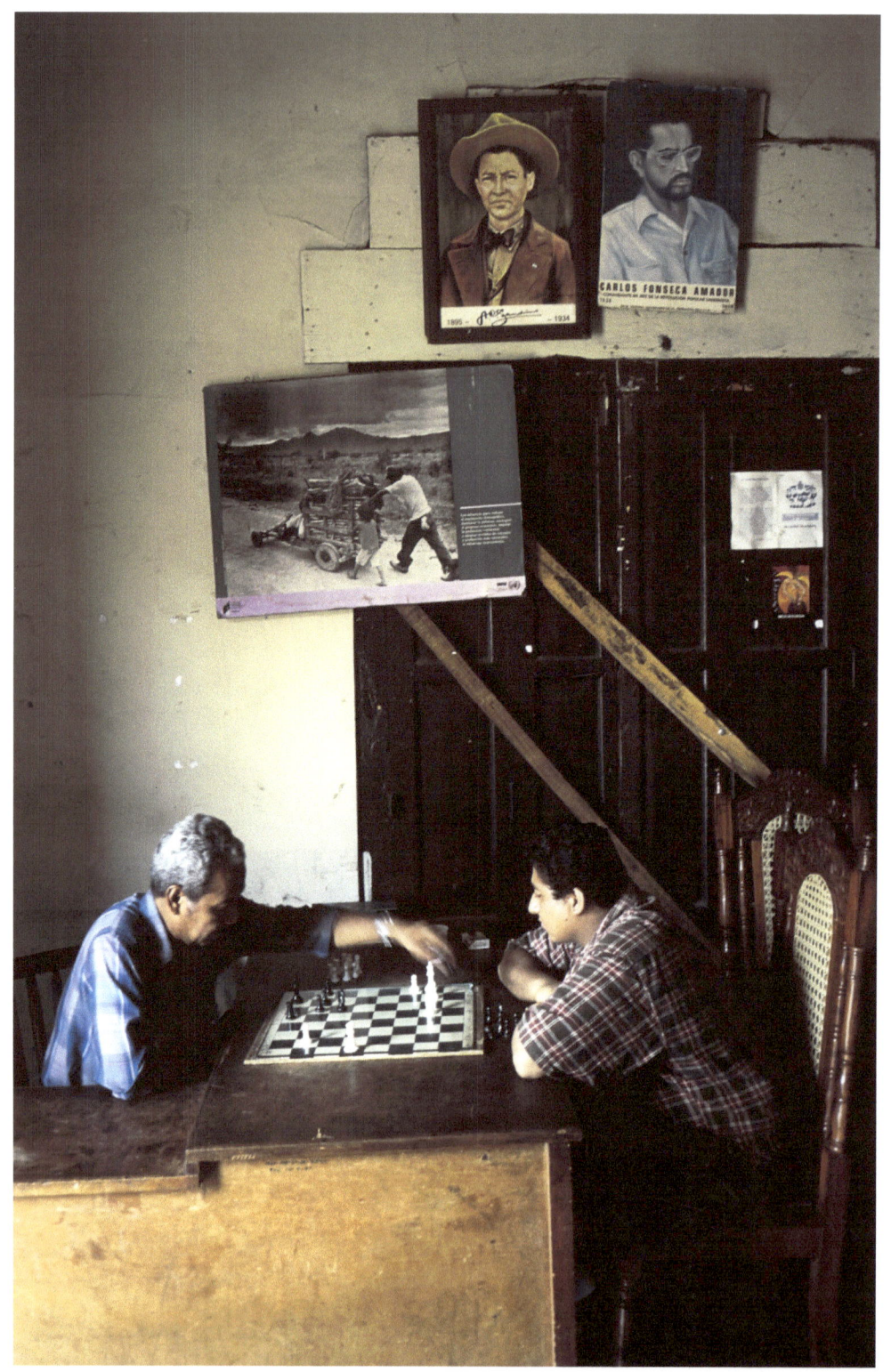

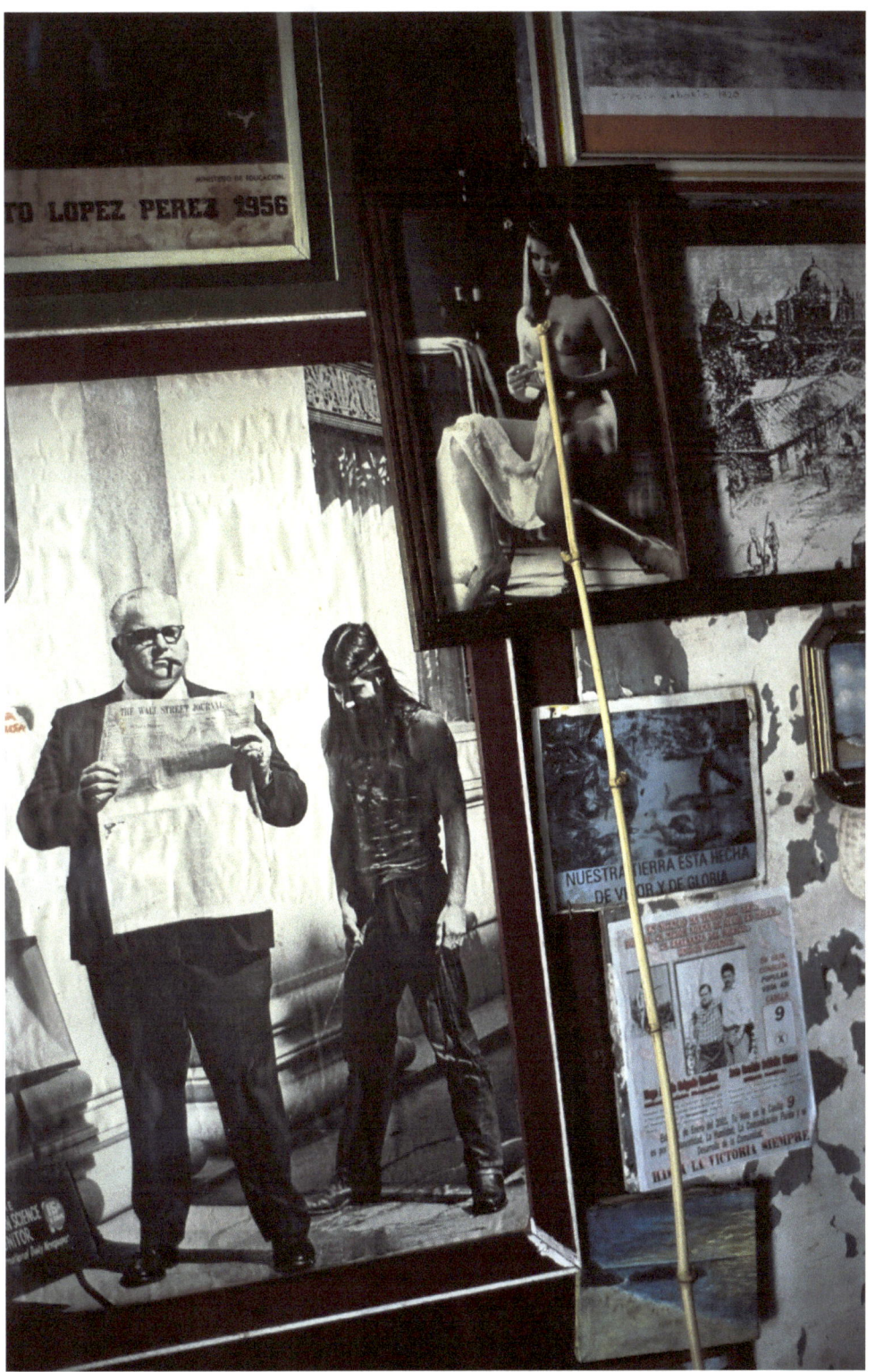

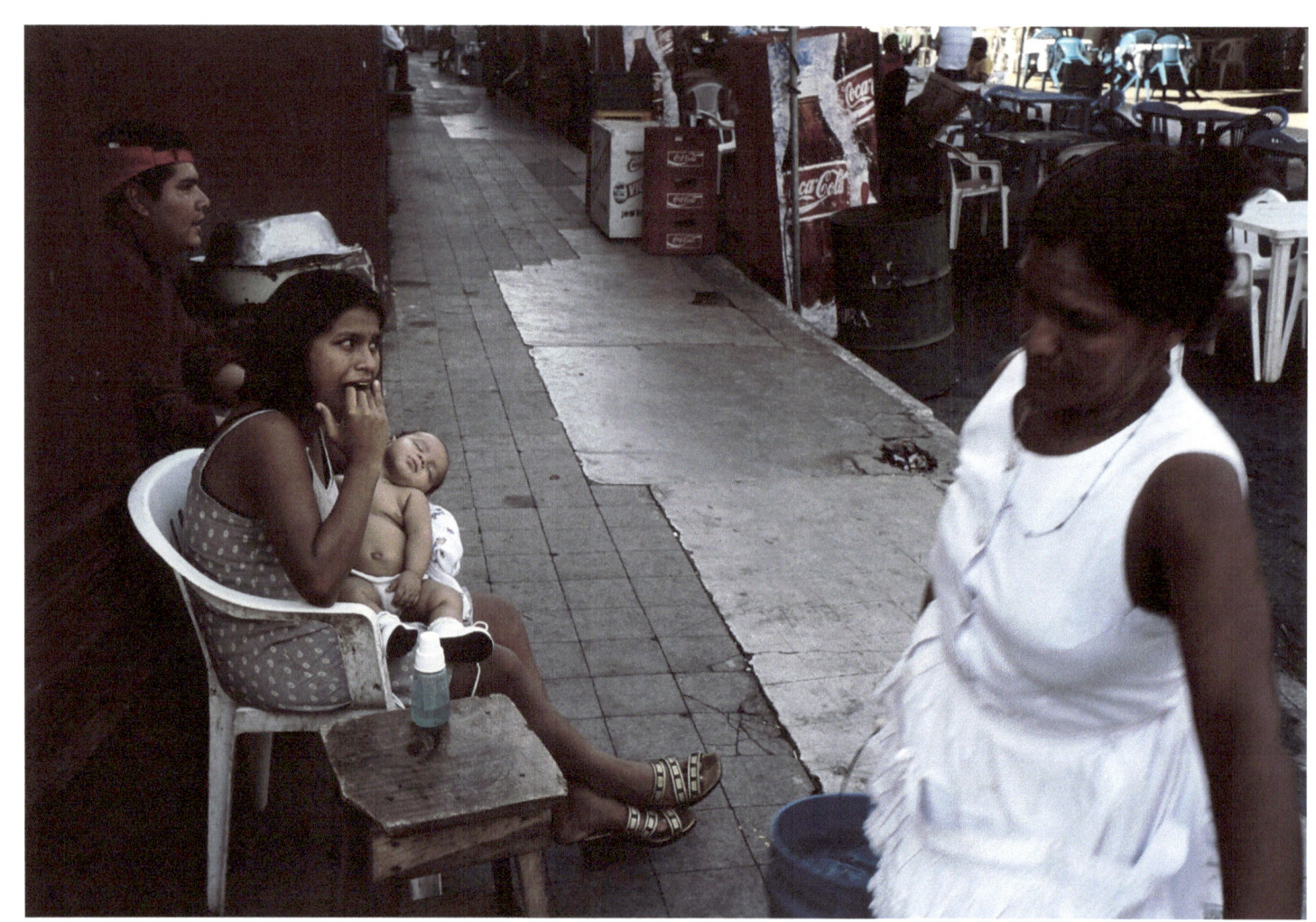

Street life in Leon

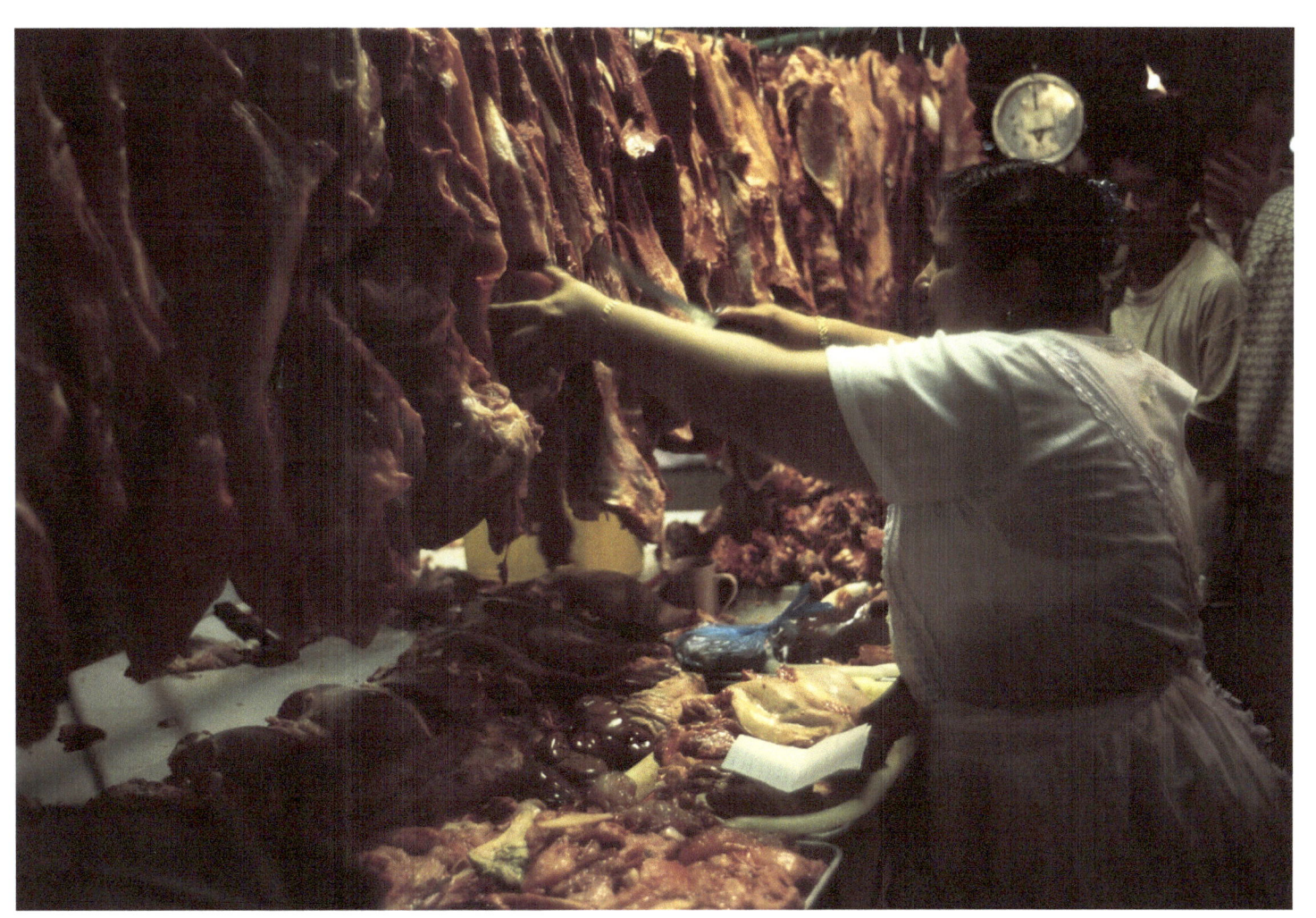

The Leon market

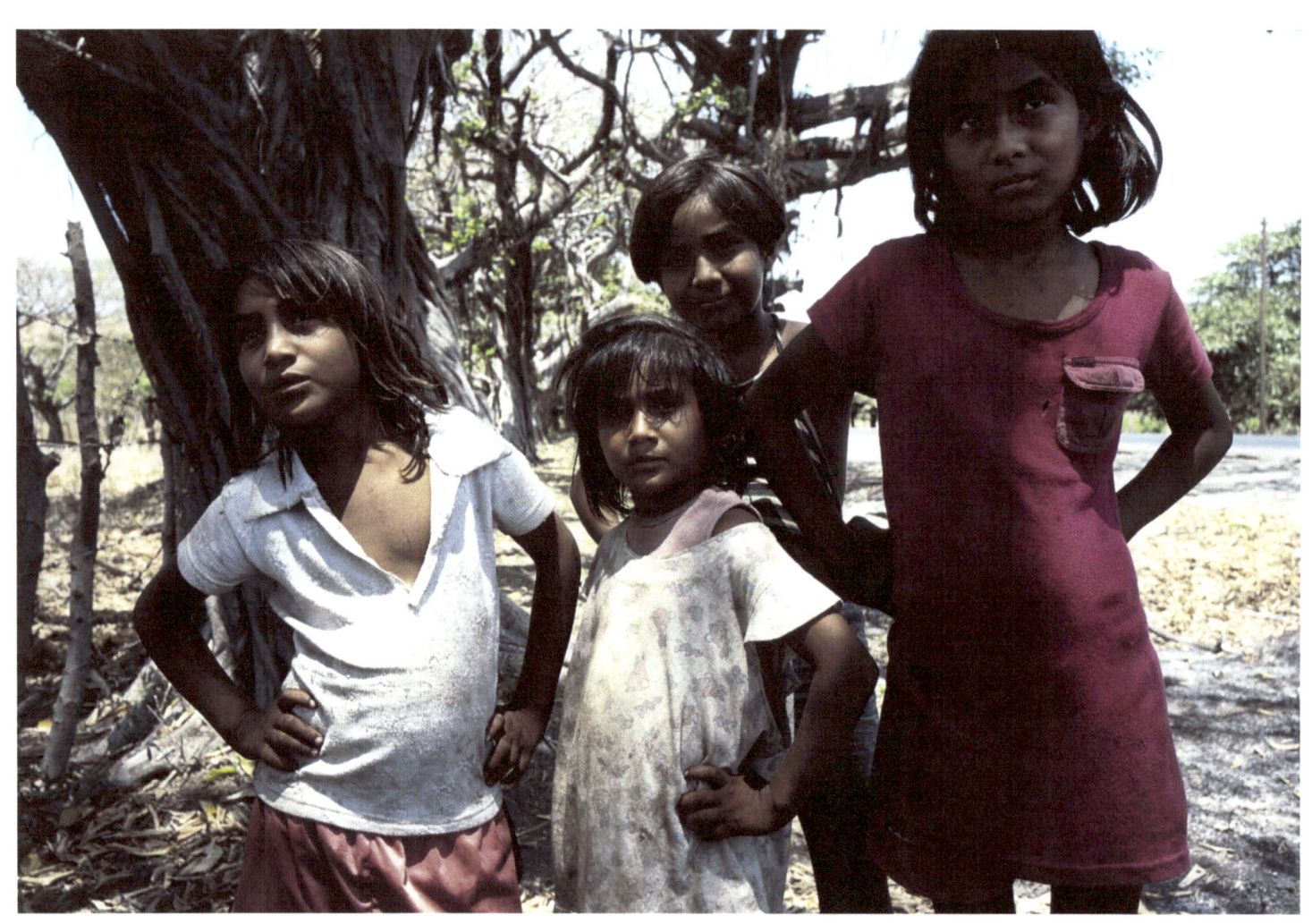
Girls living in a poor village along the Pan-American road

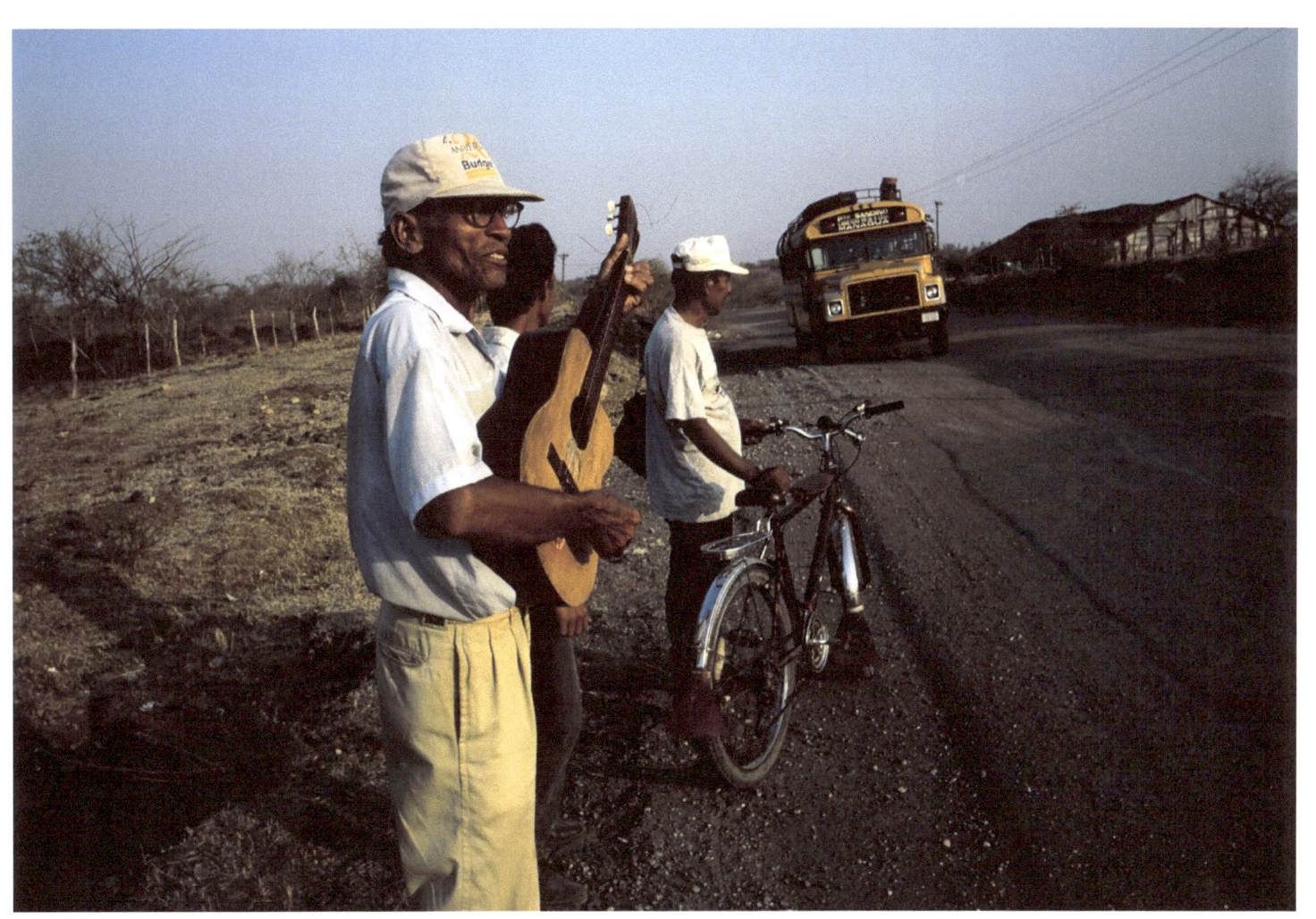

Waiting for the bus along the Pan-American road to Honduras

Honduras

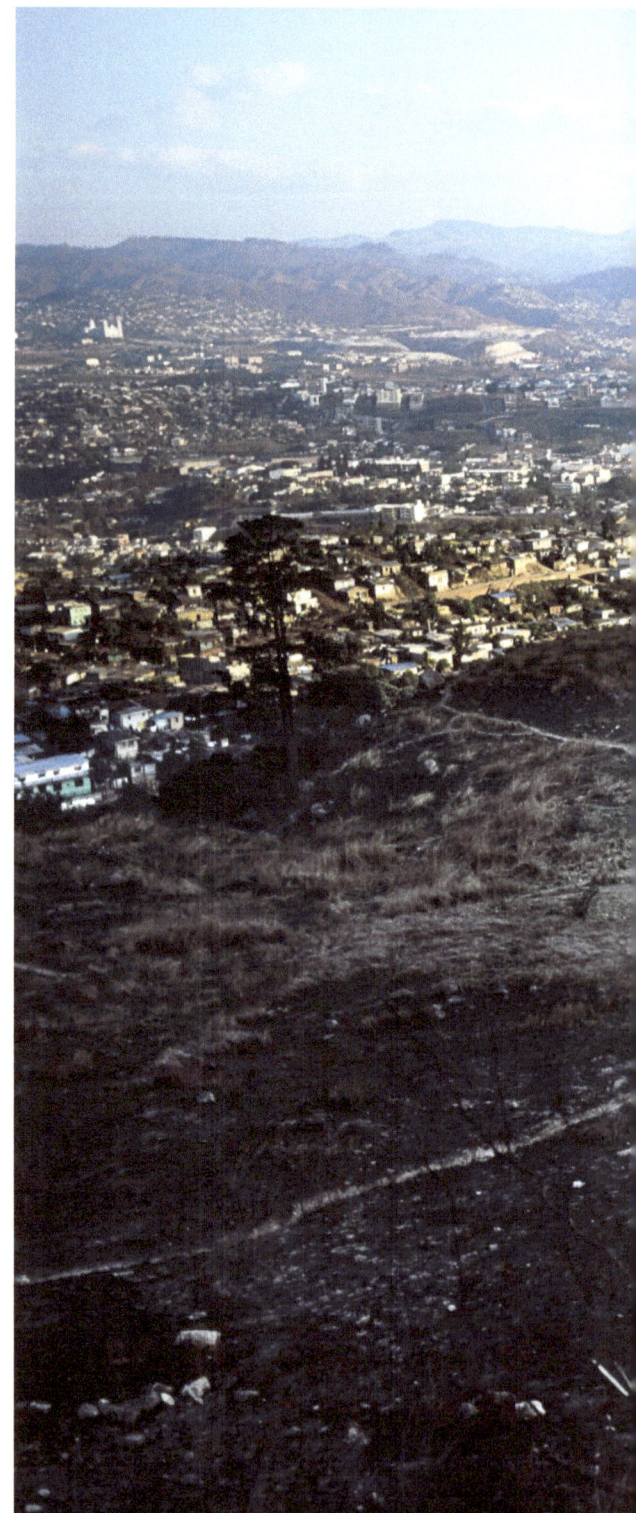

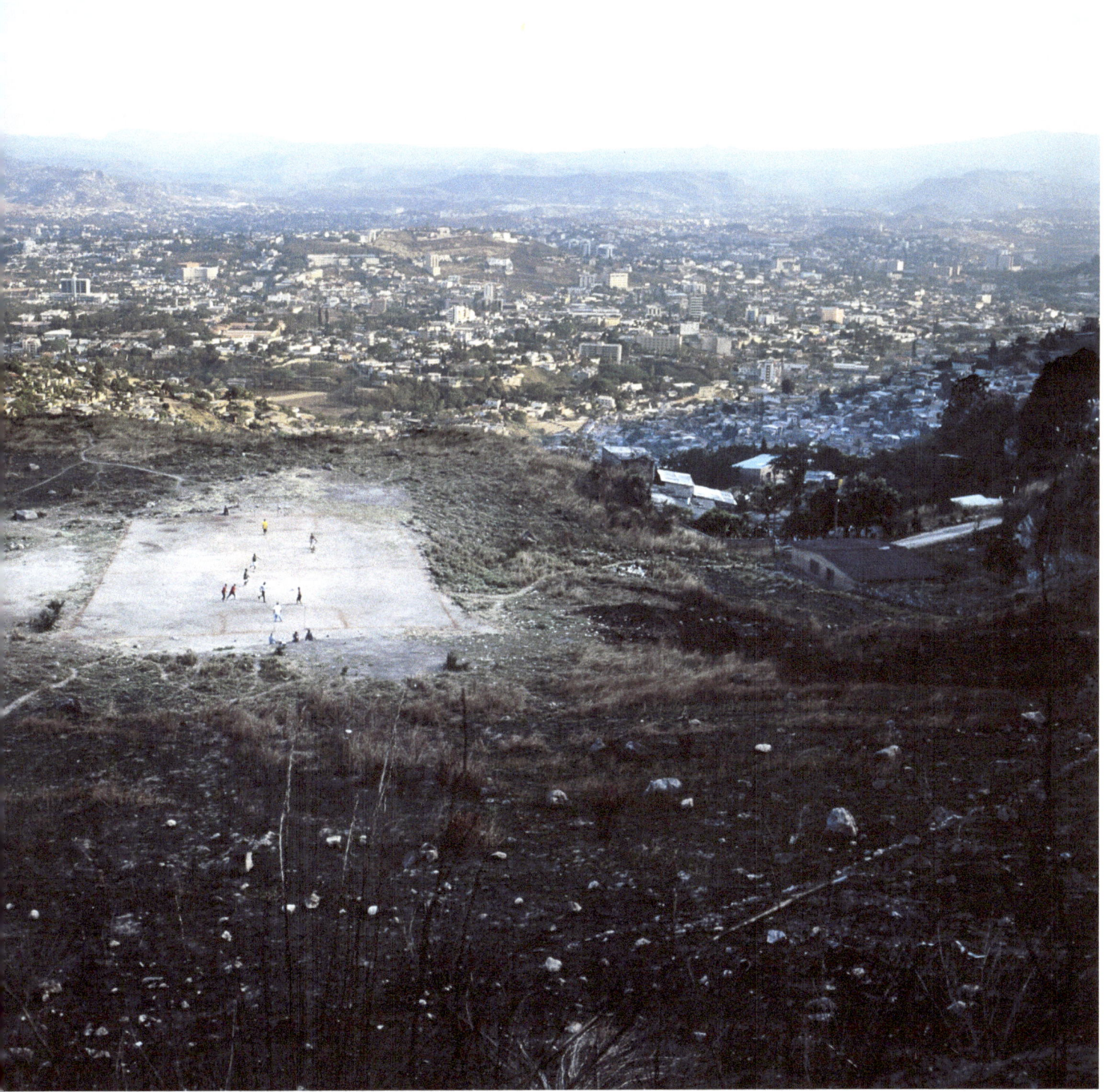

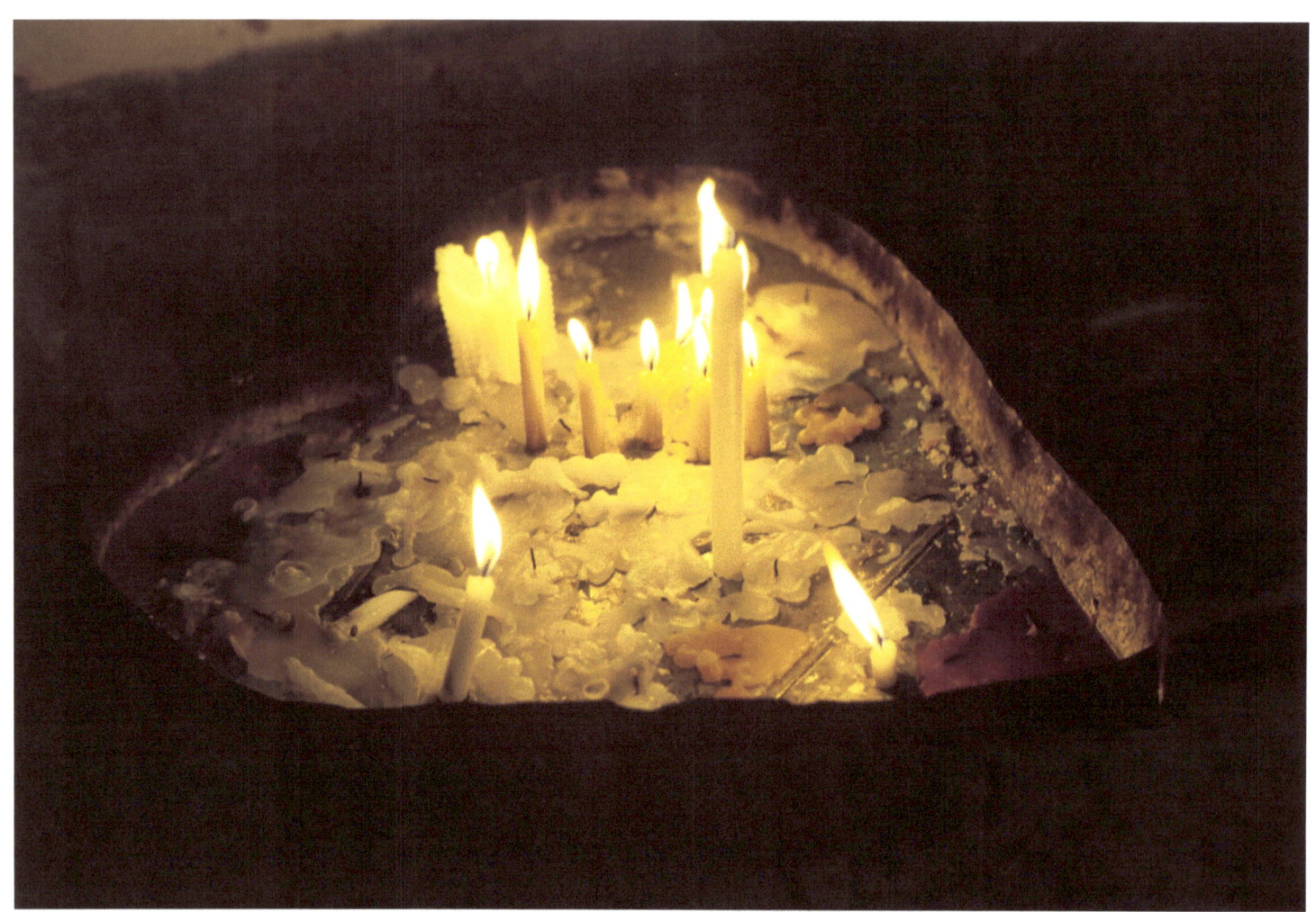

Honduras was even more tense then Nicaragua. There was not a single shop without an armed man standing guard. It was the most dangerous army in the world, far more dangerous then the criminals they were supposed to protect from.

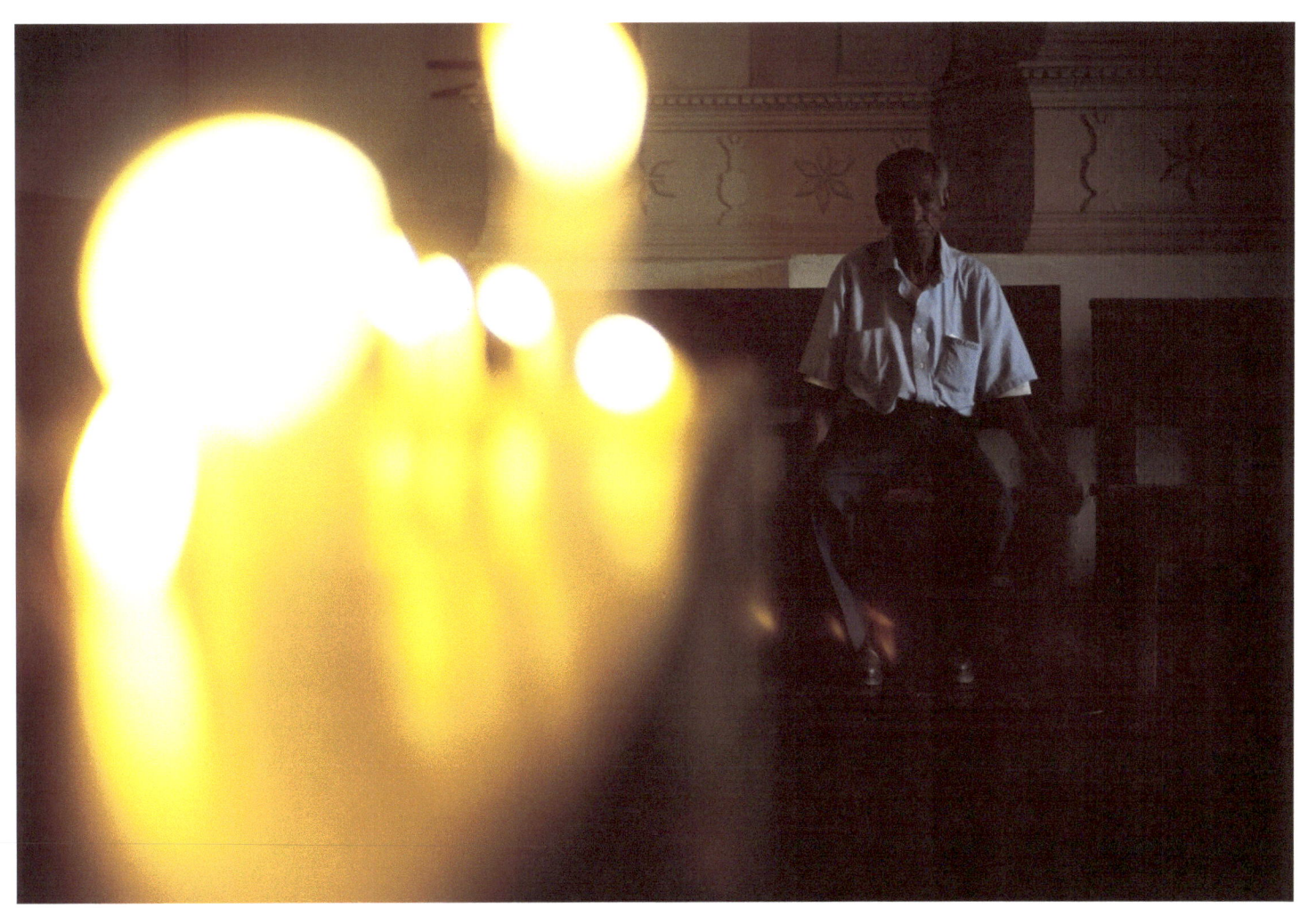

Tegucigalpa Cathedral

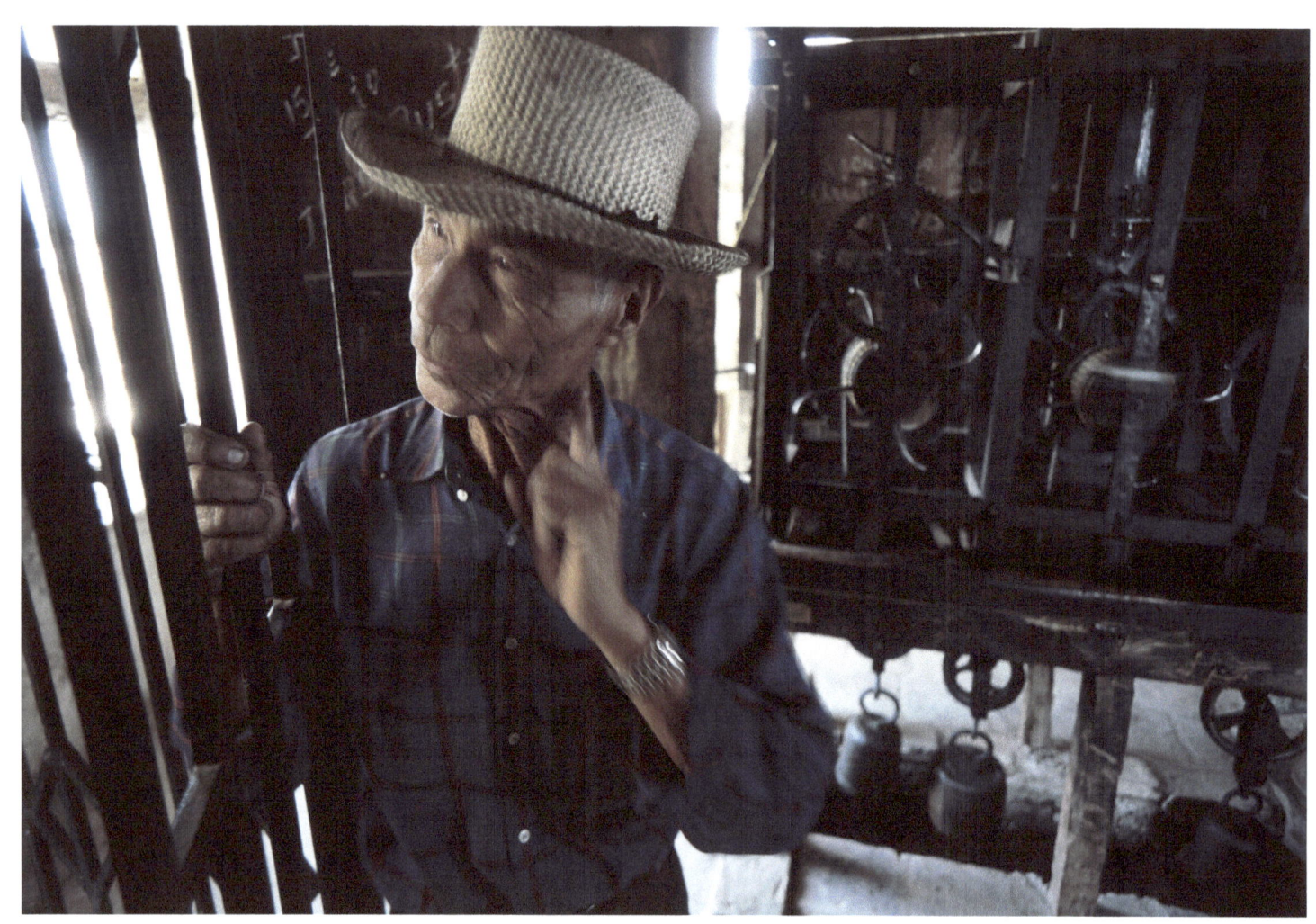

The clock tower warden in Tegucigalpa

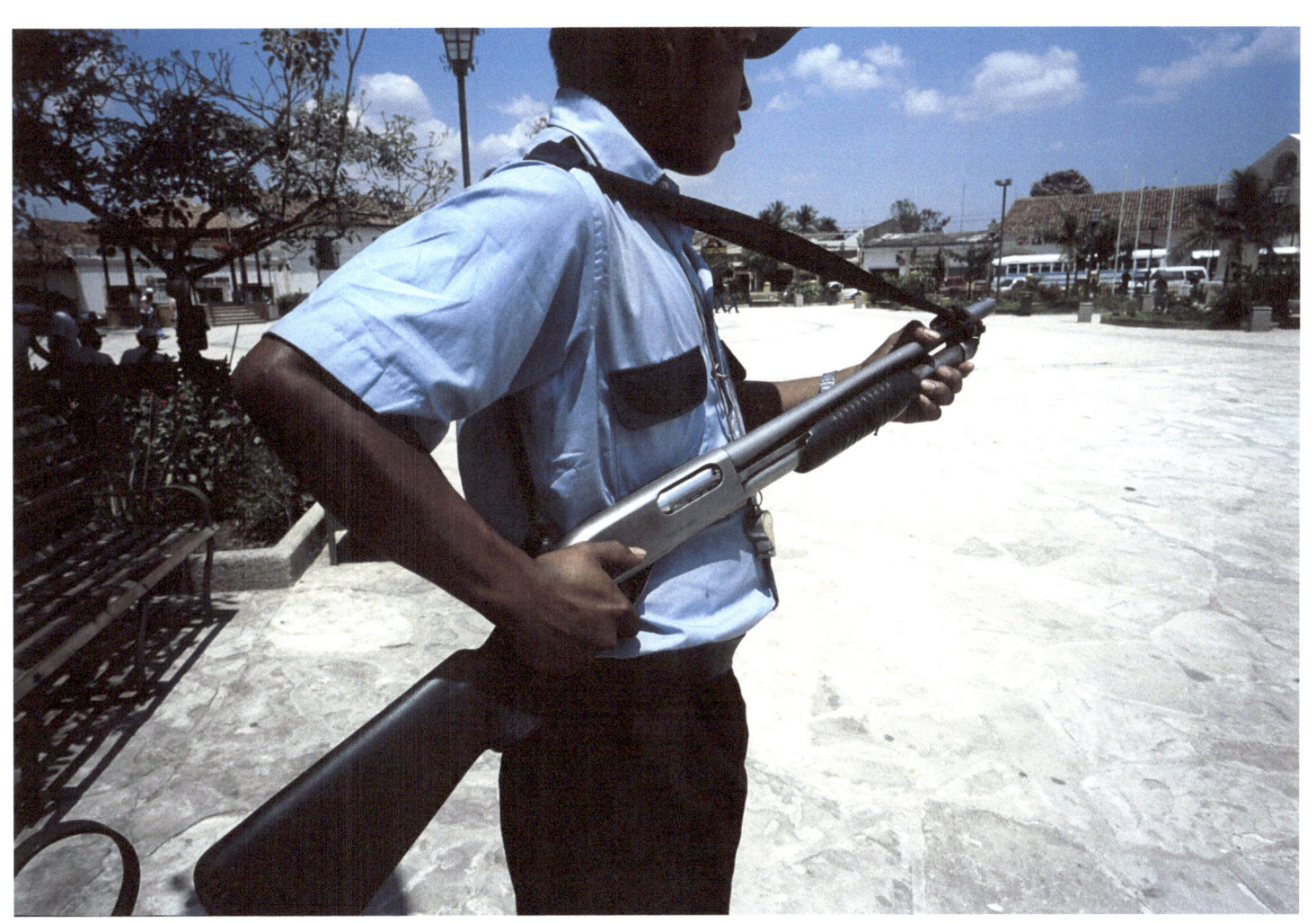

One of the countless vigilantes

El Salvador

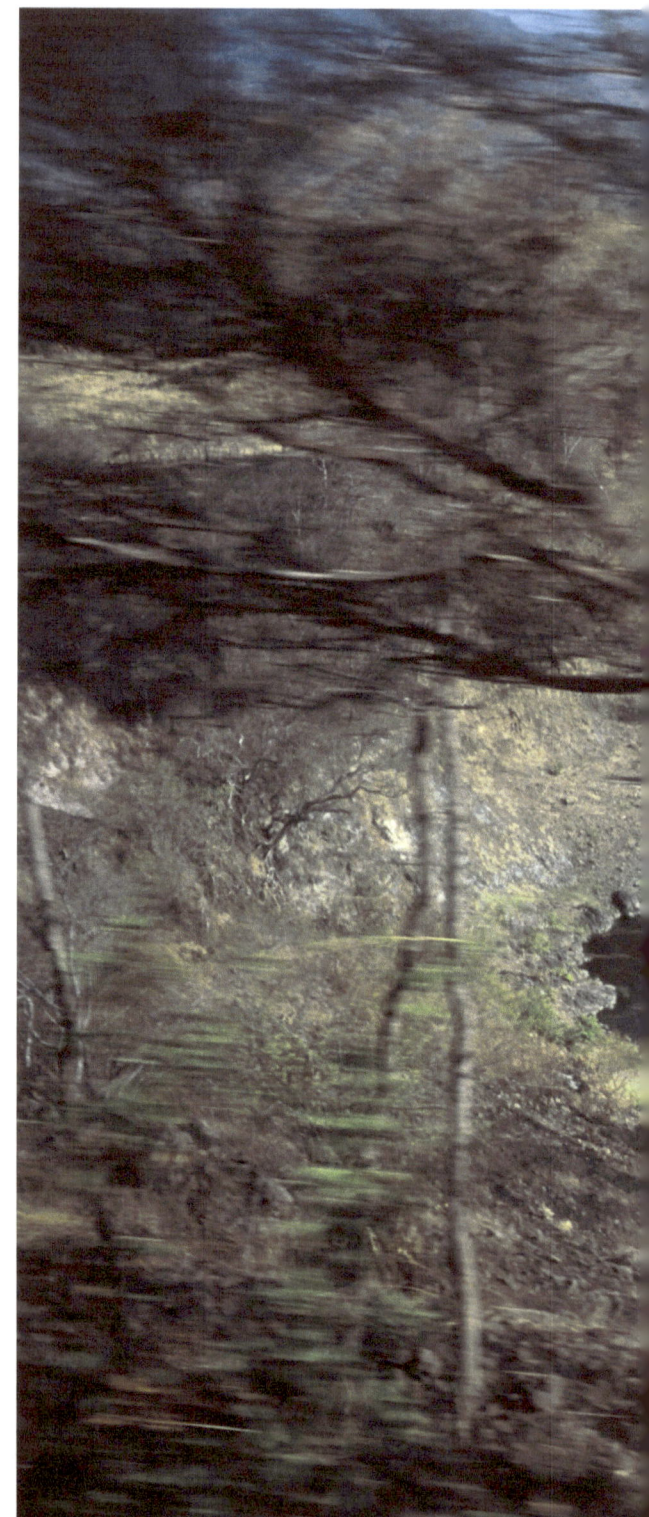

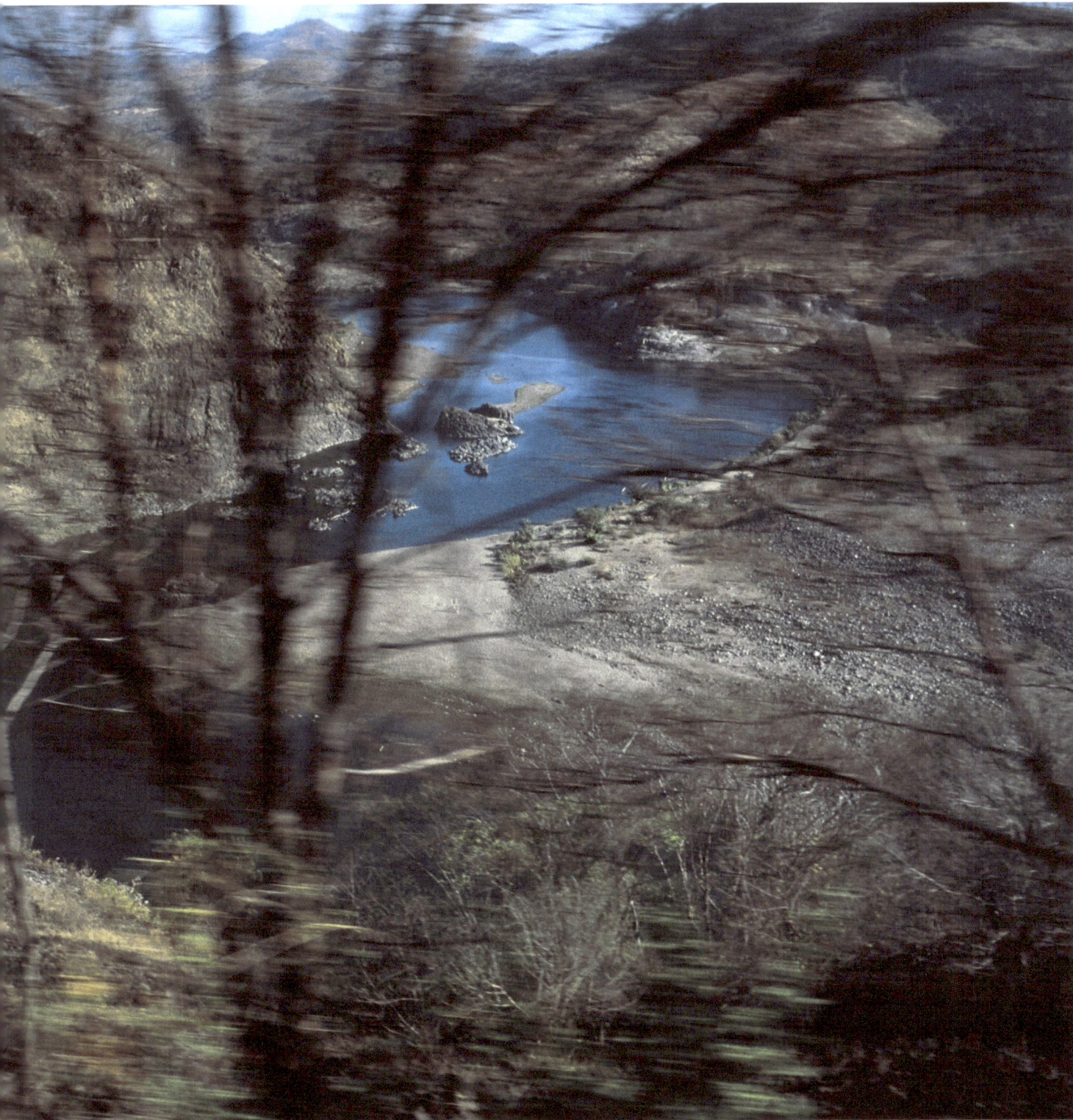

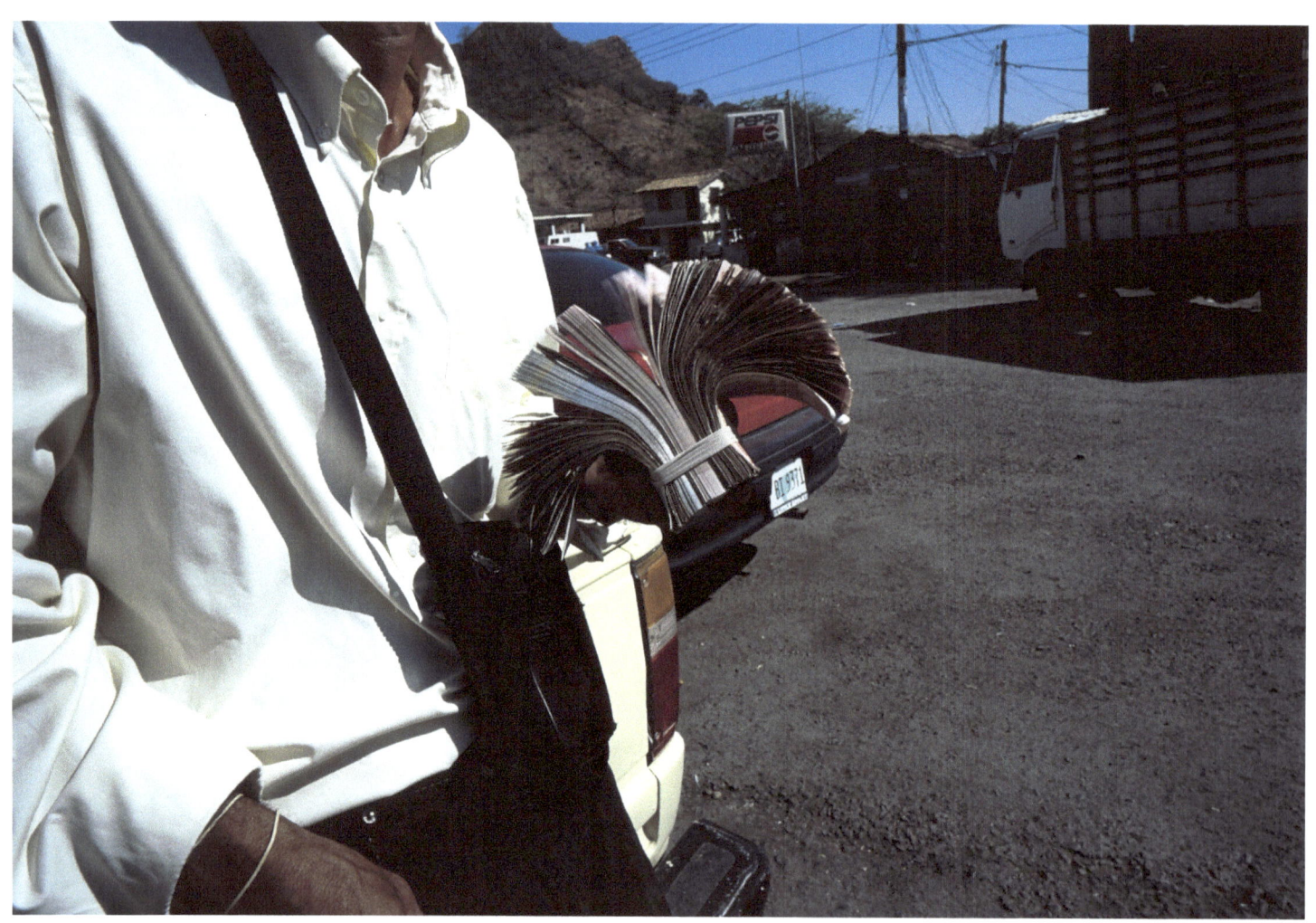

And then we got to El Salvador, the poorest country on the itinerary. Poverty was a common condition. The danger even more palpable. On average one person was kidnapped for ransom every day: only half were returned home unharmed.

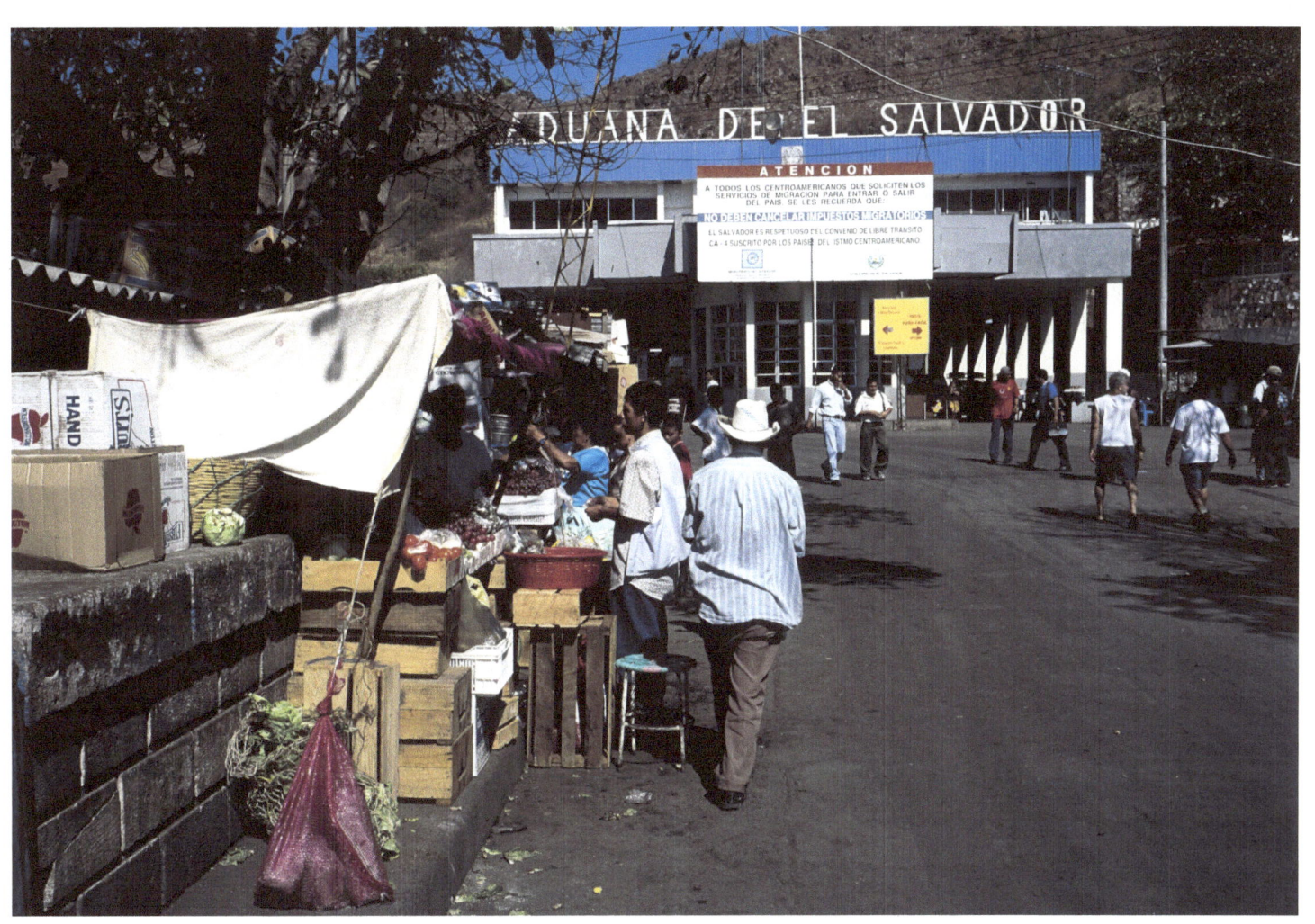
The Honduras-El Salvador border crossing

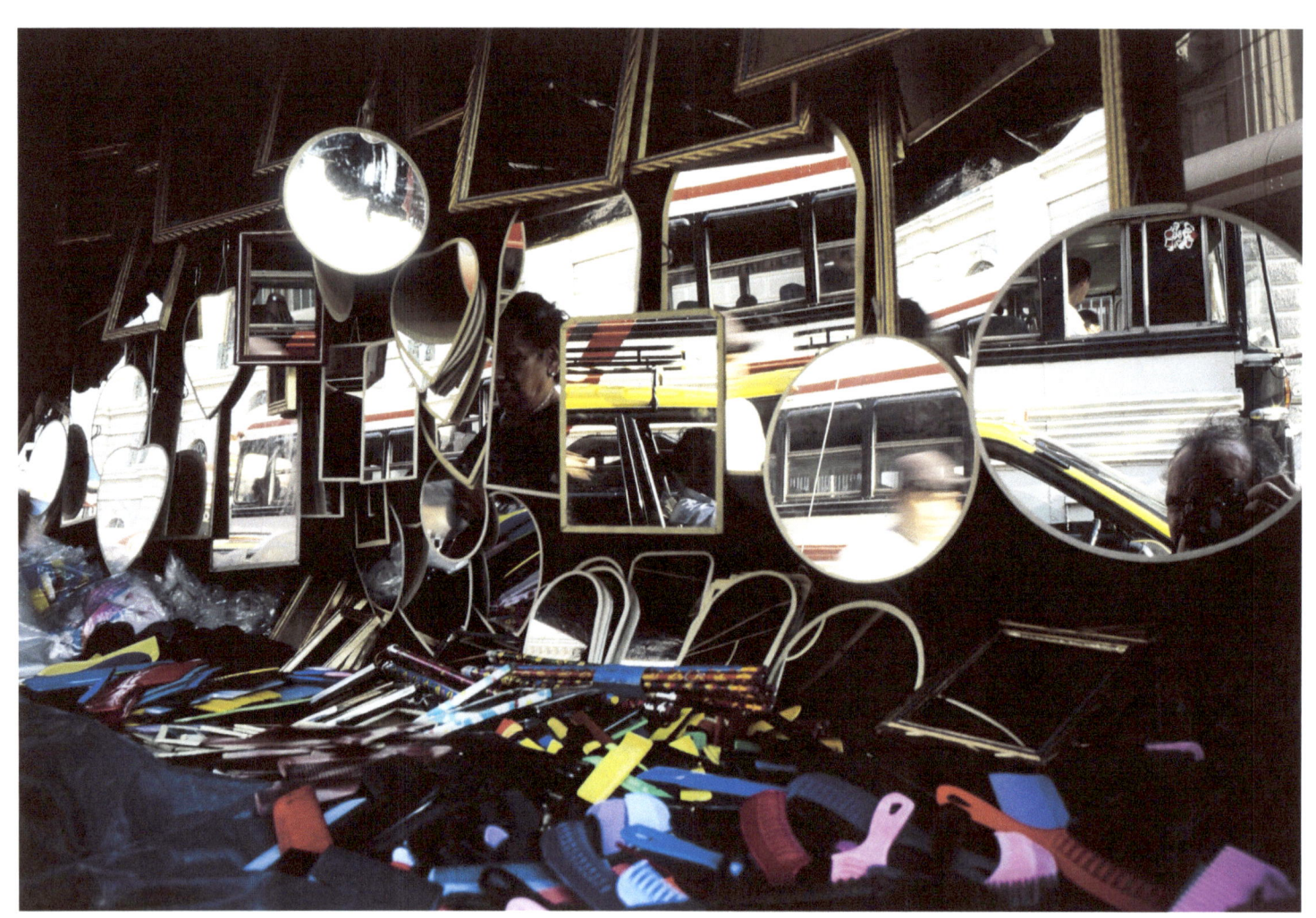

San Salvador city

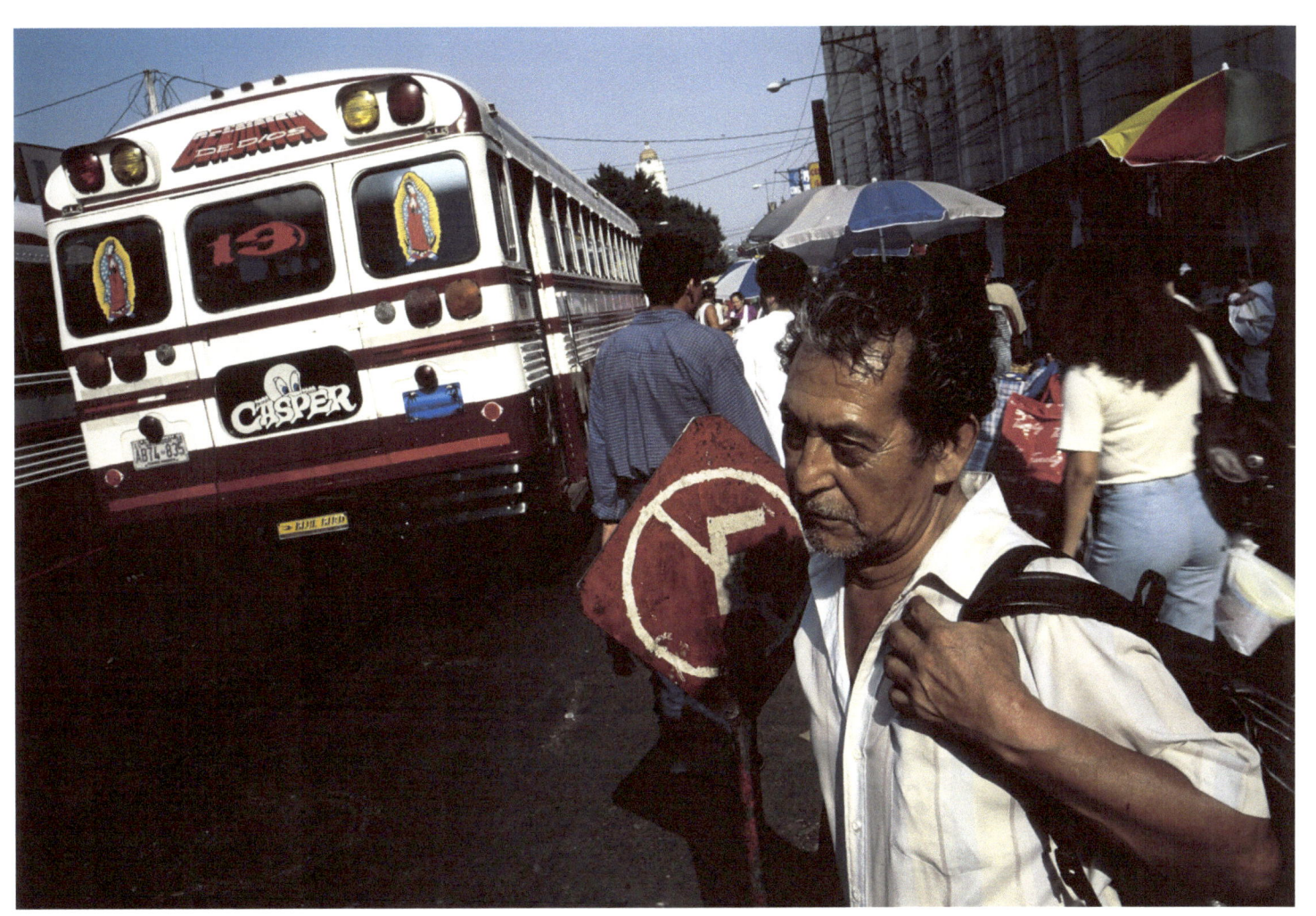

San Salvador city

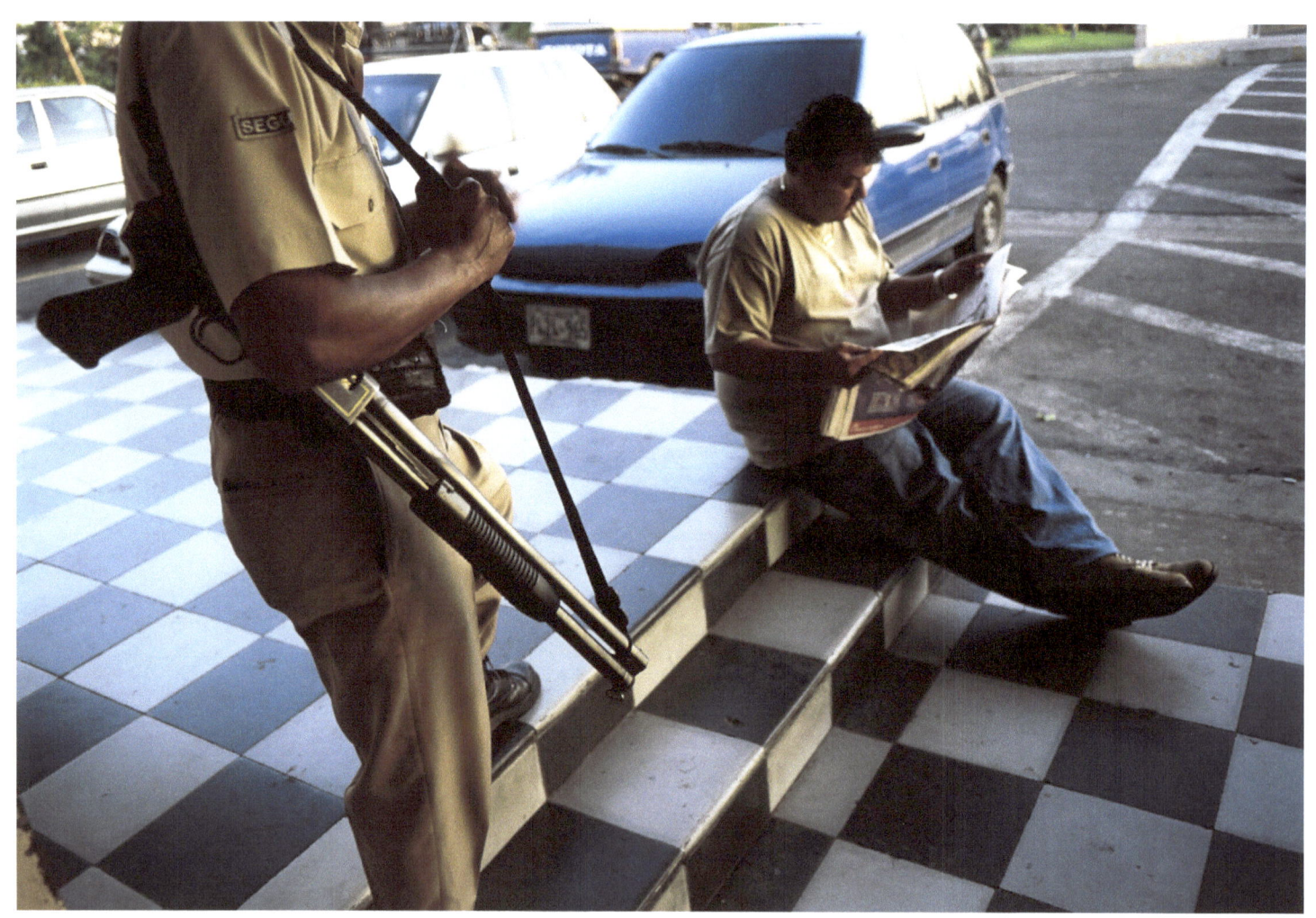

More useless "security" in San Salvador city

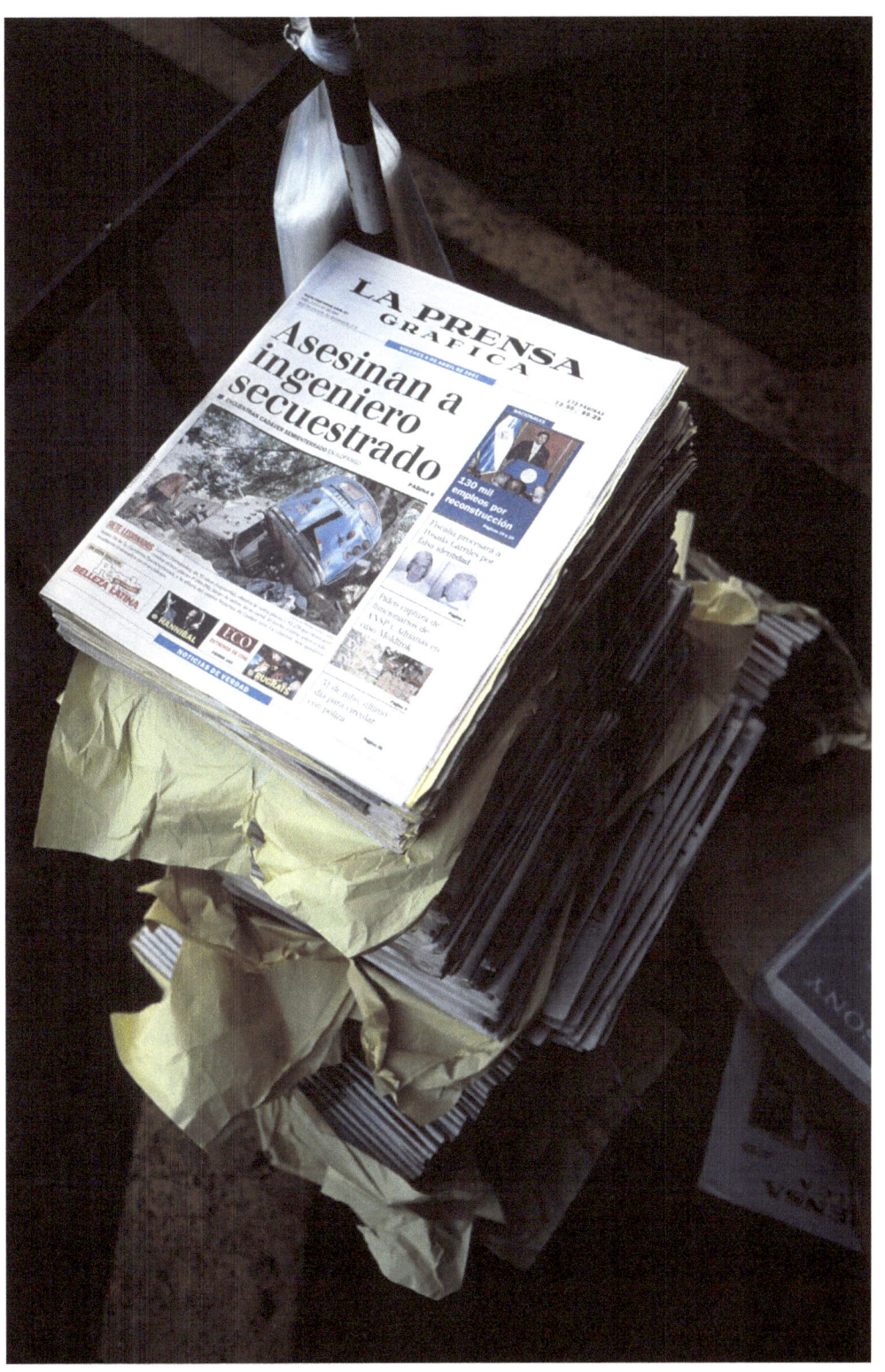

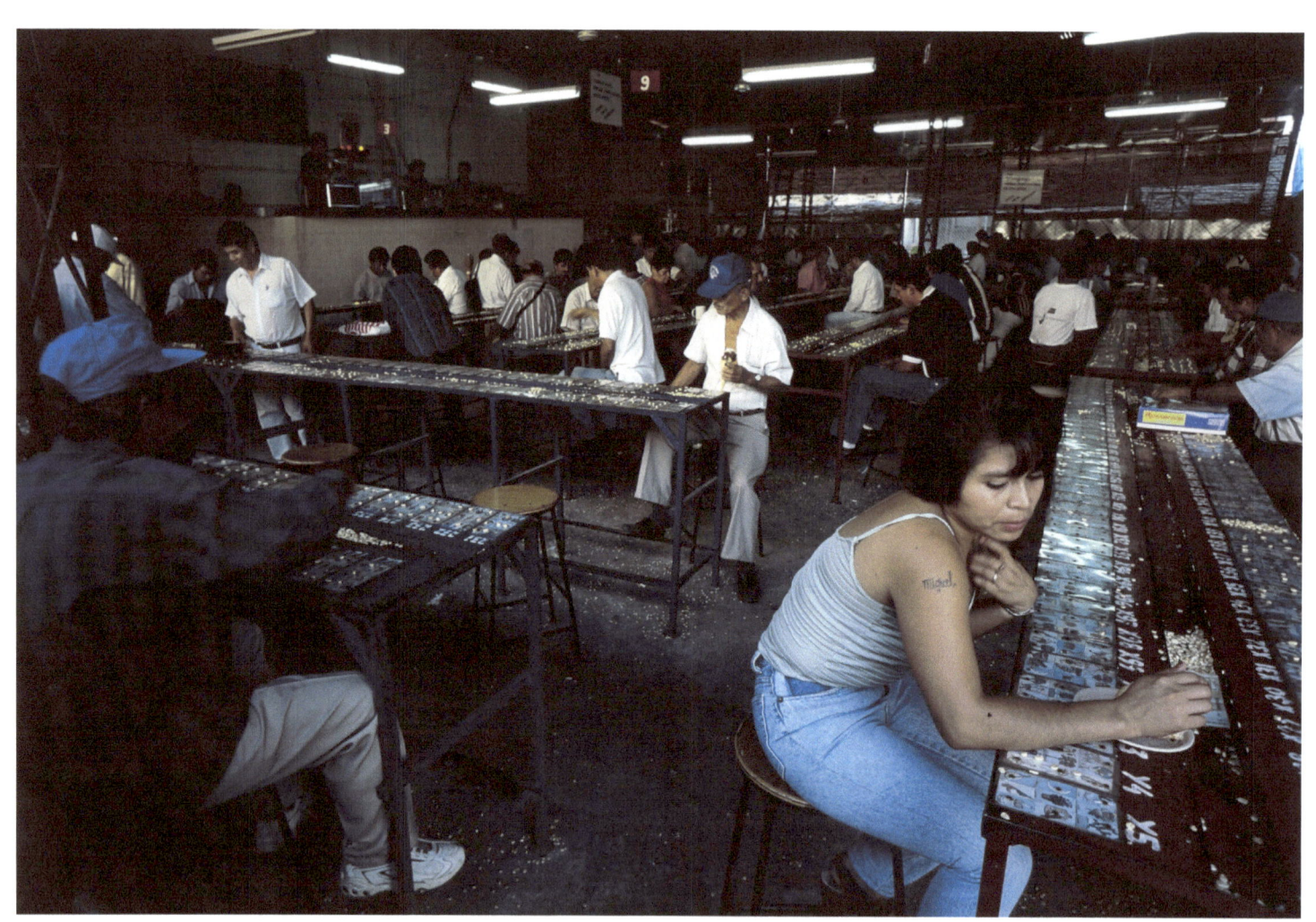
Bingo in San Salvador city

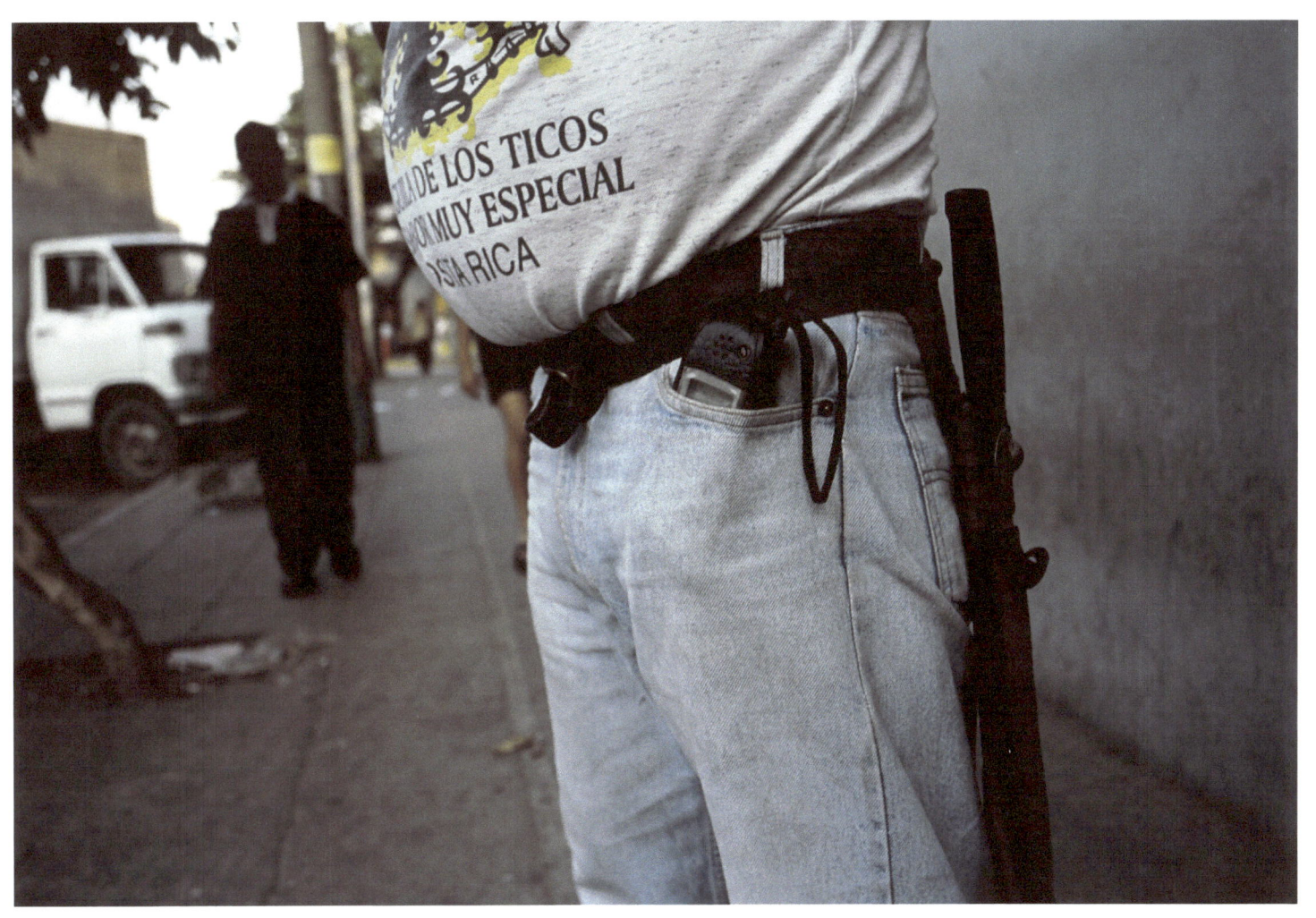
A volunteer vigilantes, not armed, in San Salvador city

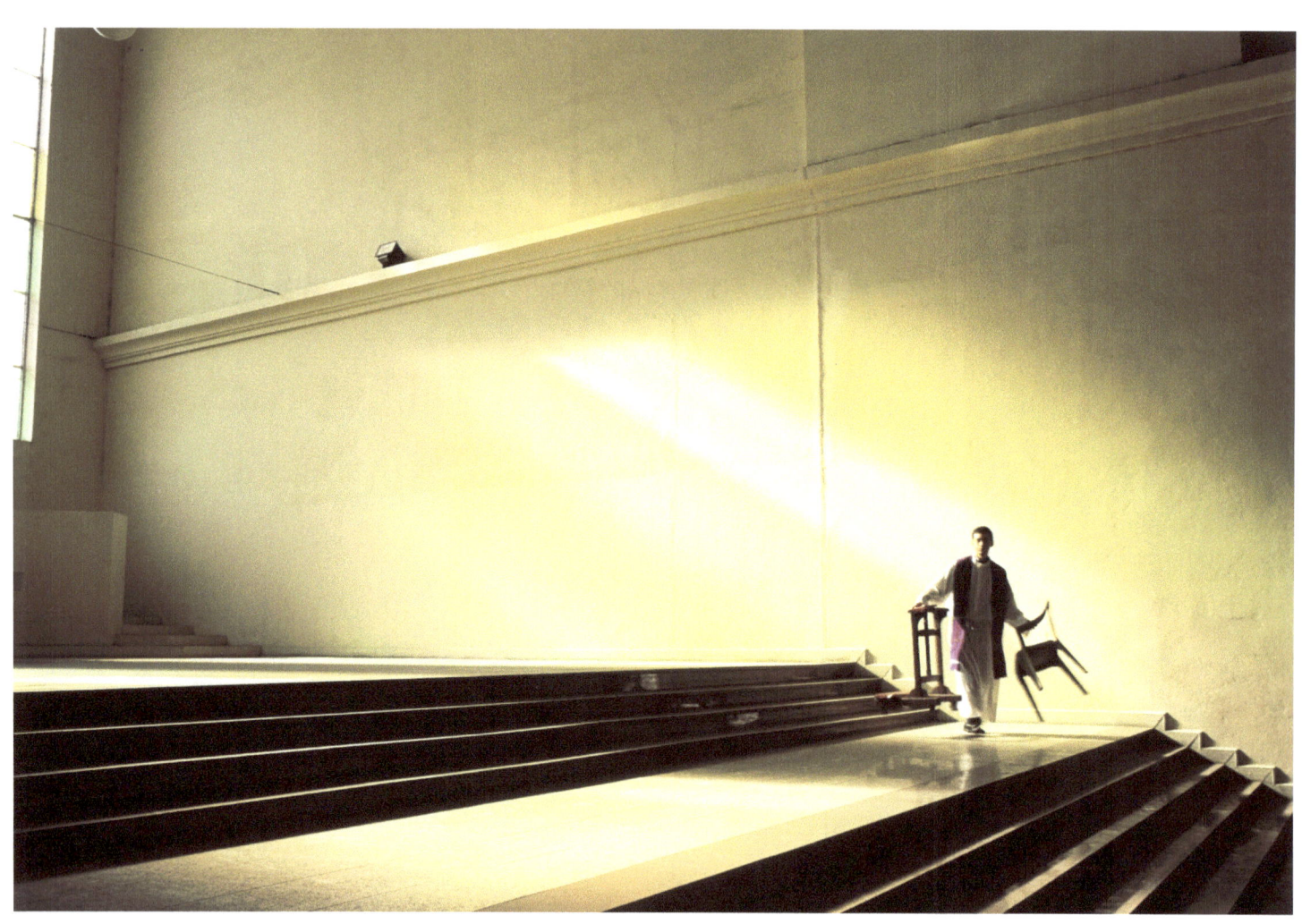

The Church, still faithful to the memory of Monsenor Romero, was playing an active social role

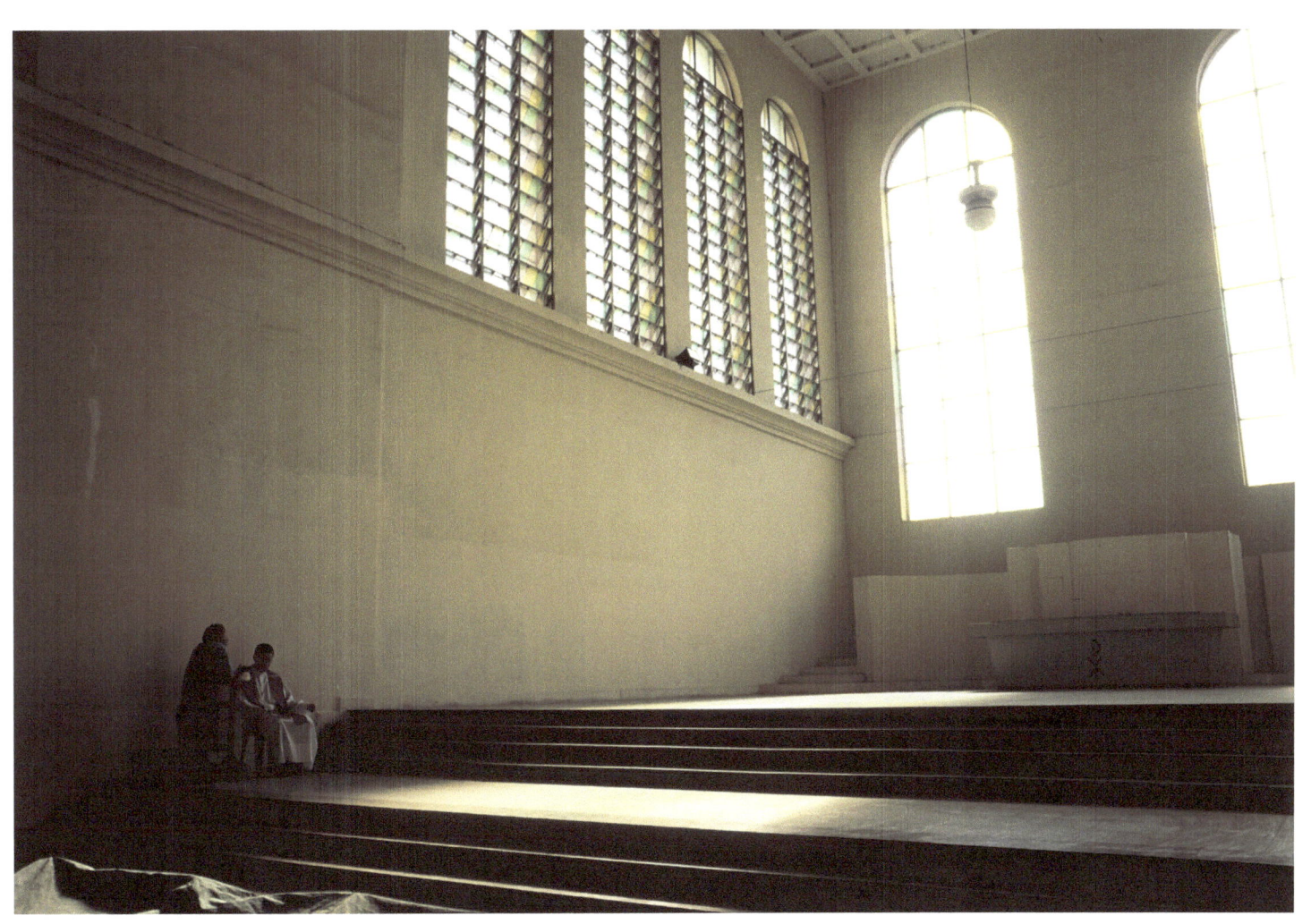
Confession in San Salvador city

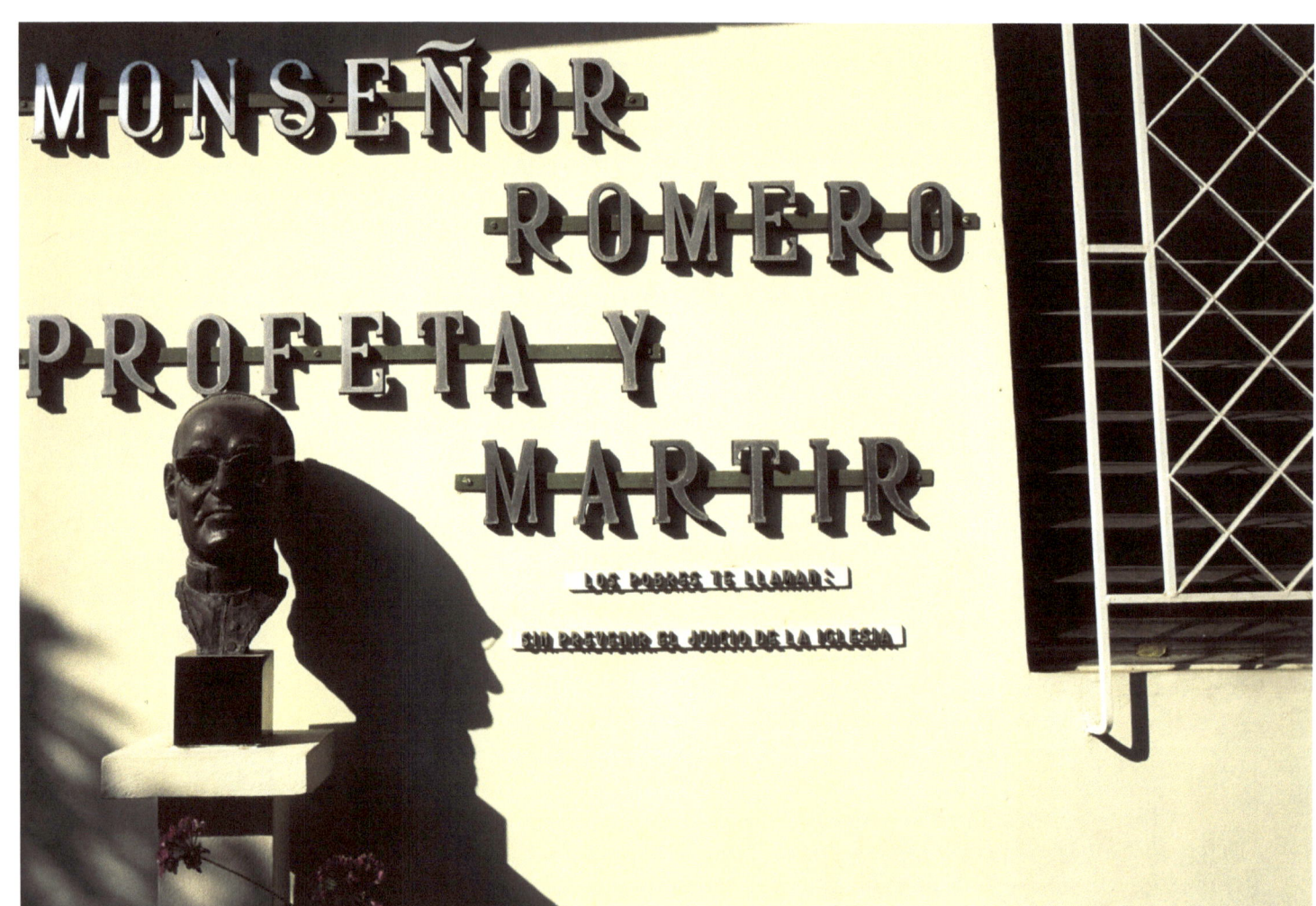

The church where Monsenor Romero was killed

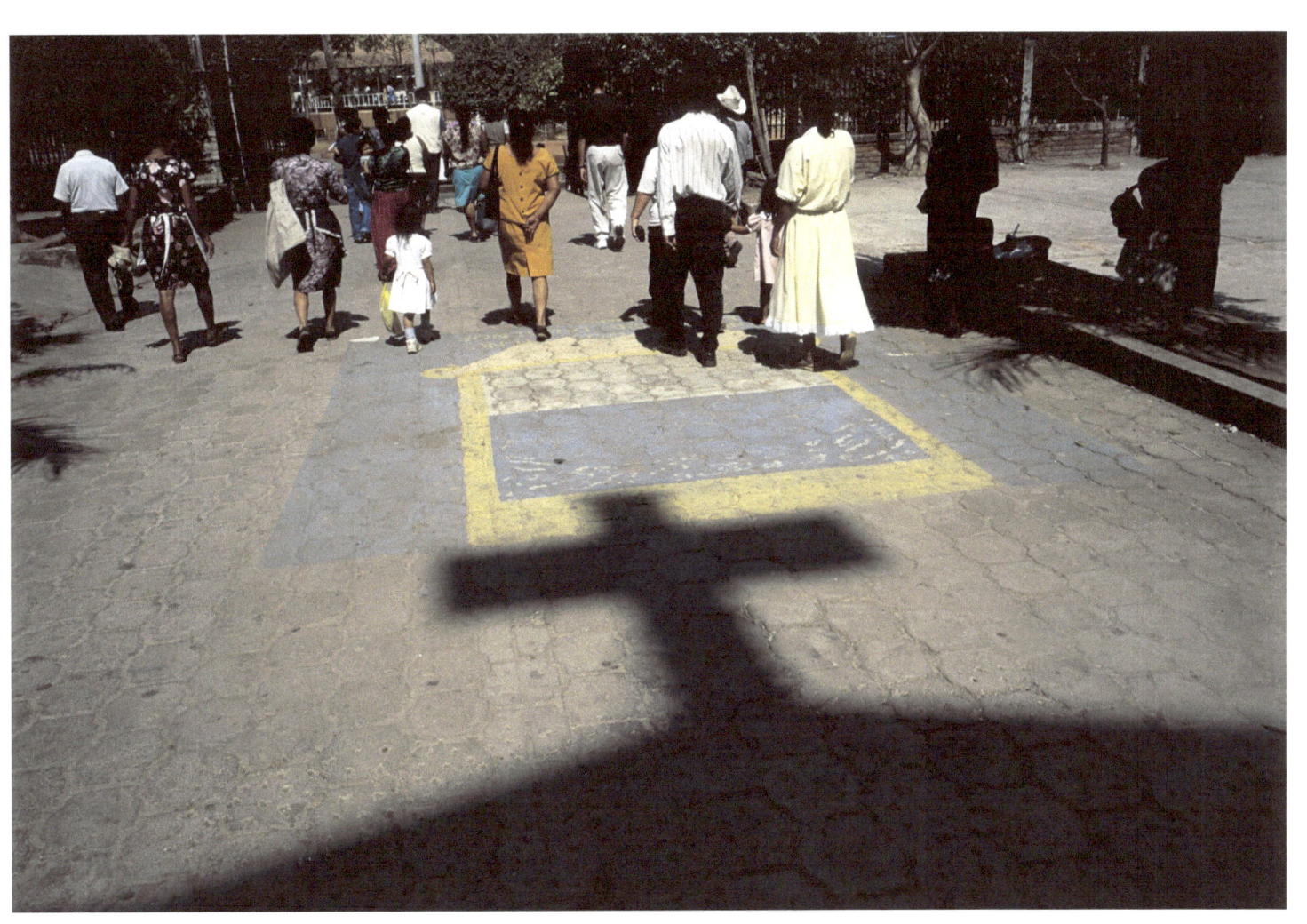

After Sunday Mass in San Salvador city

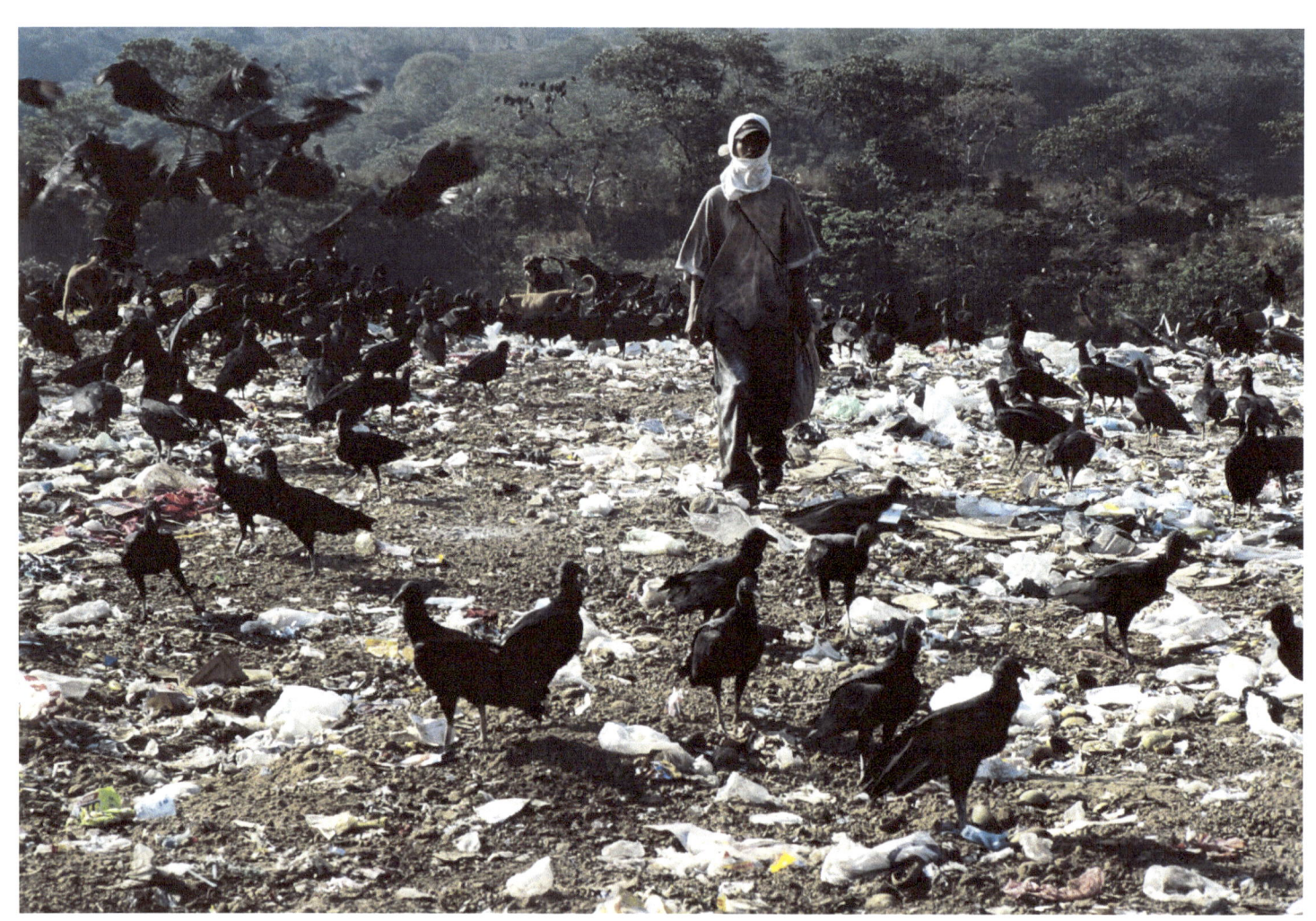
The waste dump of San Salvador, as crowded as the city itself

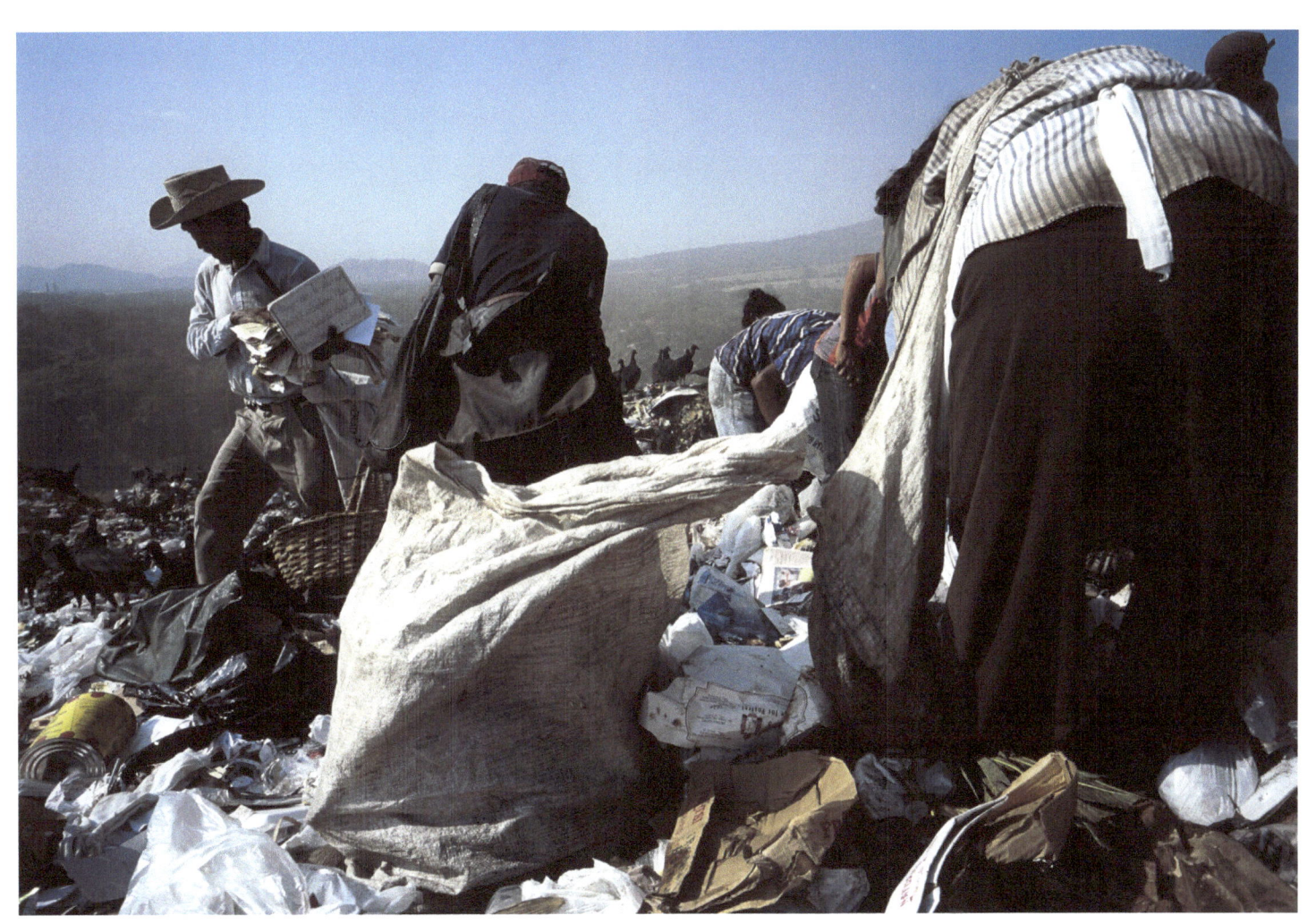

The waste dump of San Salvador

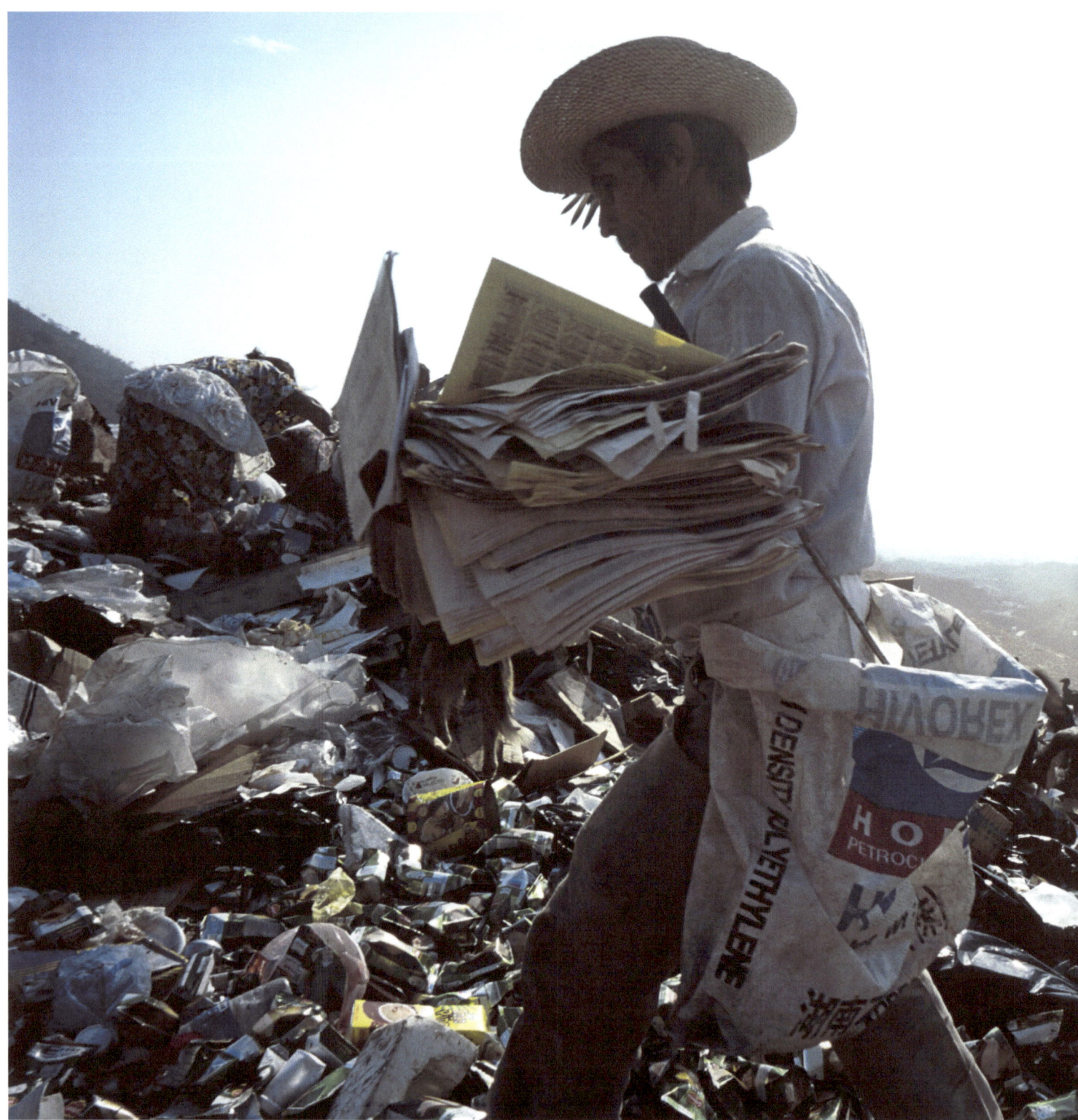

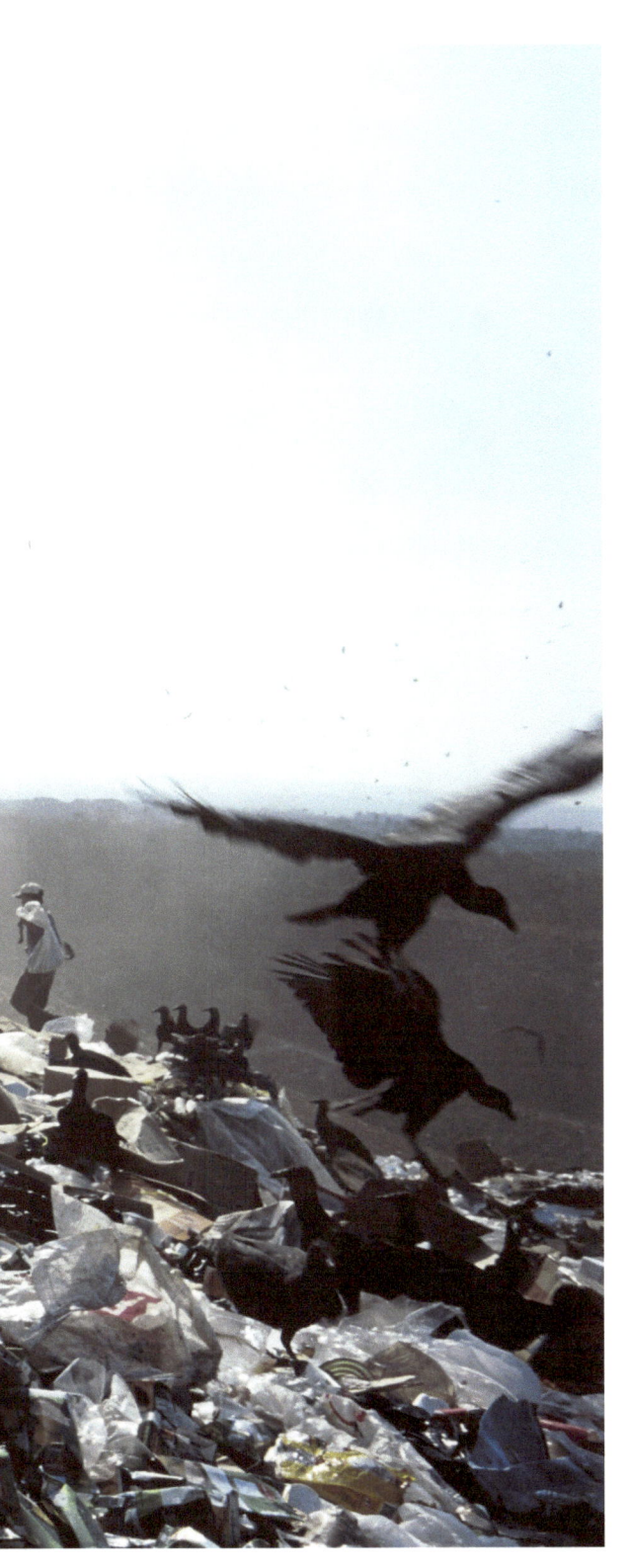

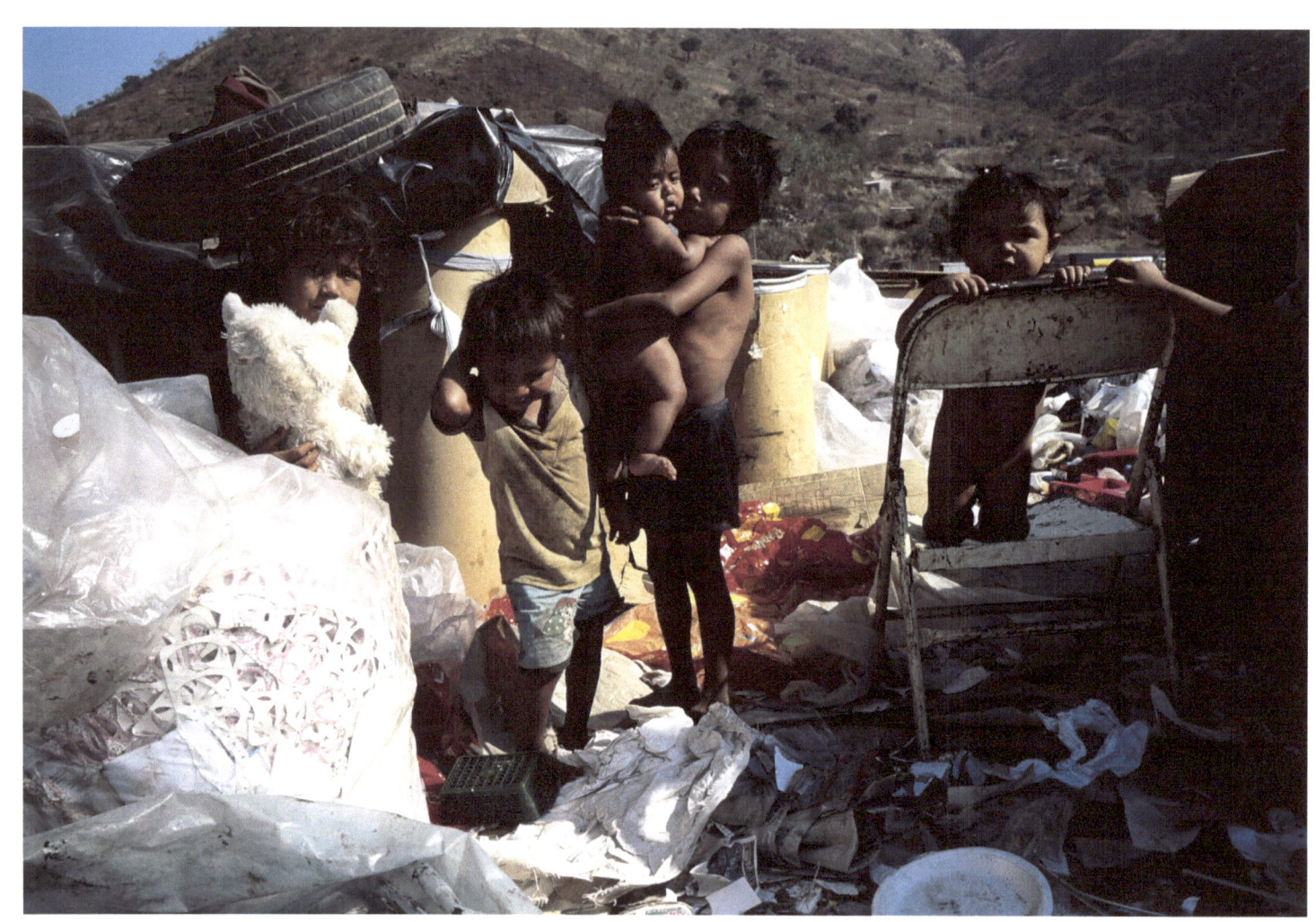
The waste dump of San Salvador

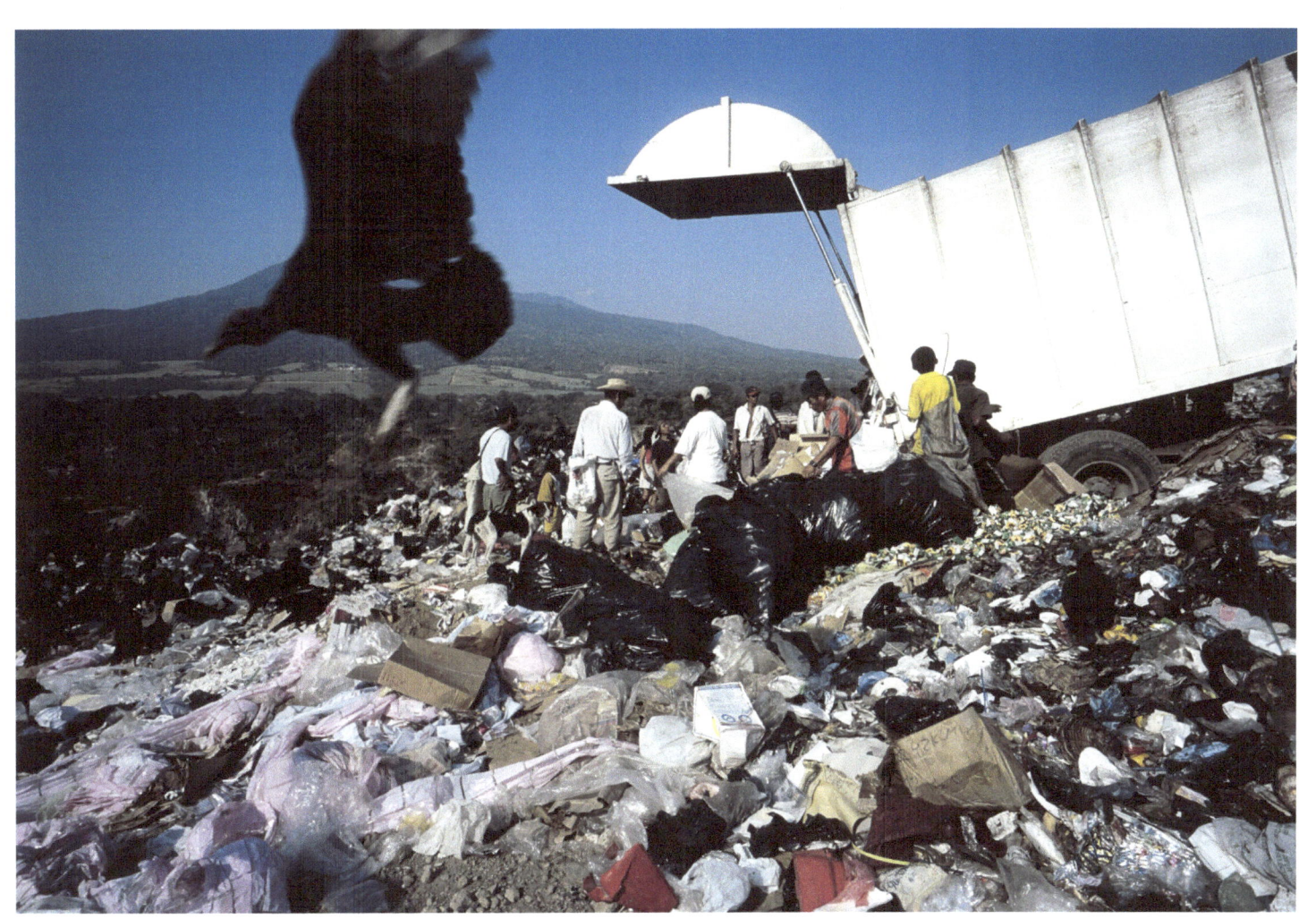
The waste dump of San Salvador

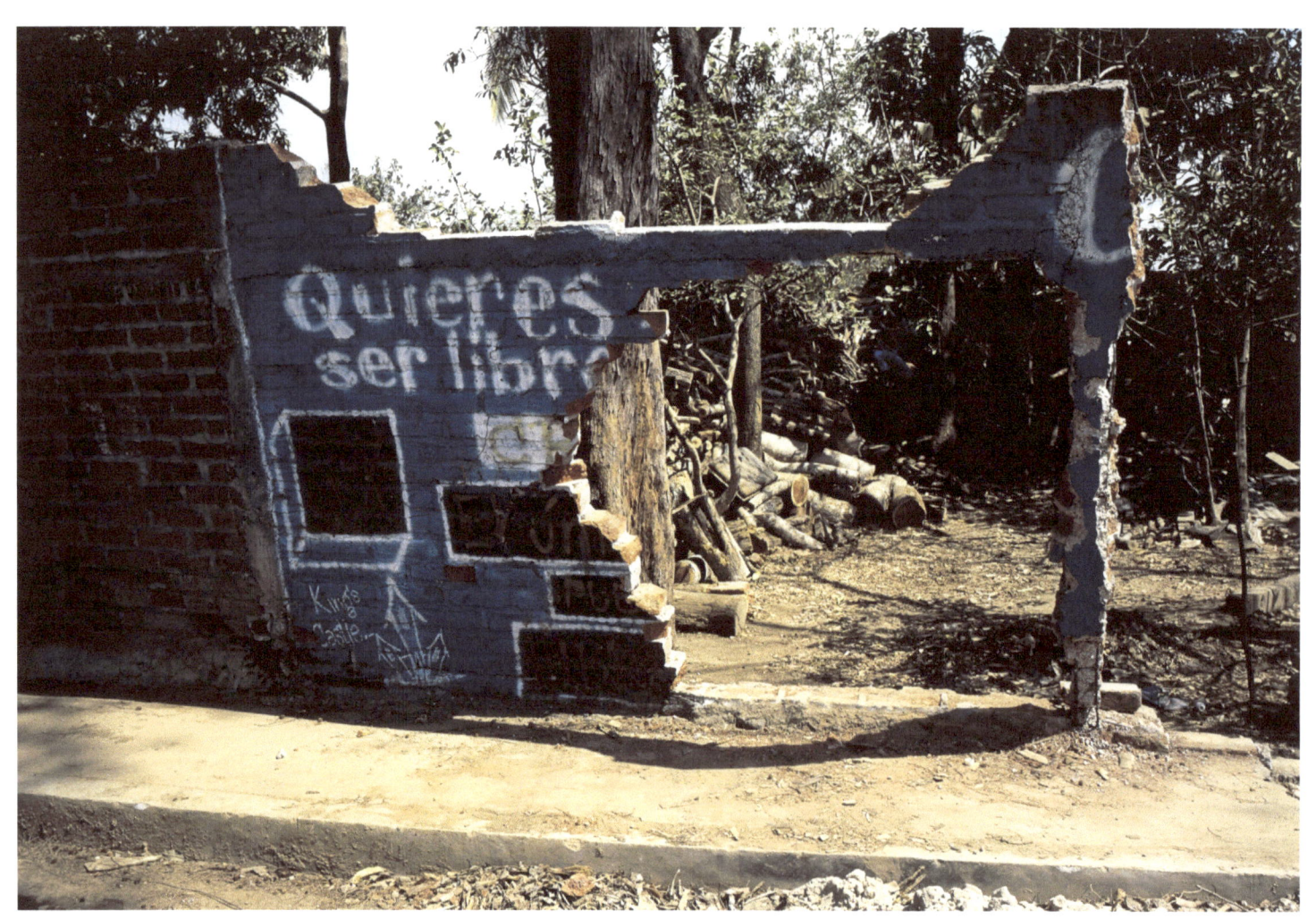

Santa Ana, just after an earthquake

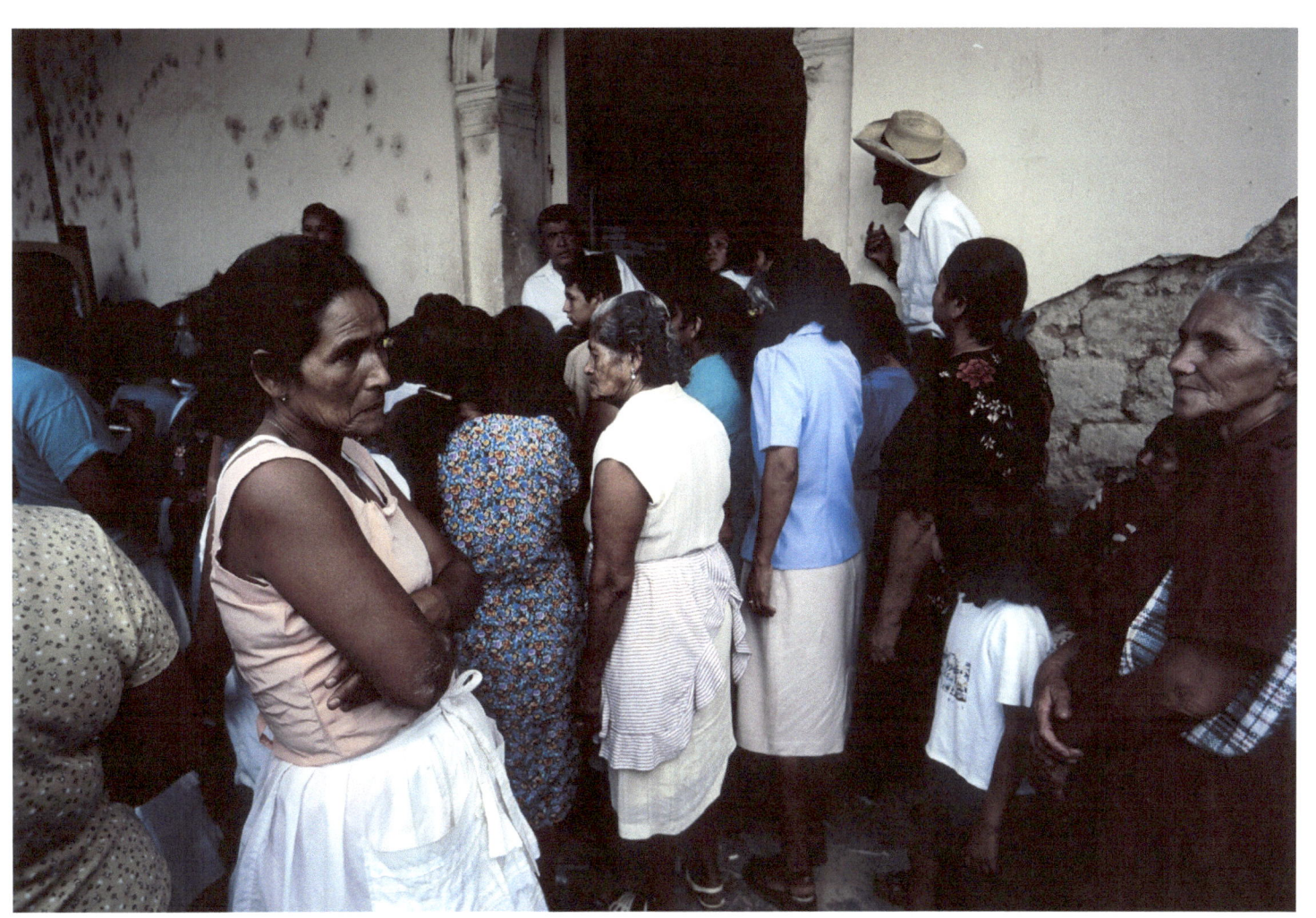

Santa Ana, awaiting help after the earthquake

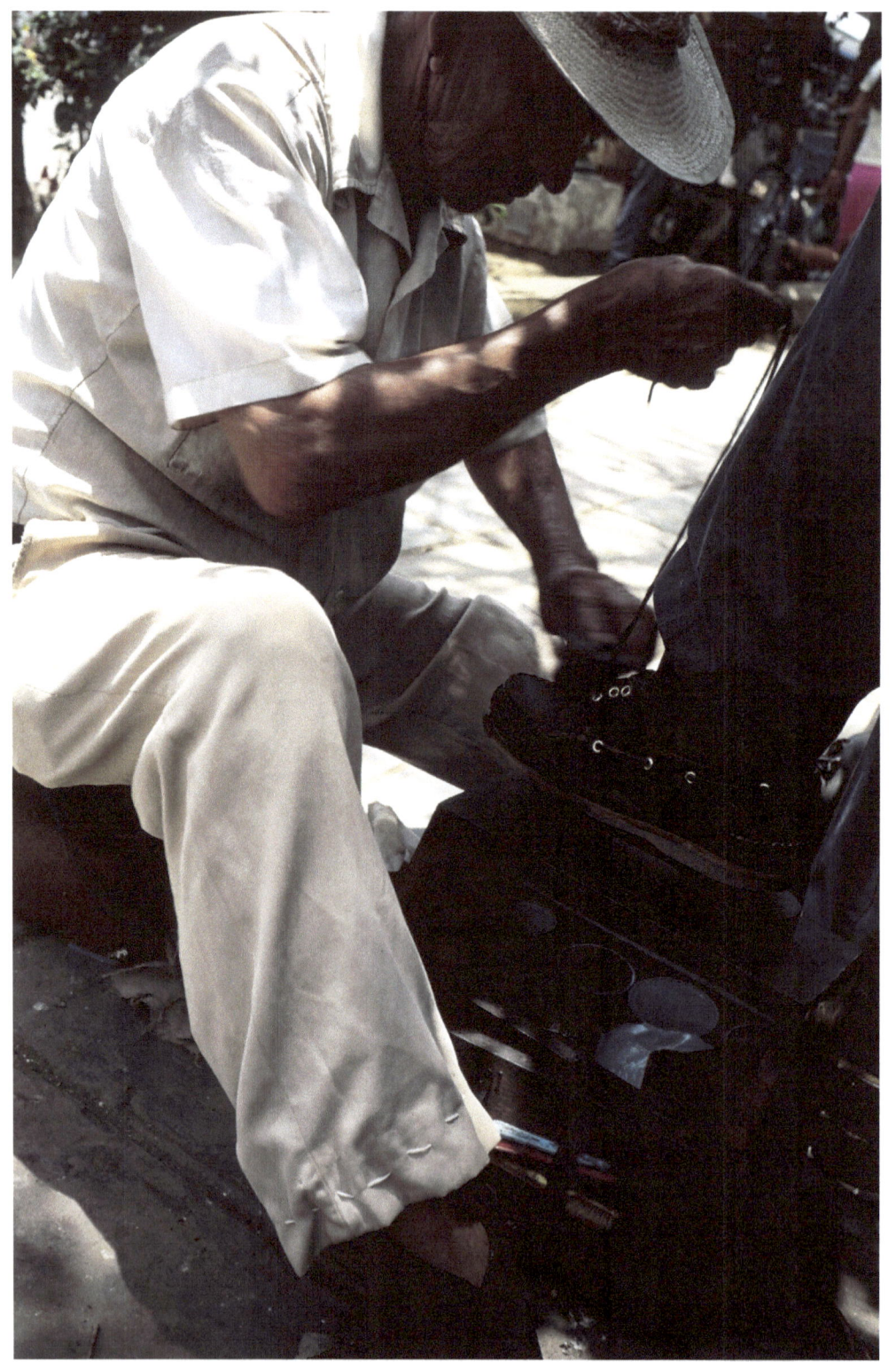

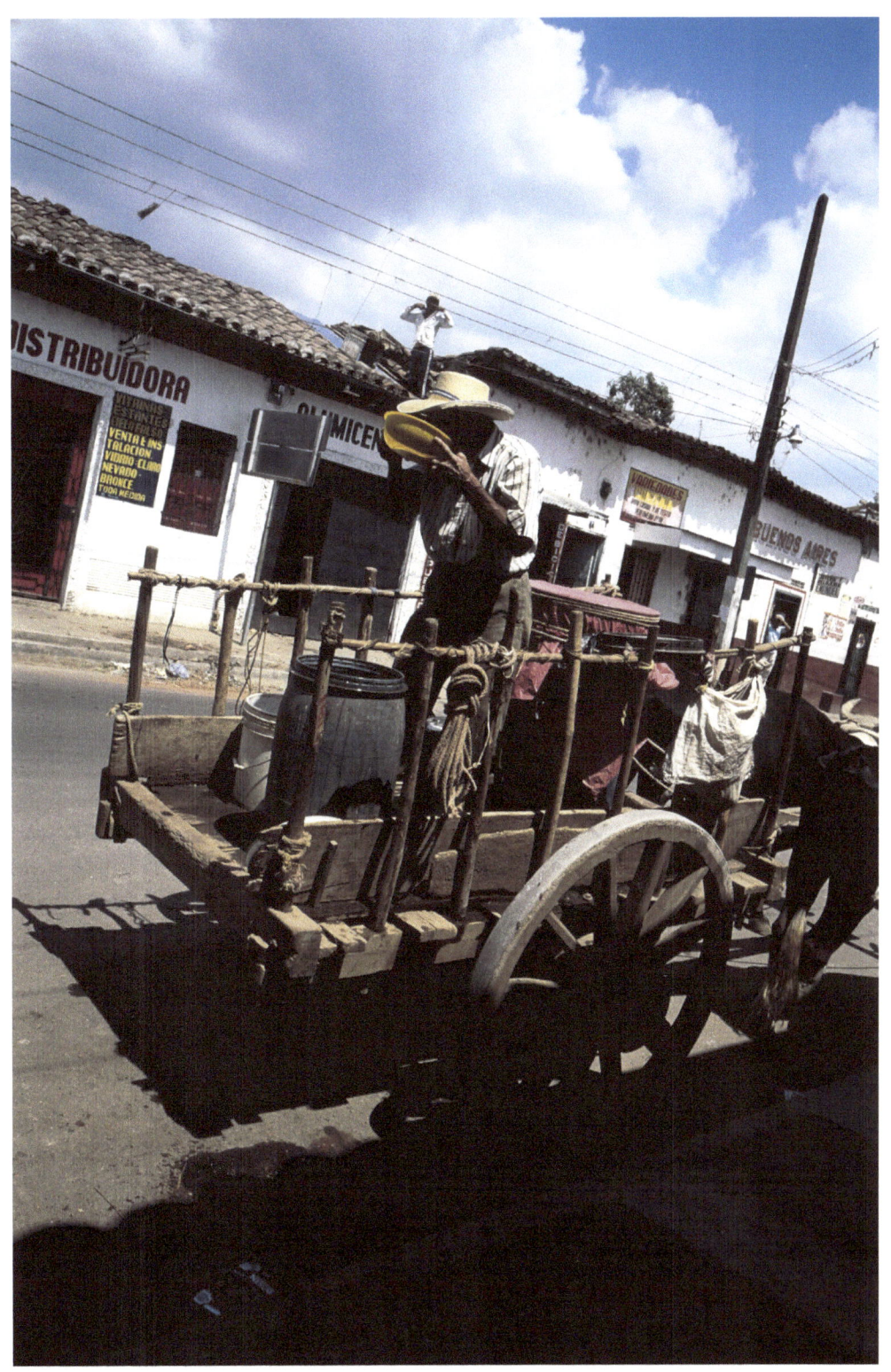

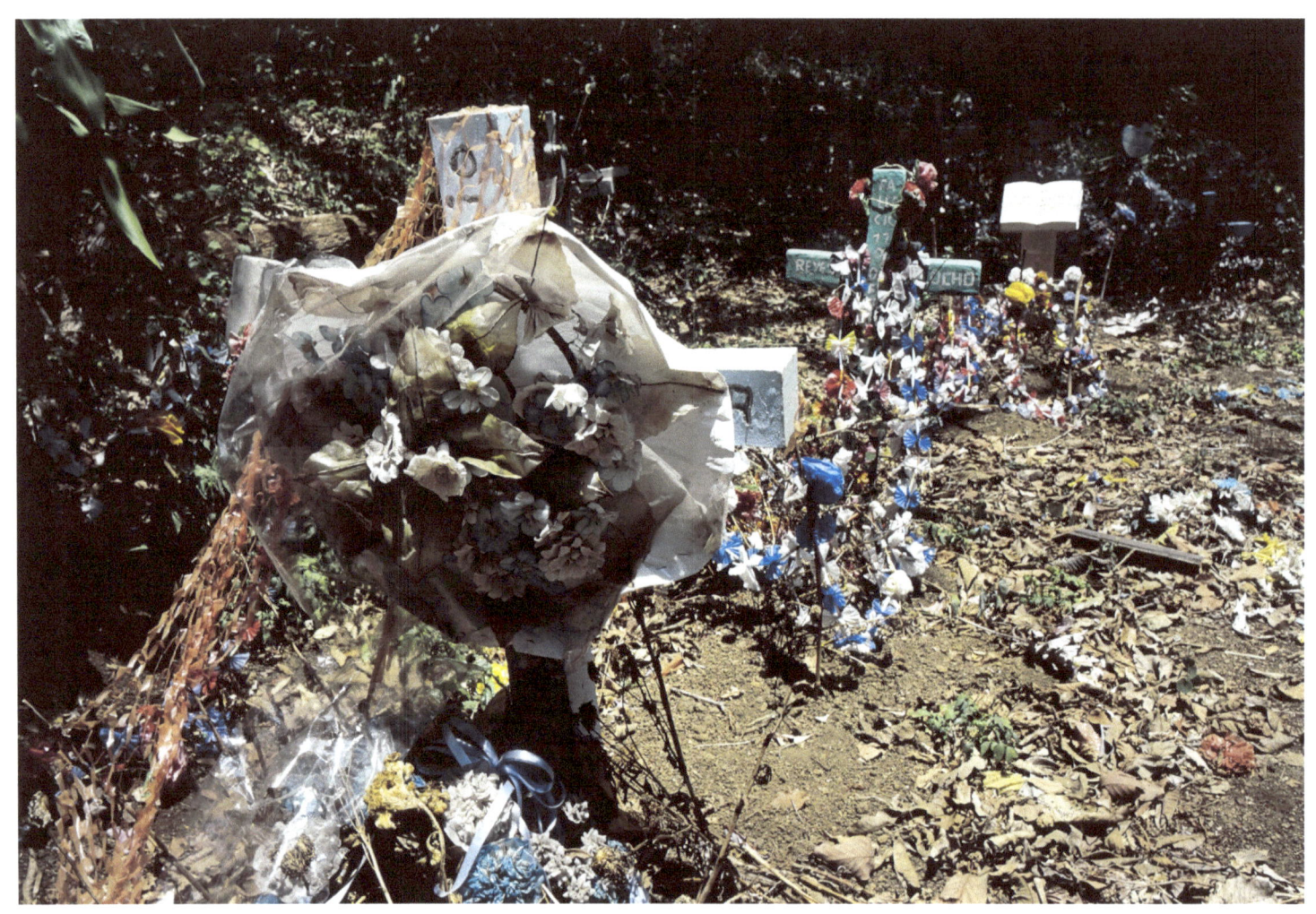

(Previous pages) In Santa Ana, I asked the shoeshine man: "What did you do before?" "Guerrillero.."

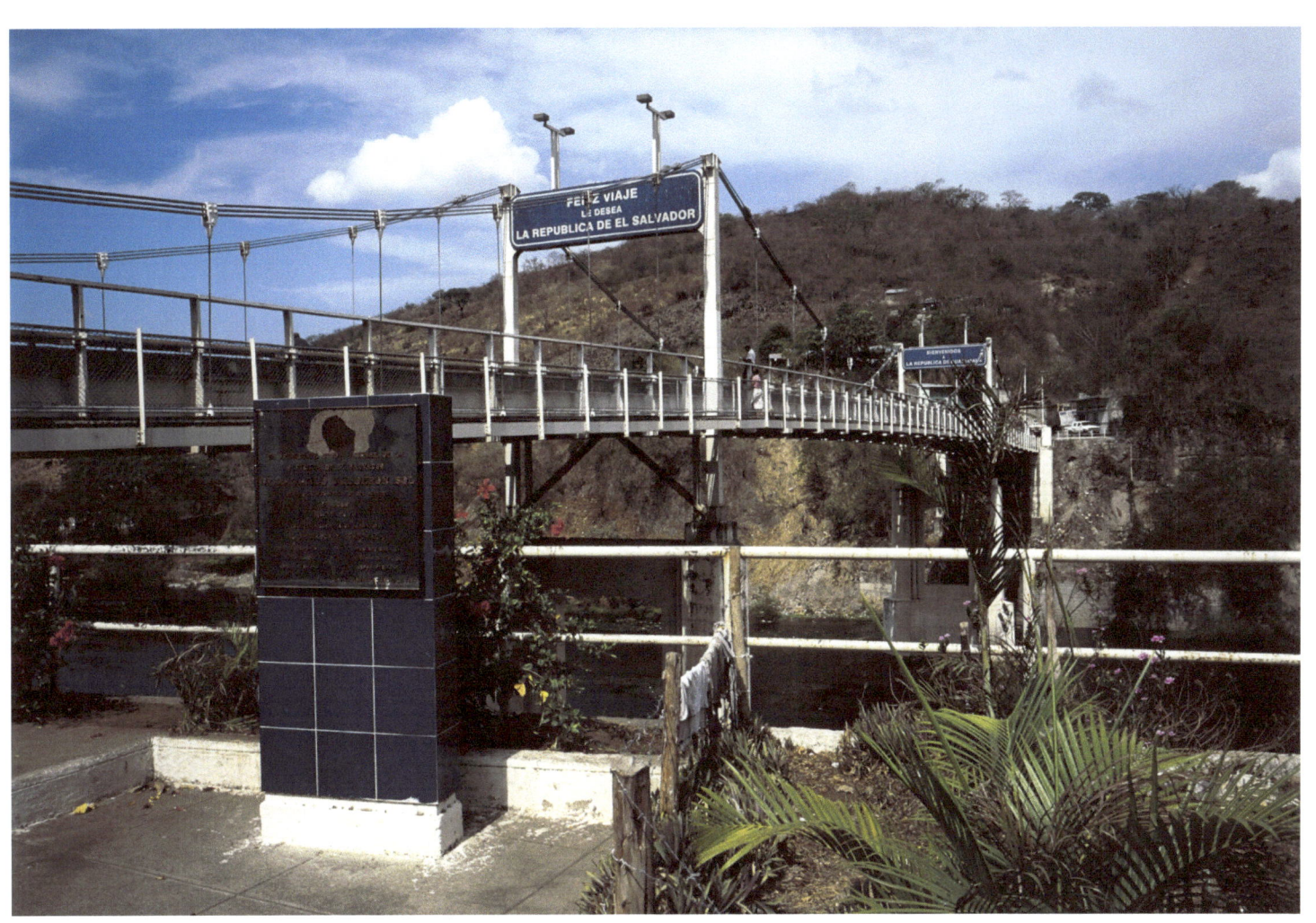

El Salvador and Guatemala border bridge

Guatemala

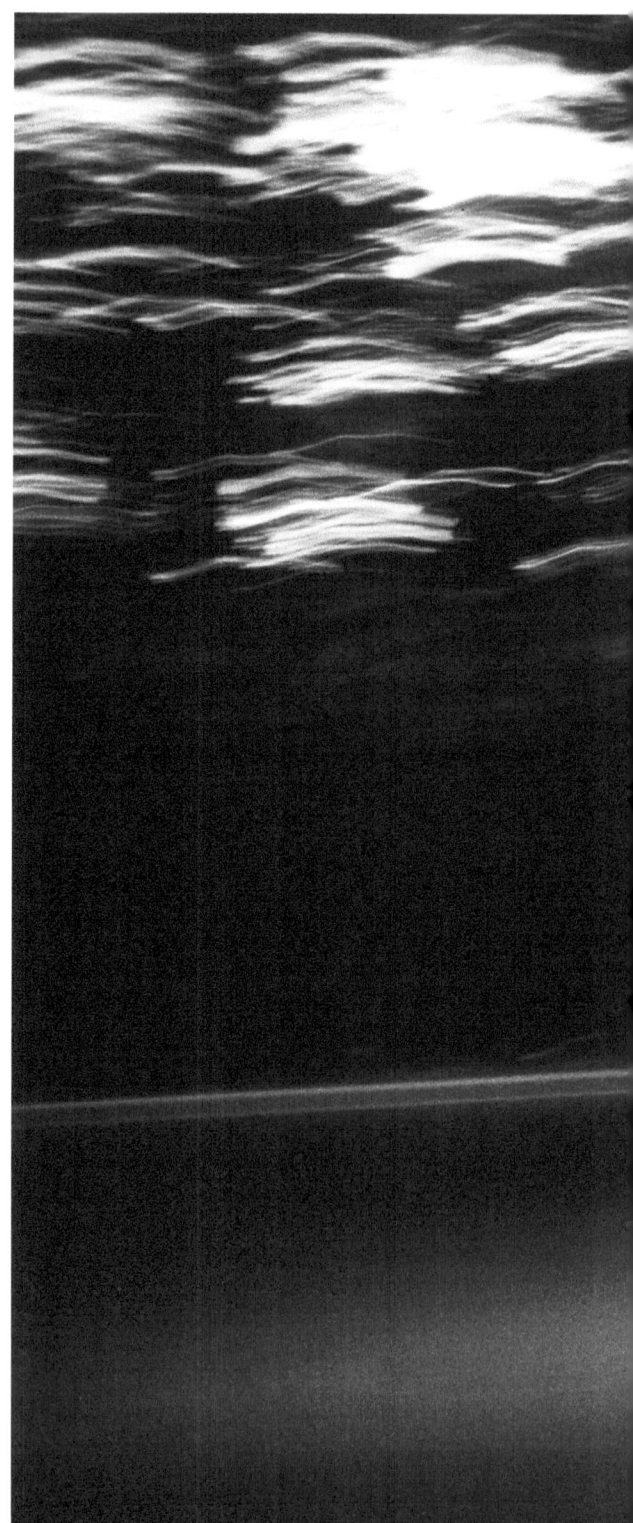

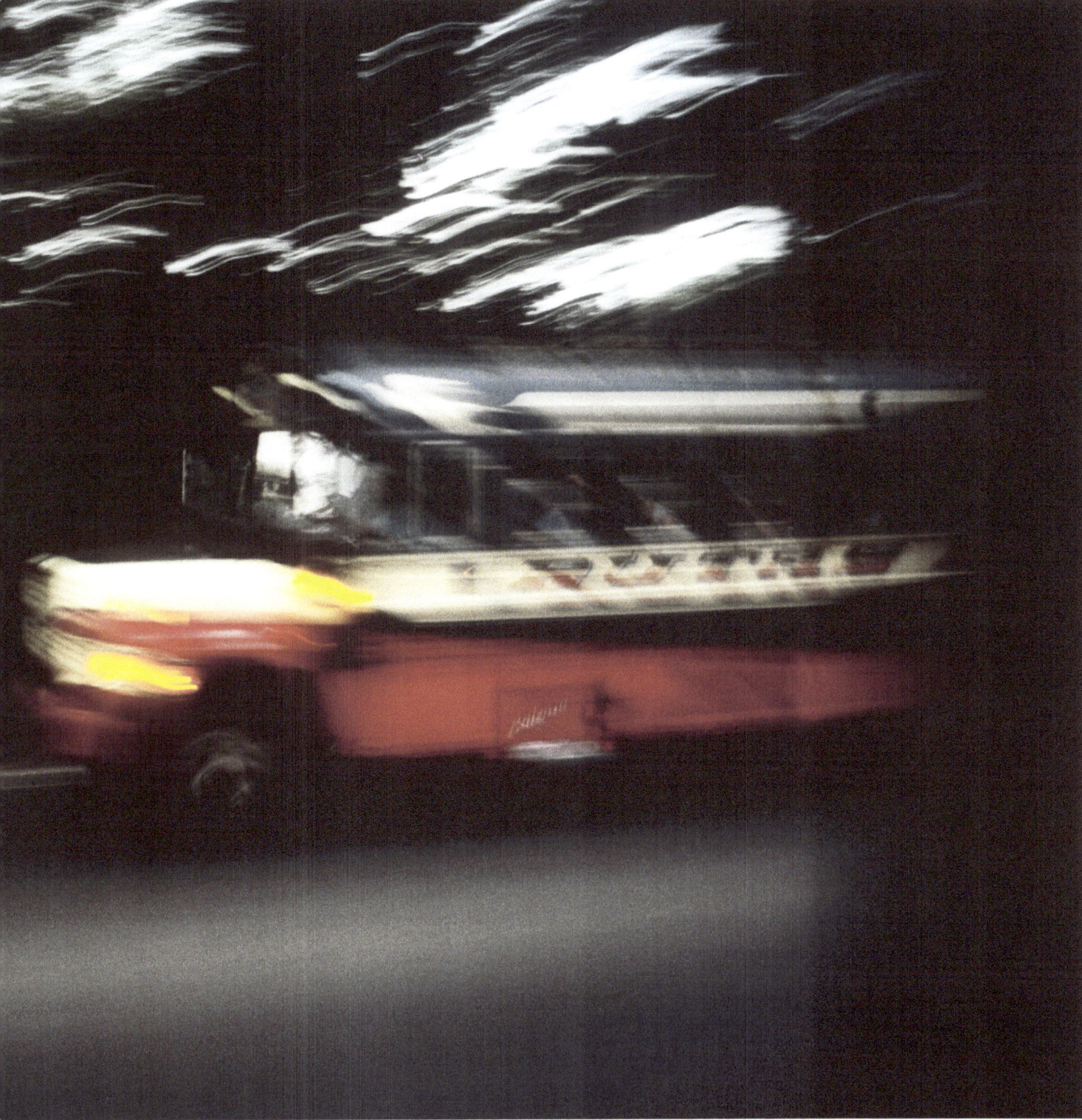

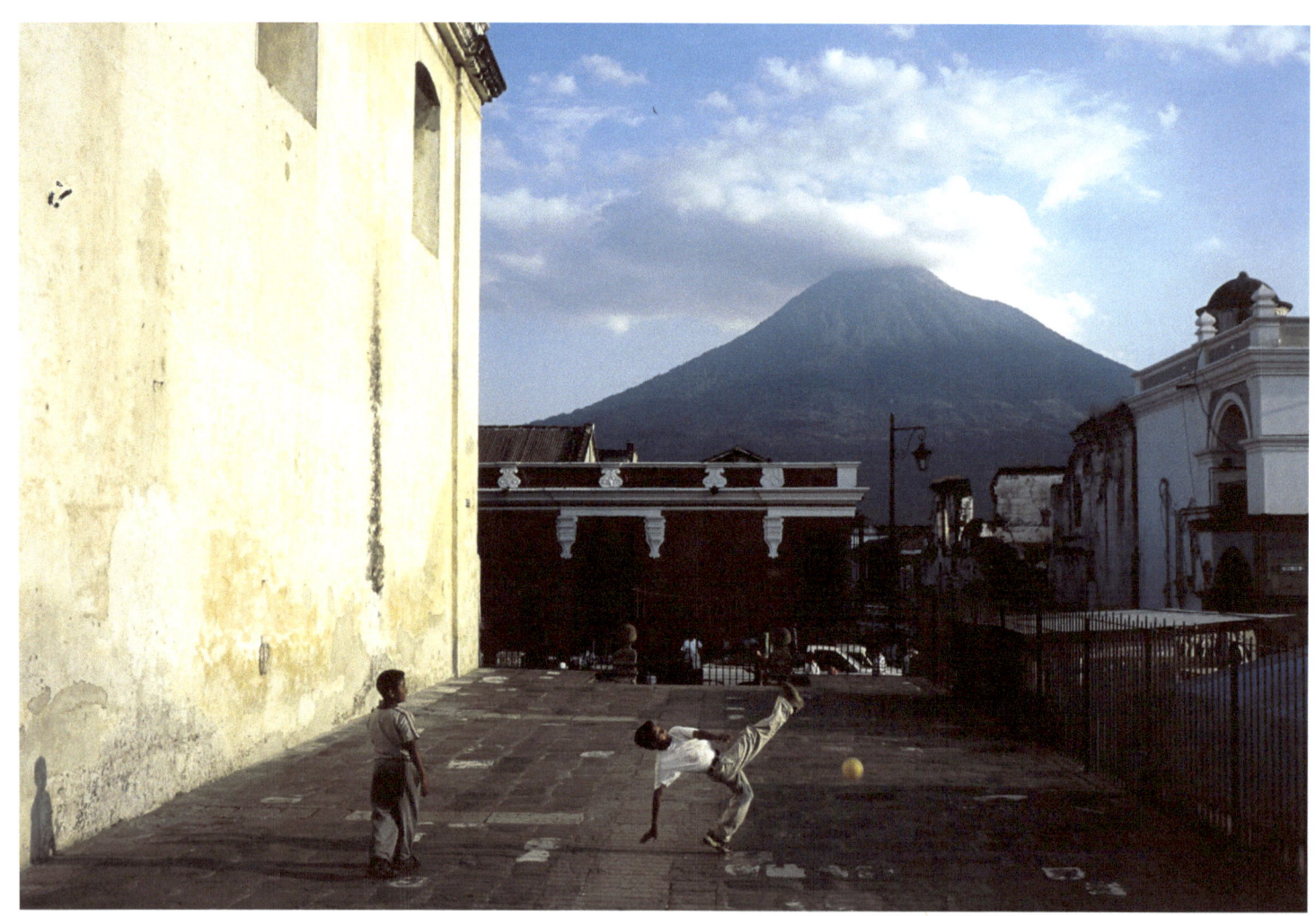

We arrived in Guatemala during the Semana Santa (Easter Holy Week). This is the climax for the most syncretic society in Latin America, when Christianity and Mayan animism mix, react and explode in incense smoke.

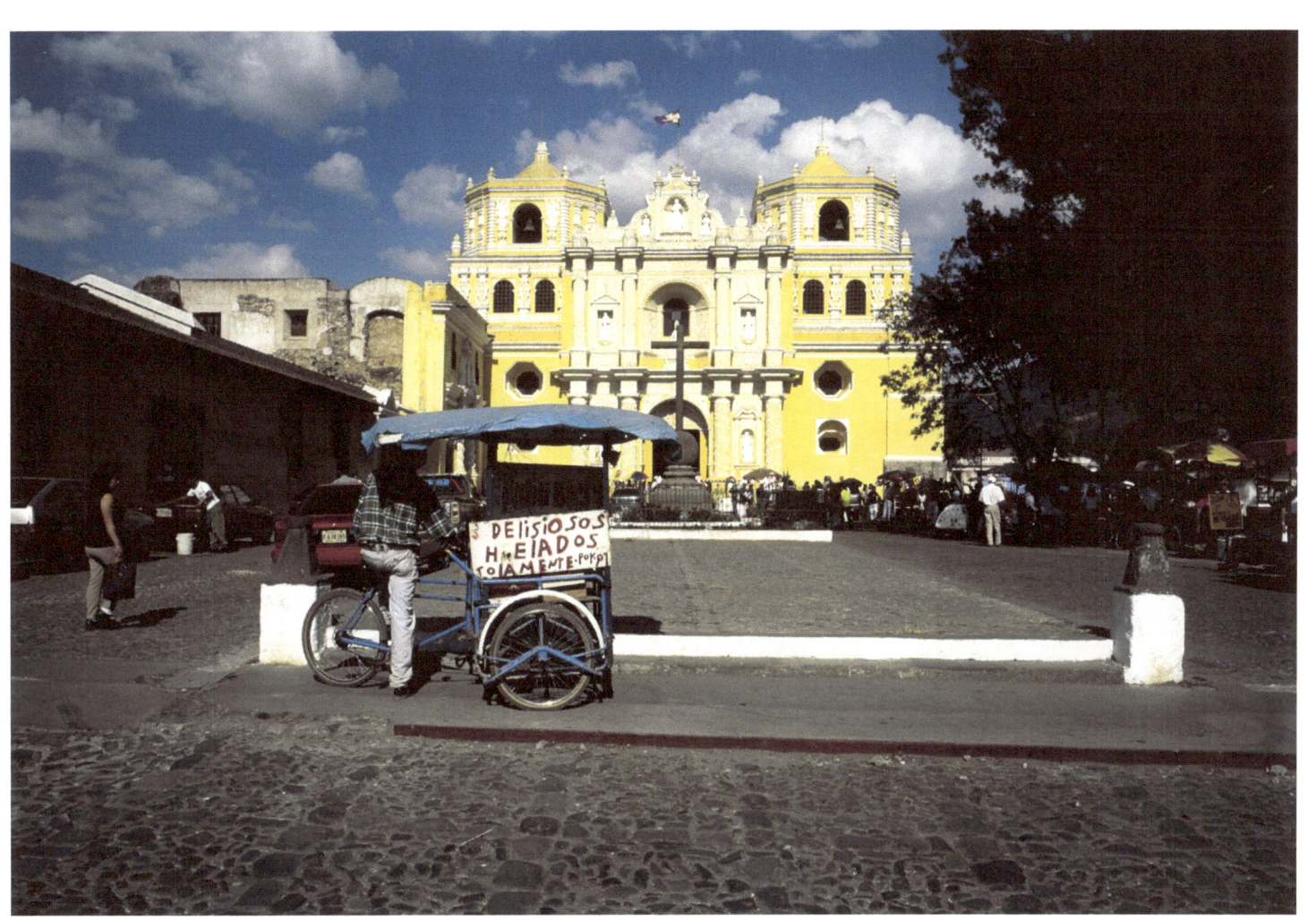

Antigua Guatemala

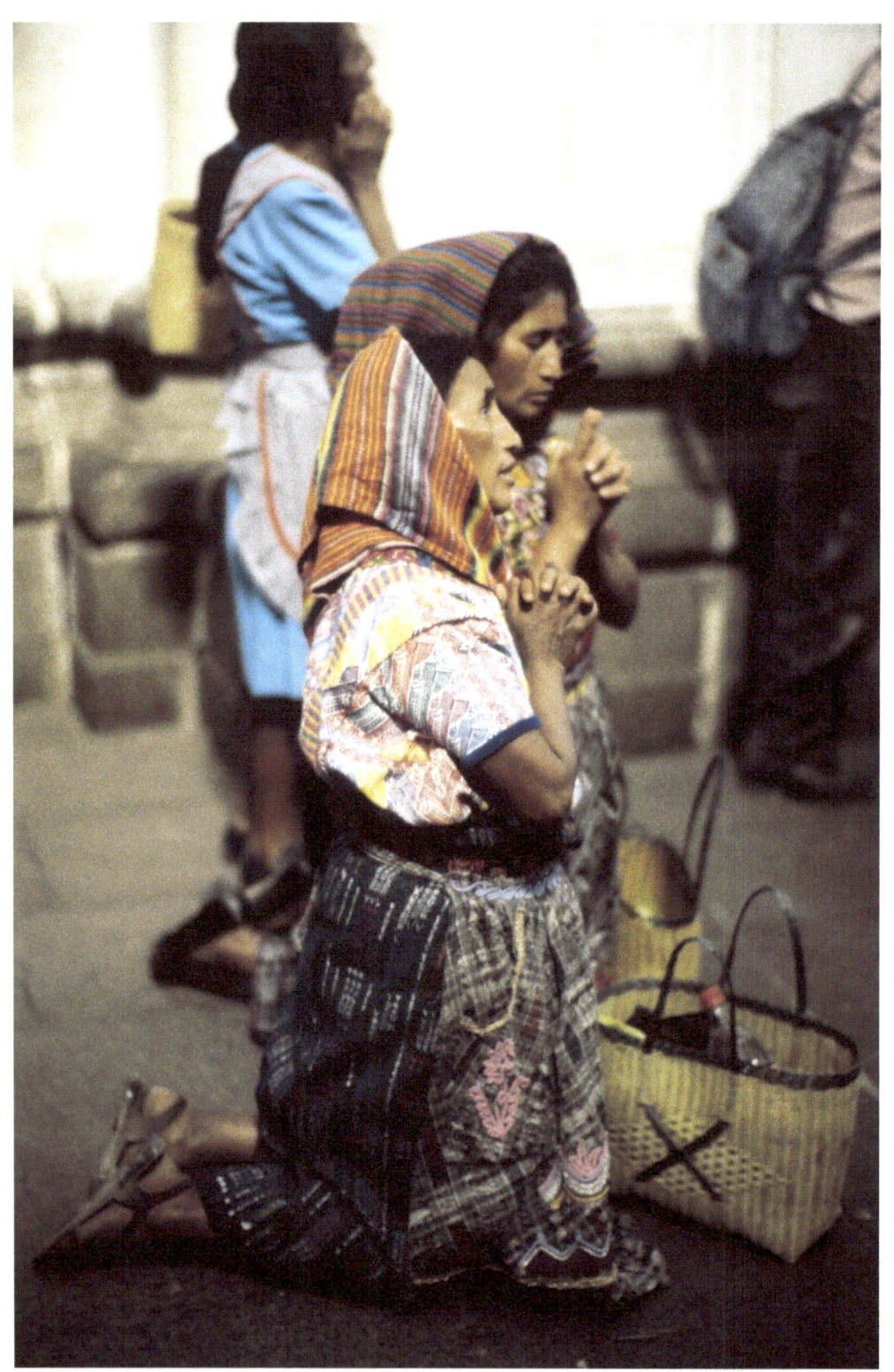

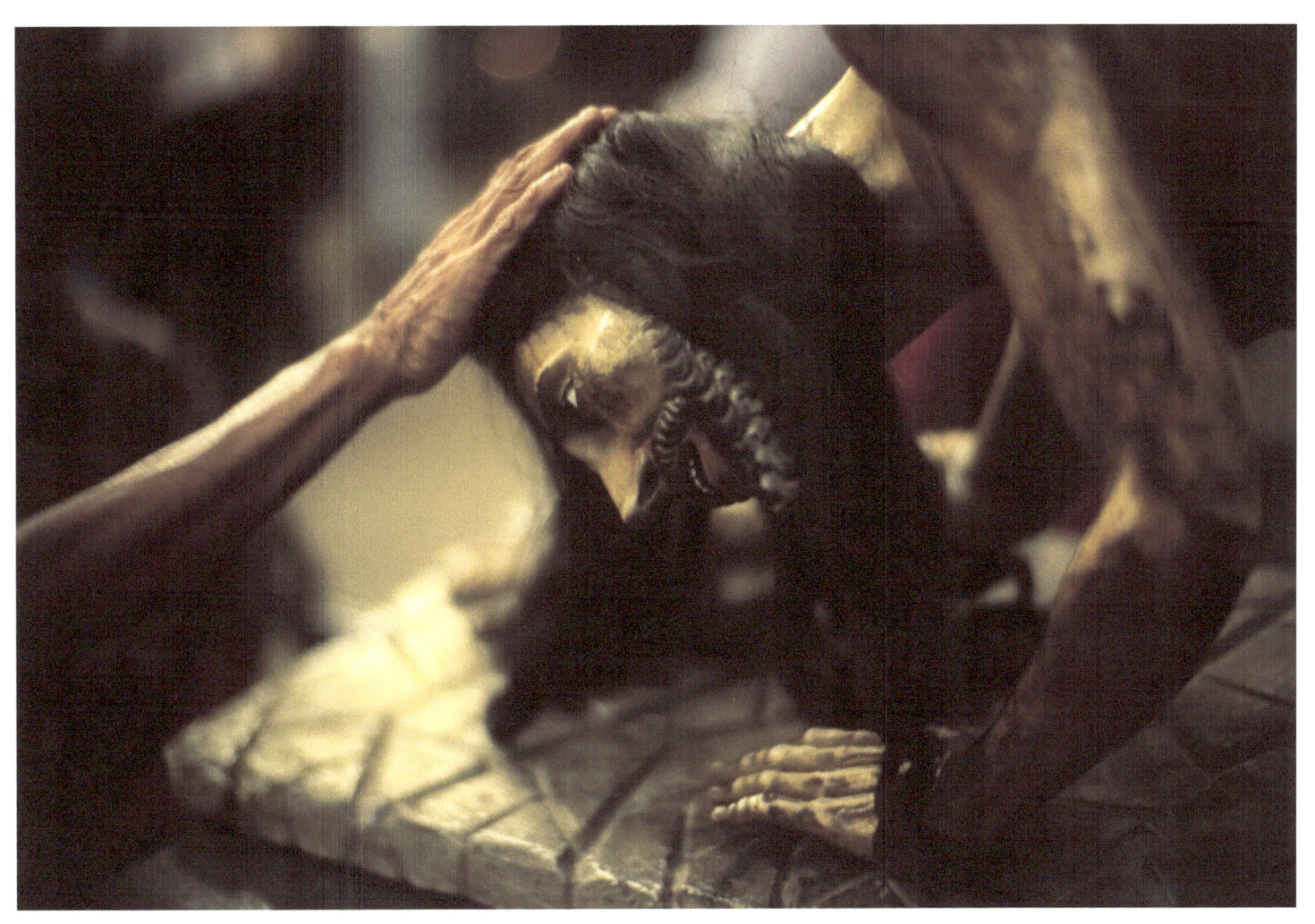

Antigua Guatemala, prayer in the city Cathedral

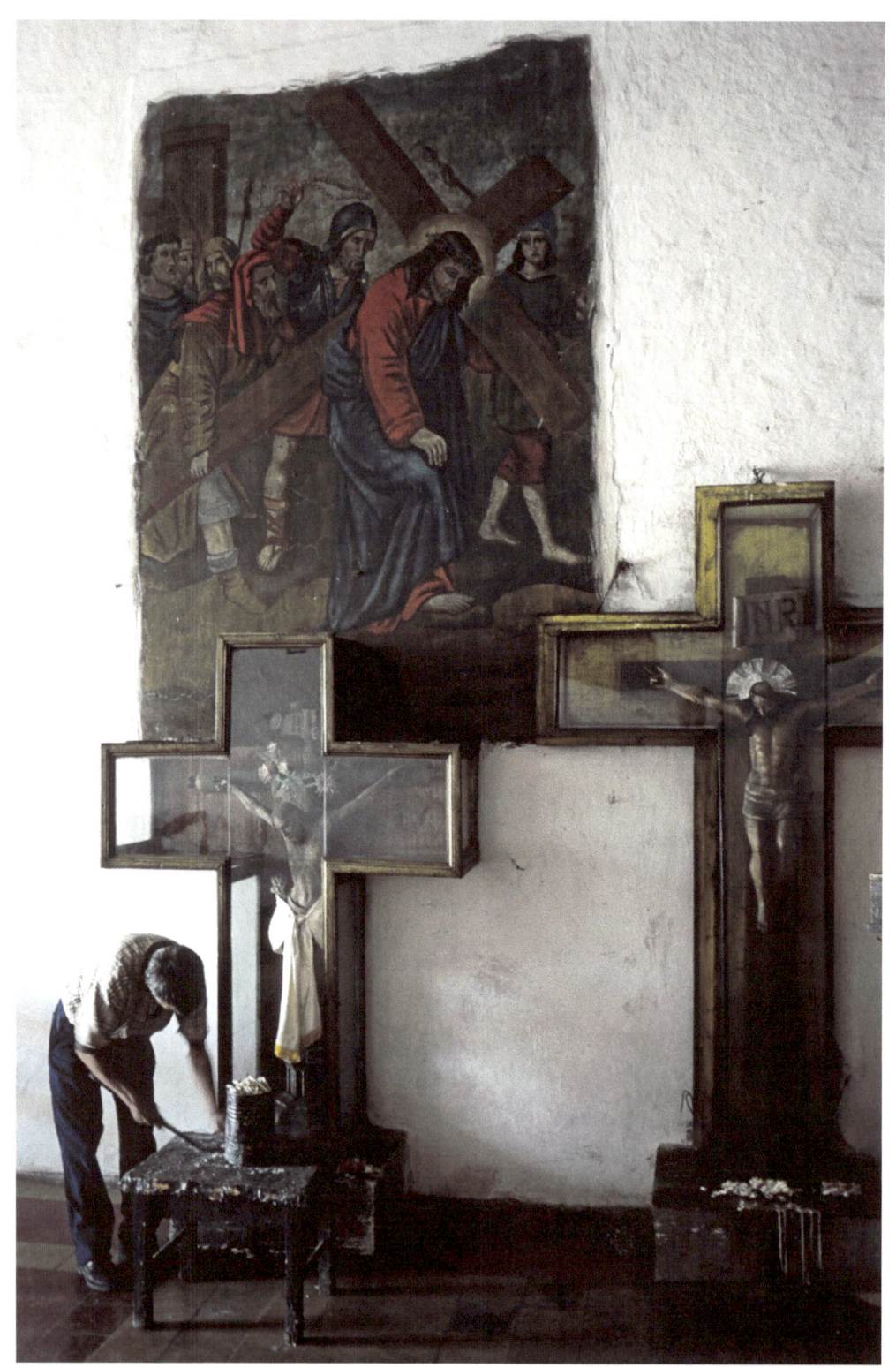

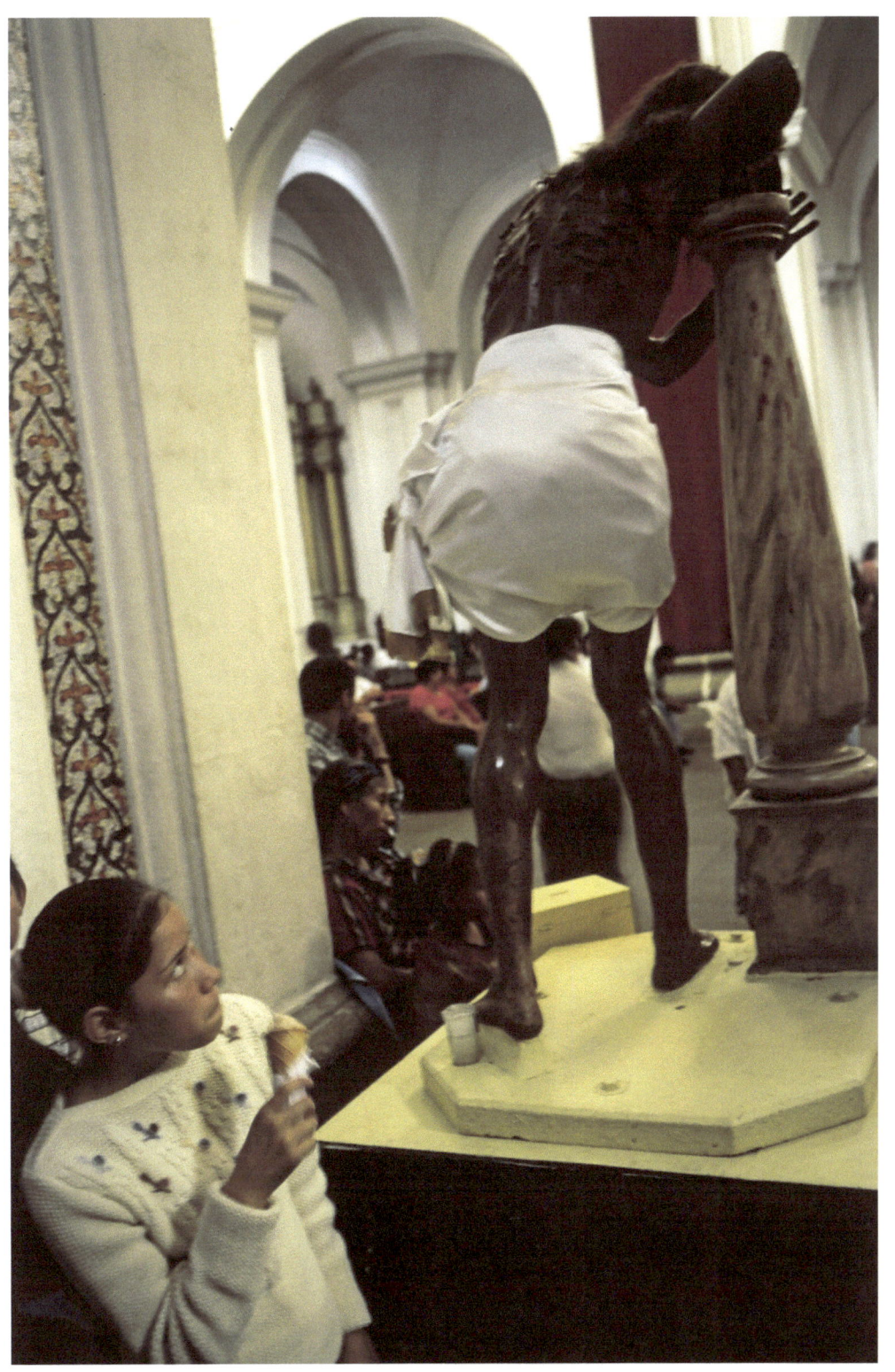

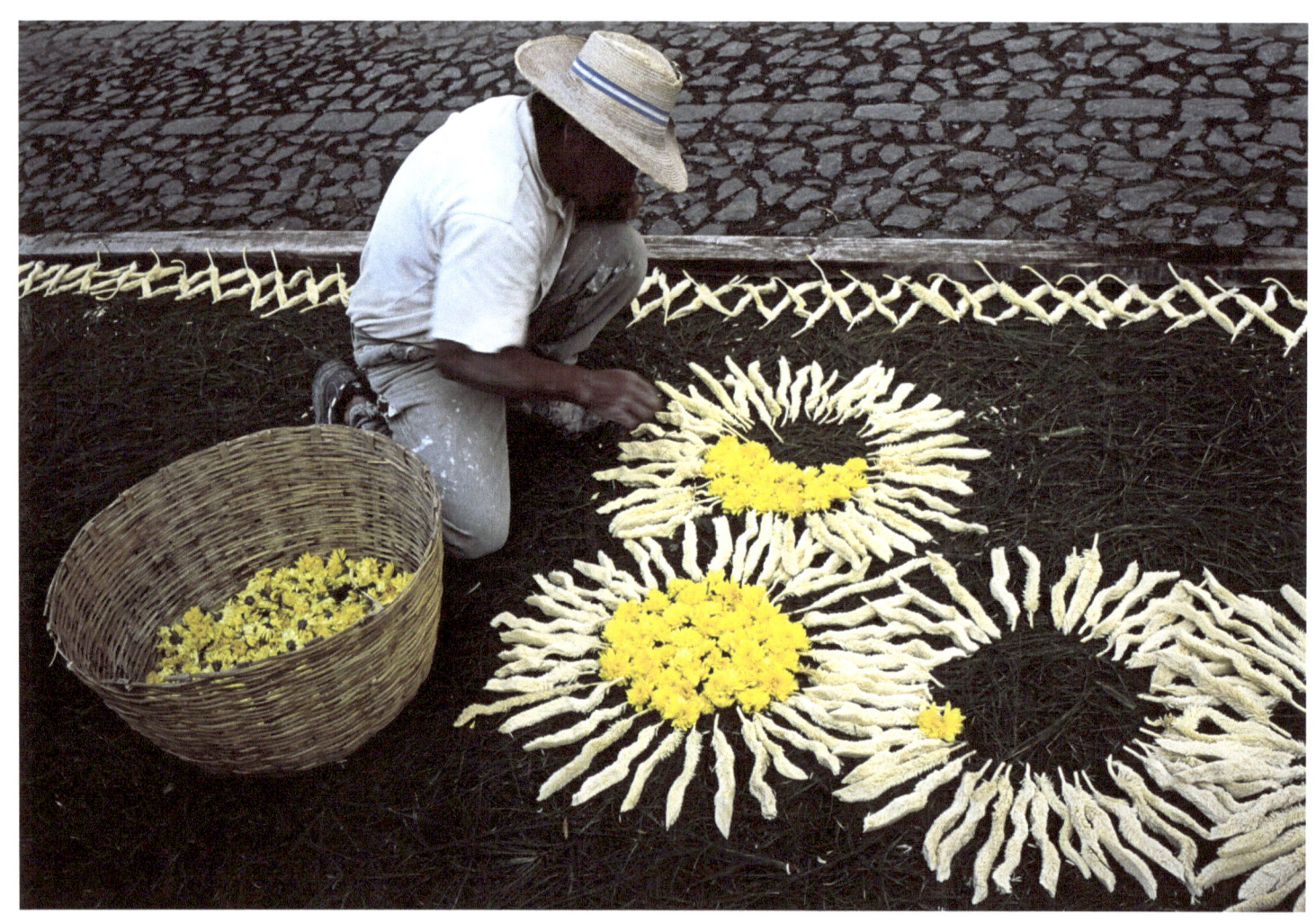

Antigua Guatemala, Semana Santa procession, flowerbed preparation

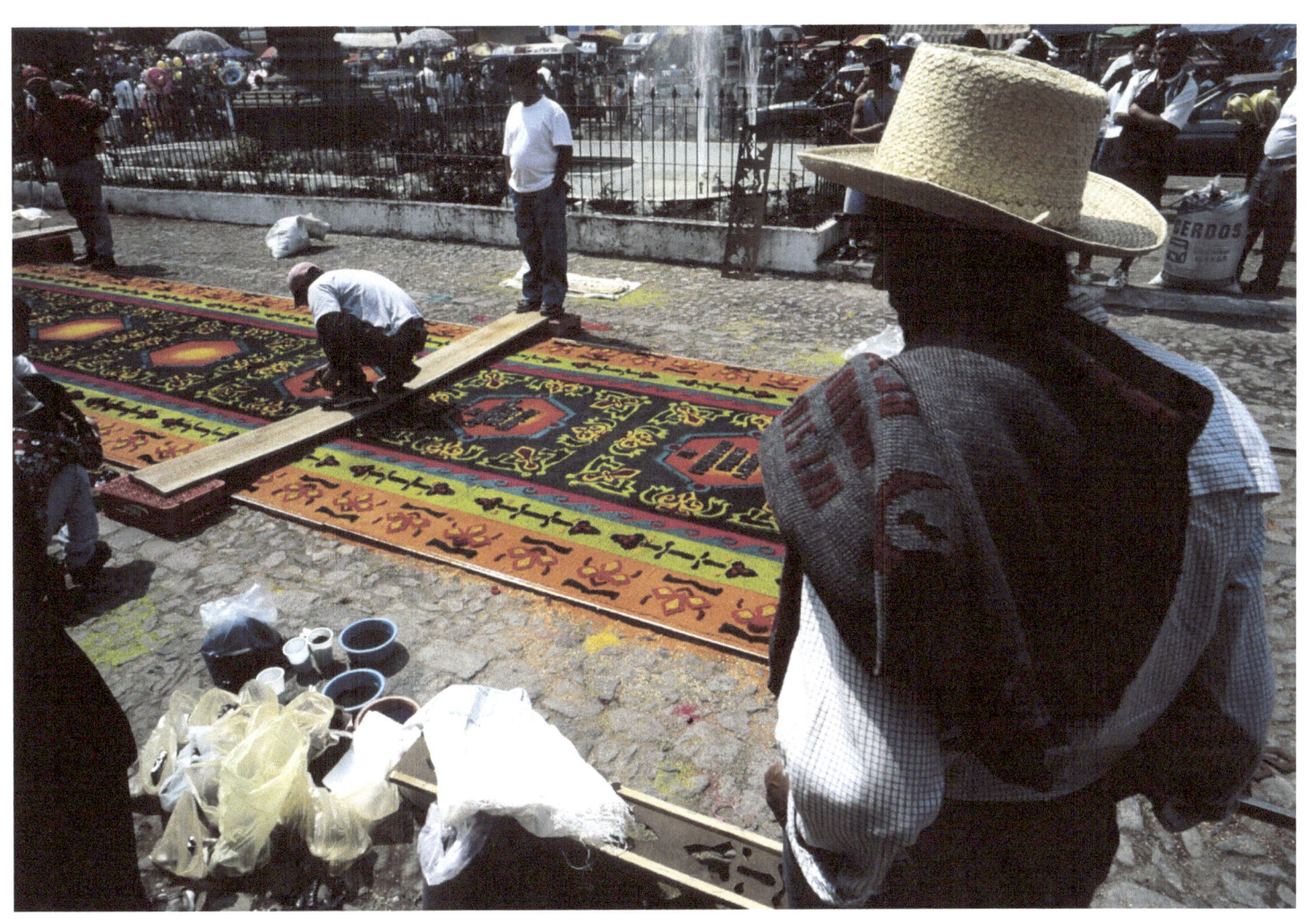

Antigua Guatemala, Semana Santa procession, flowerbed preparation

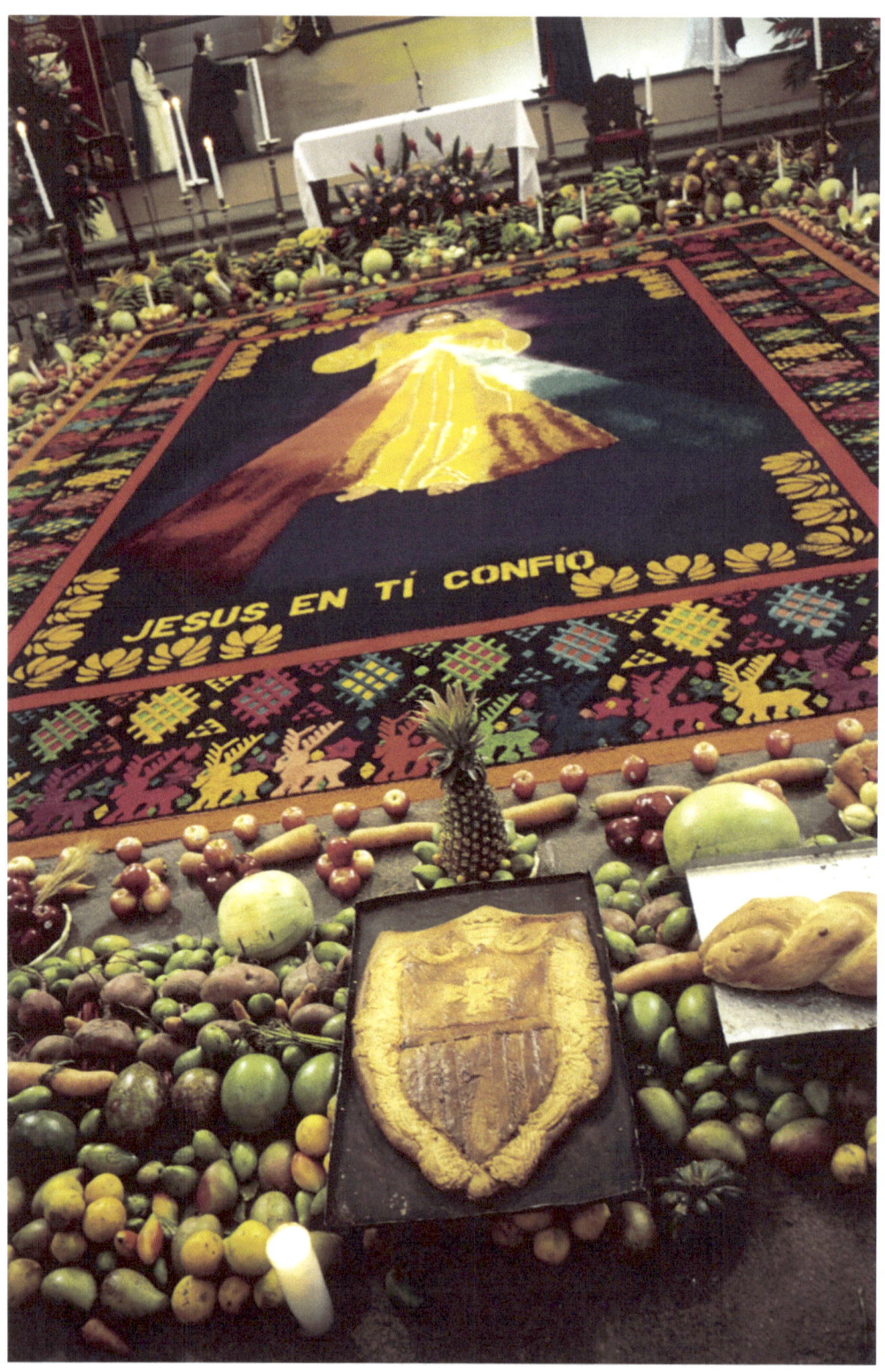

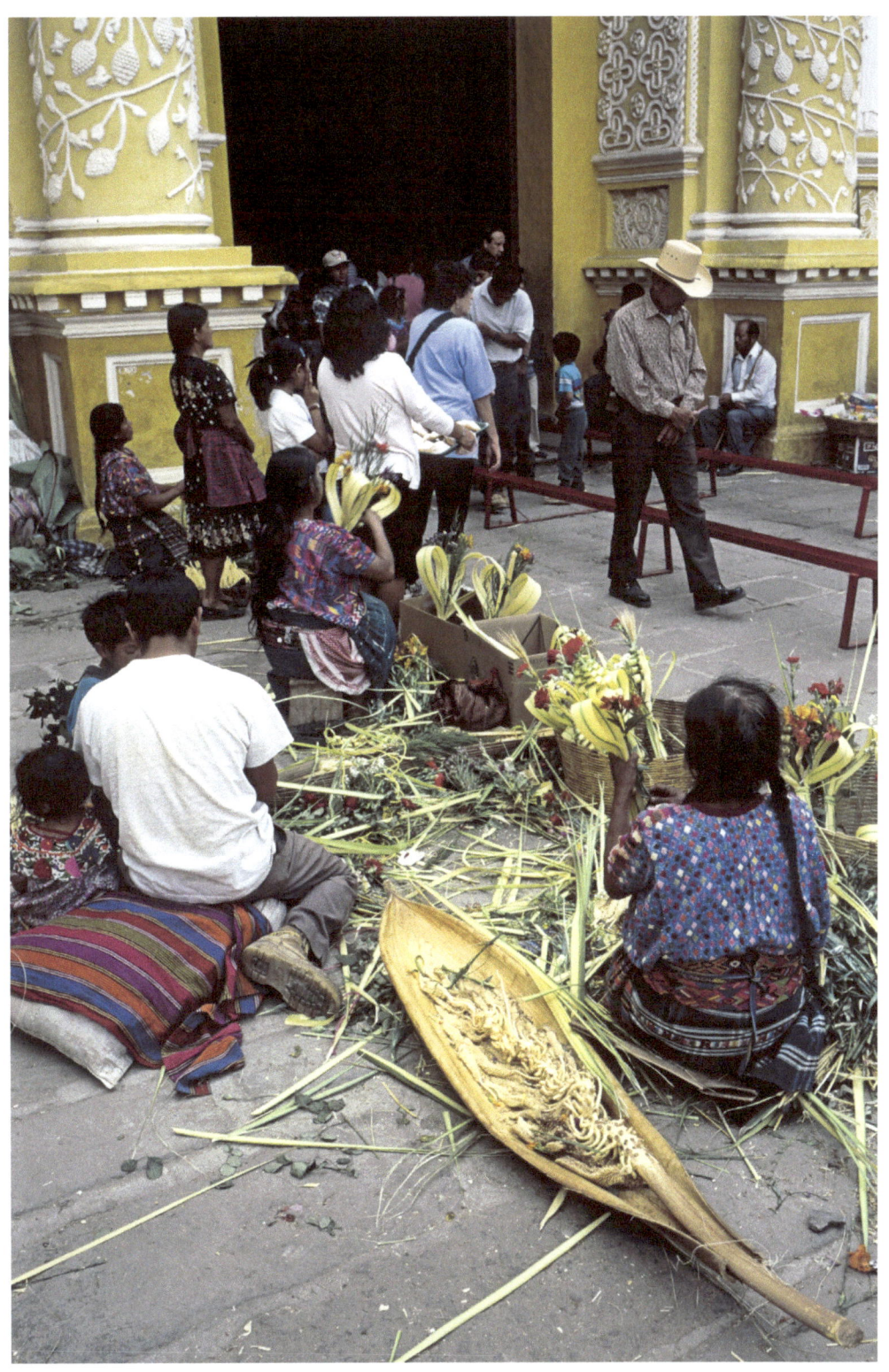

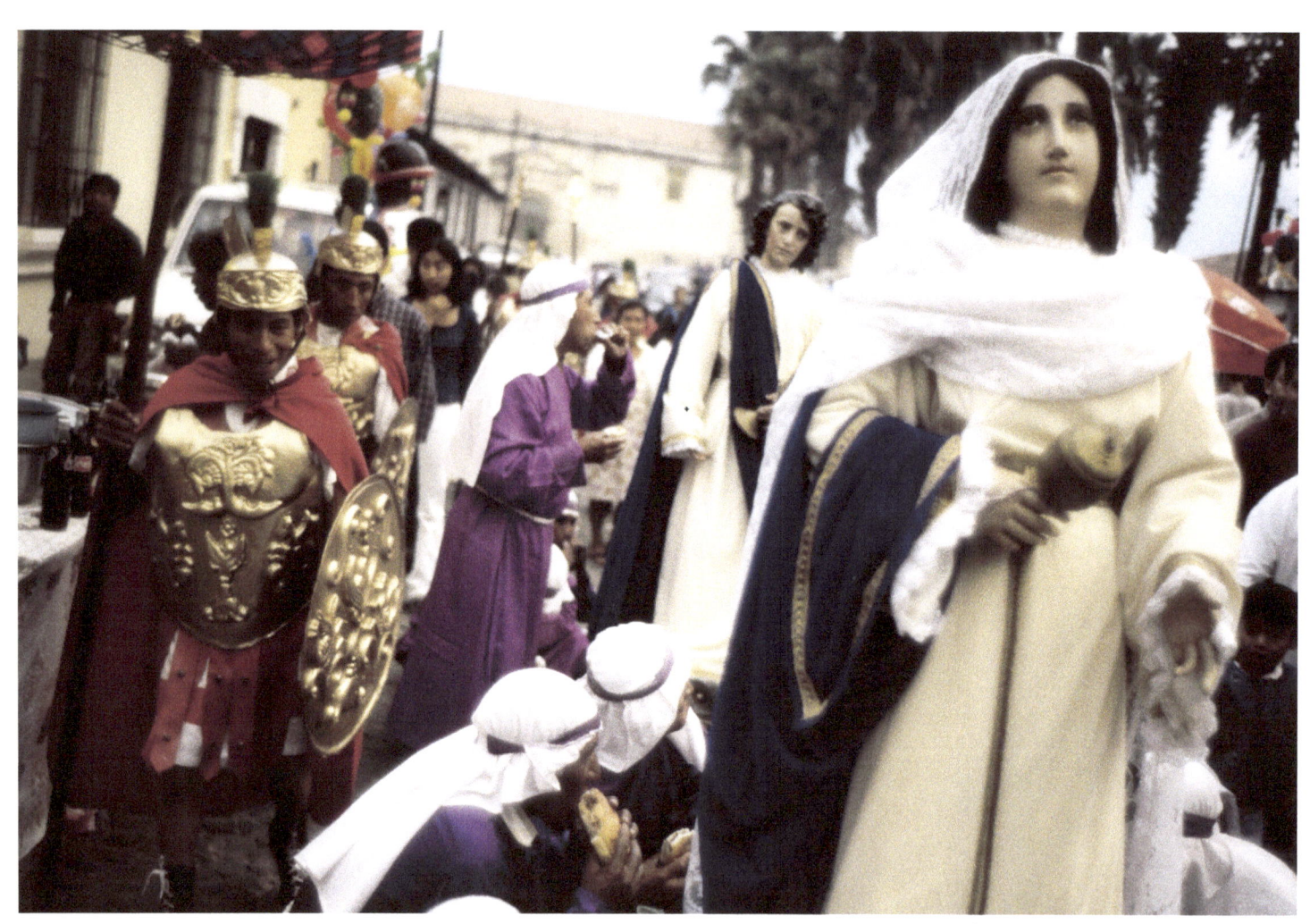
Antigua Guatemala, Semana Santa procession

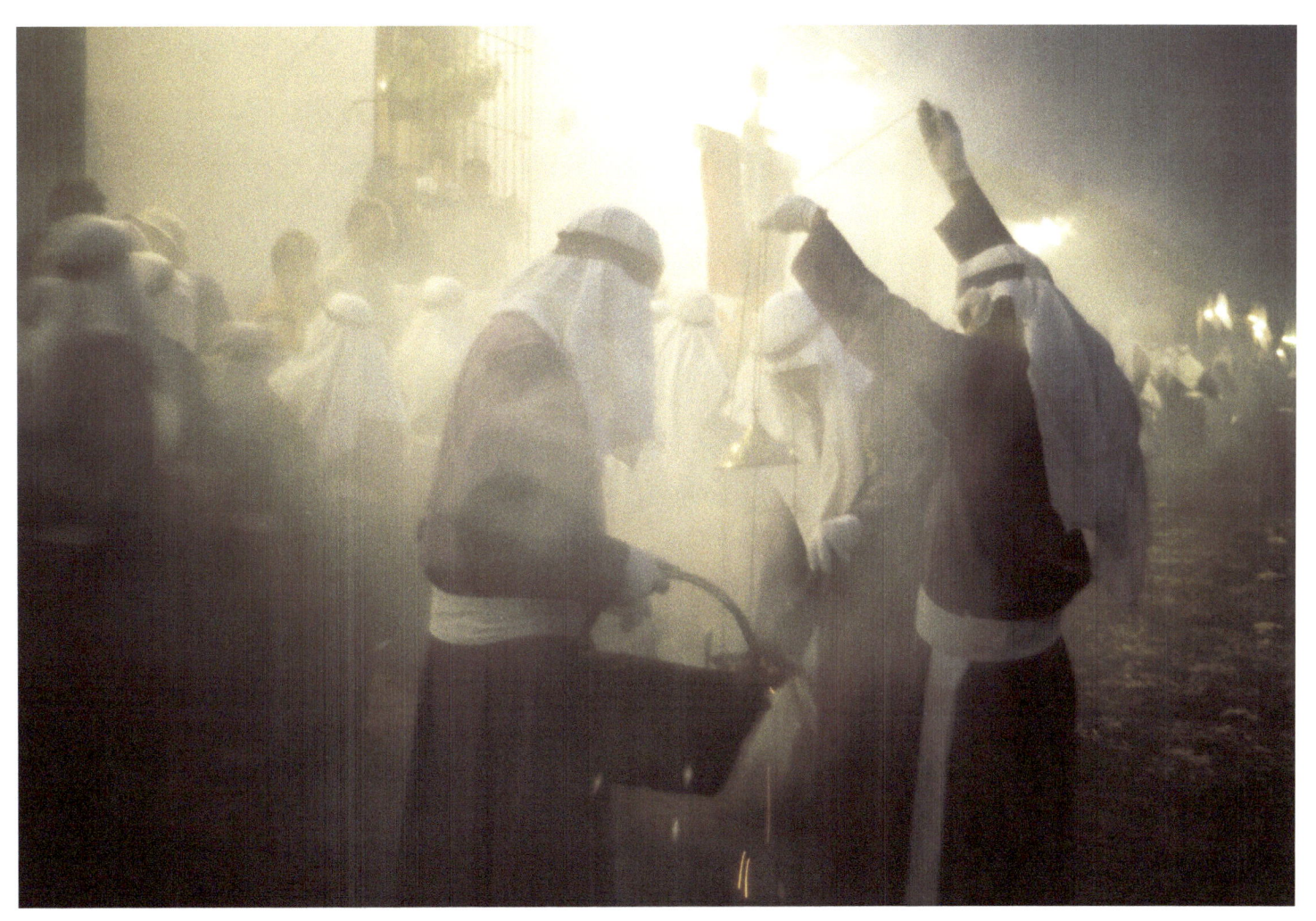
Antigua Guatemala, Semana Santa procession

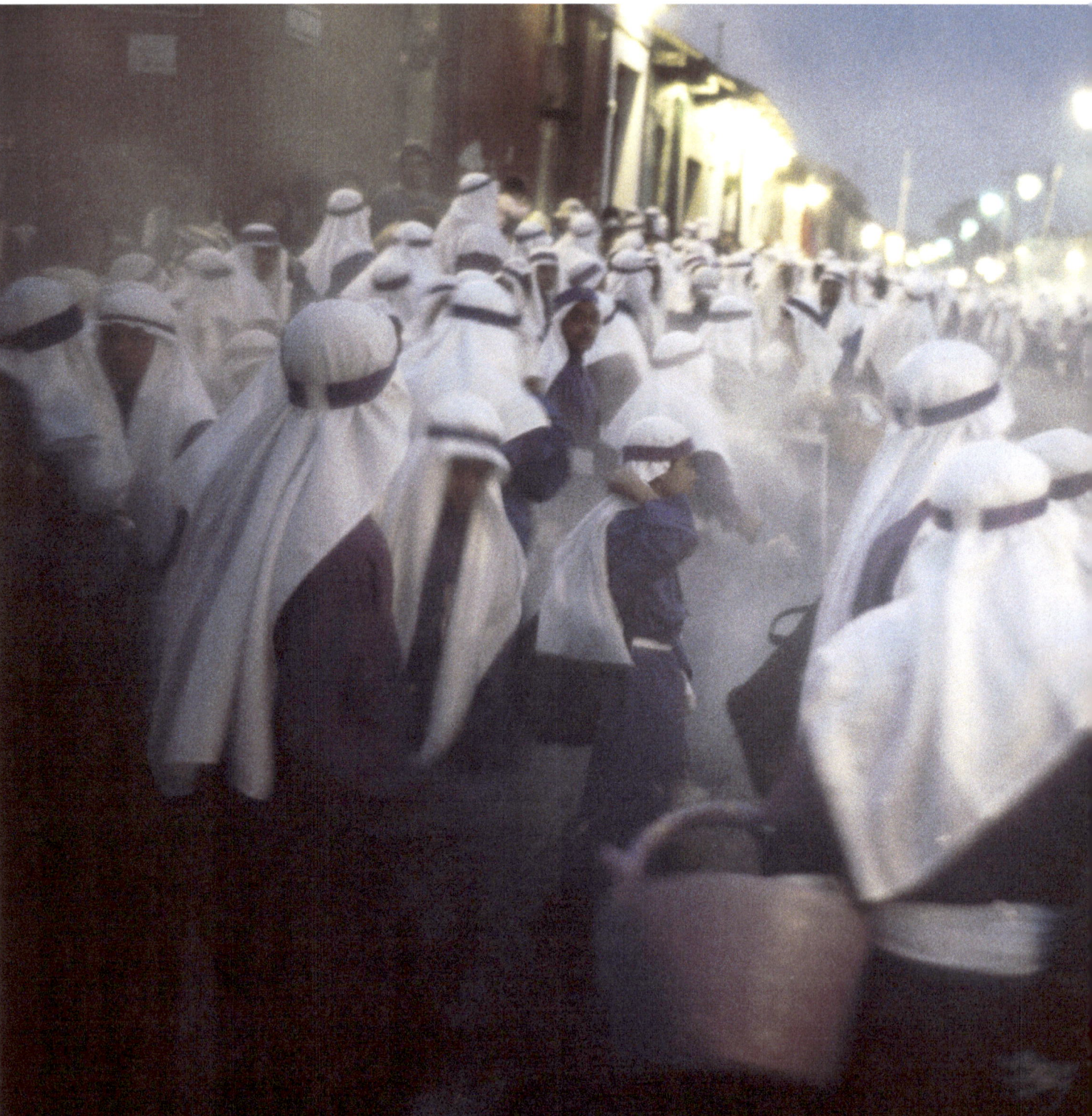

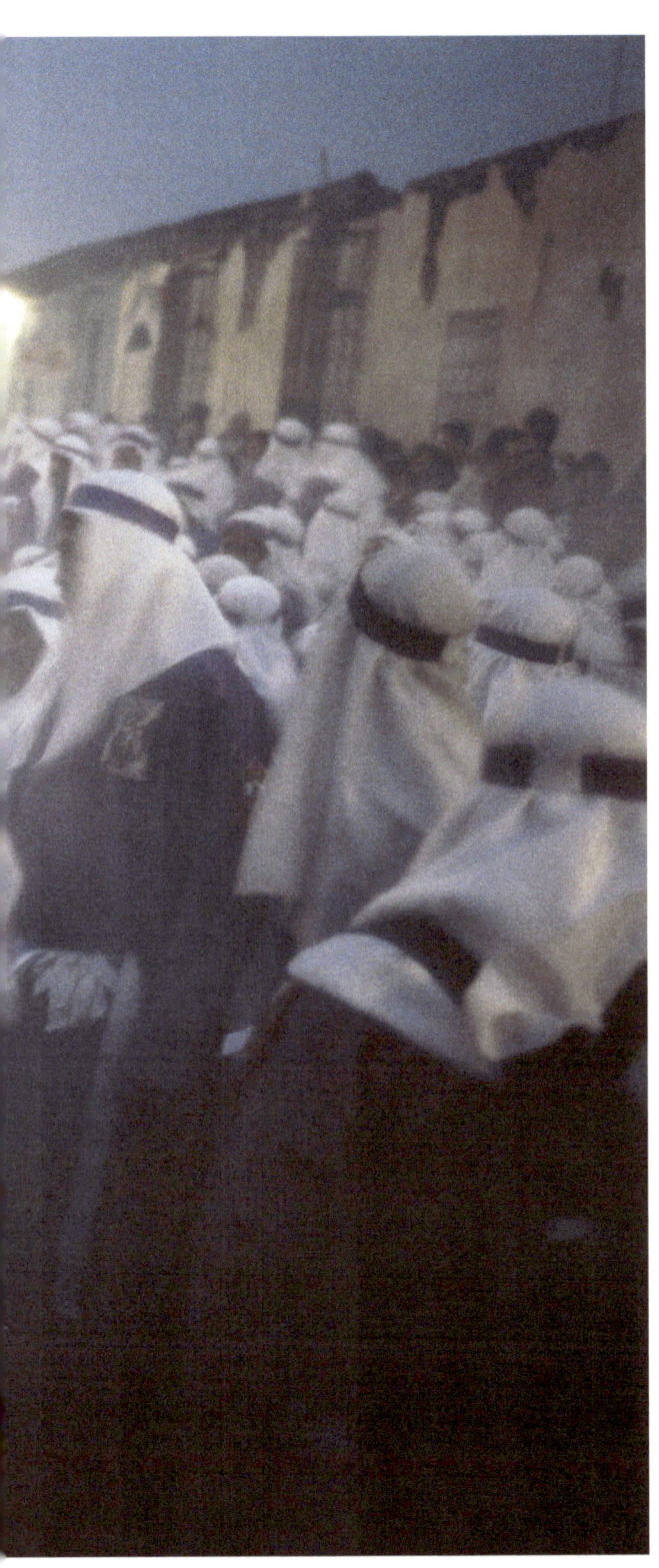

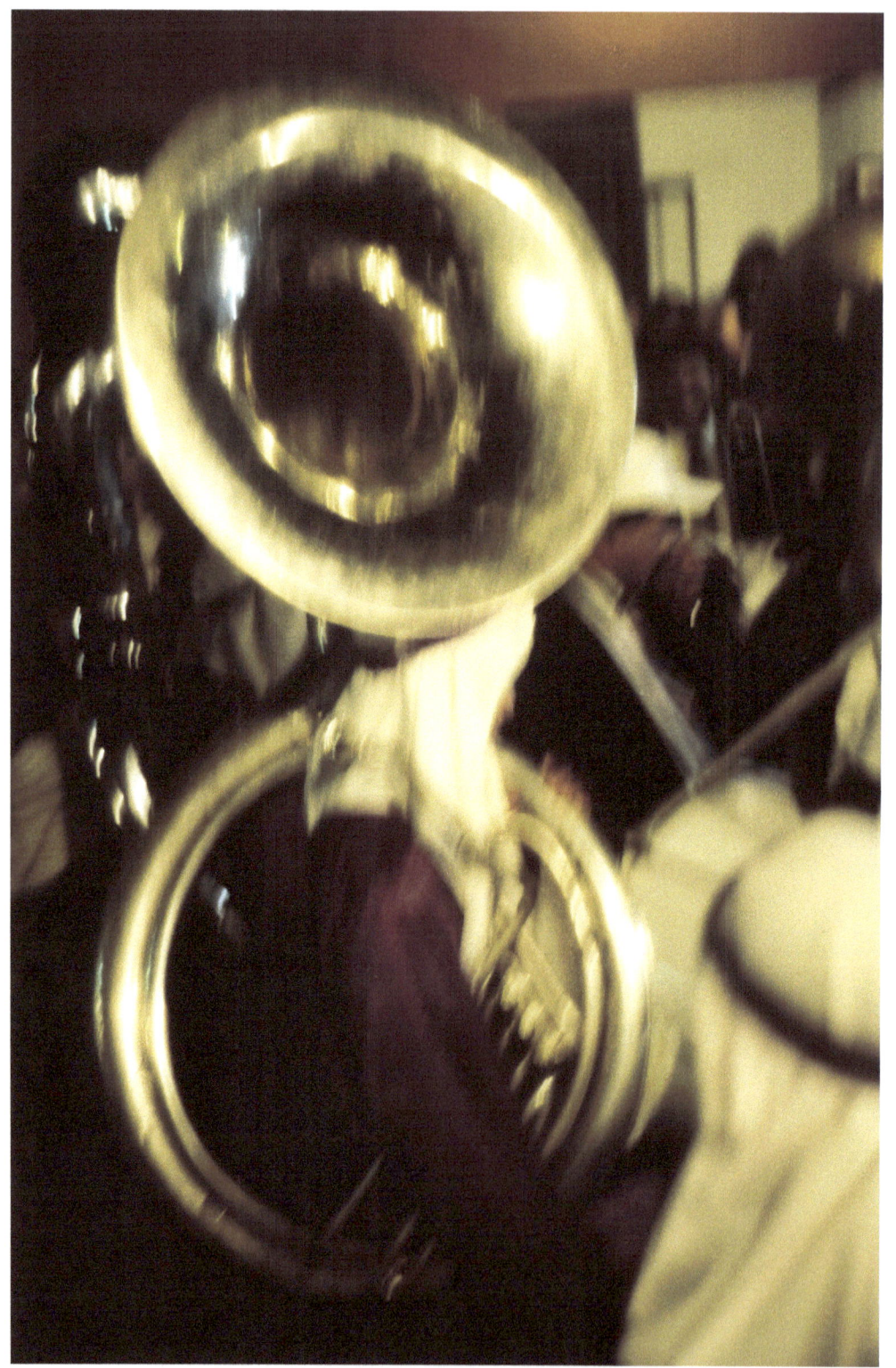

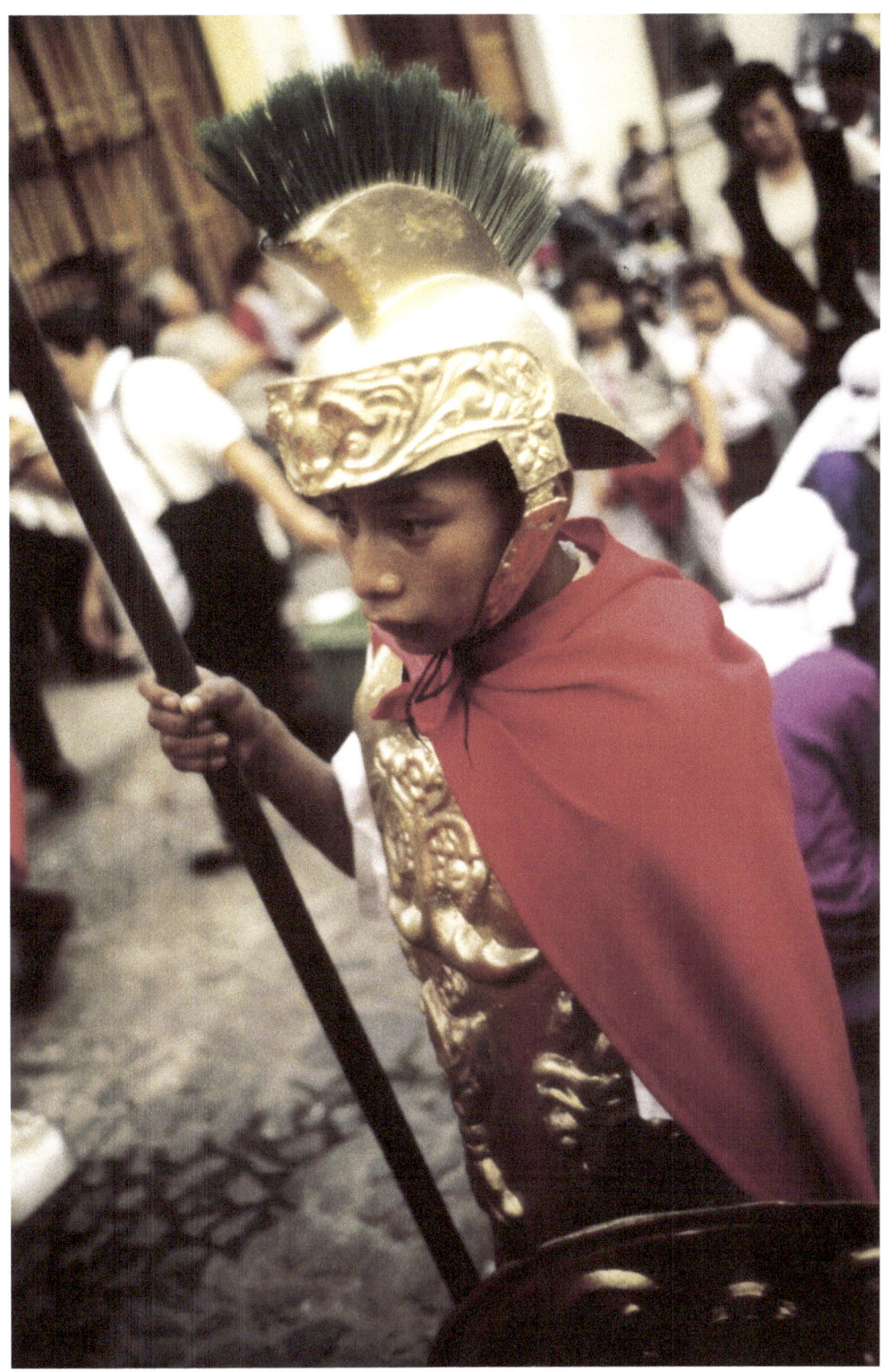

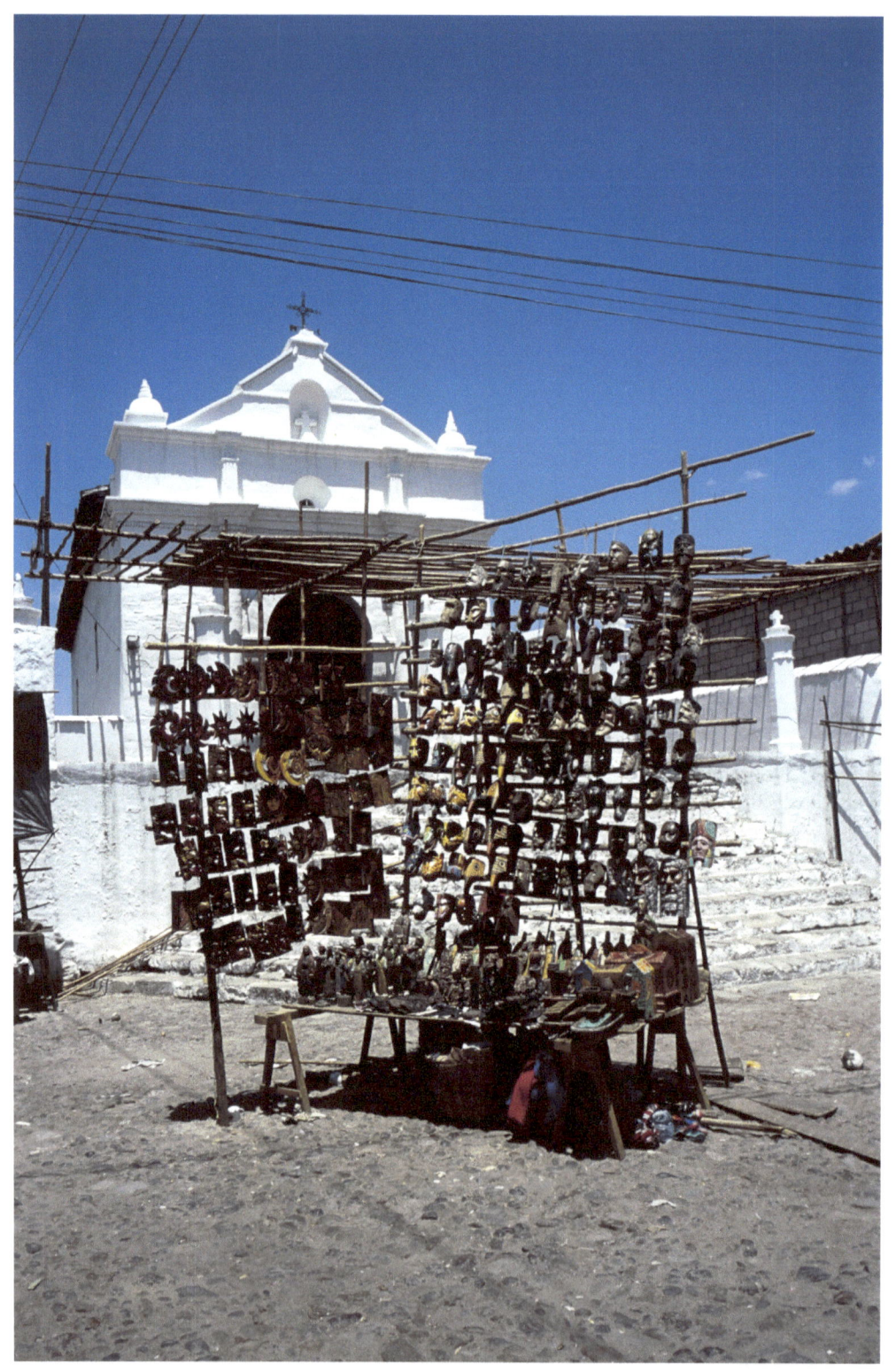

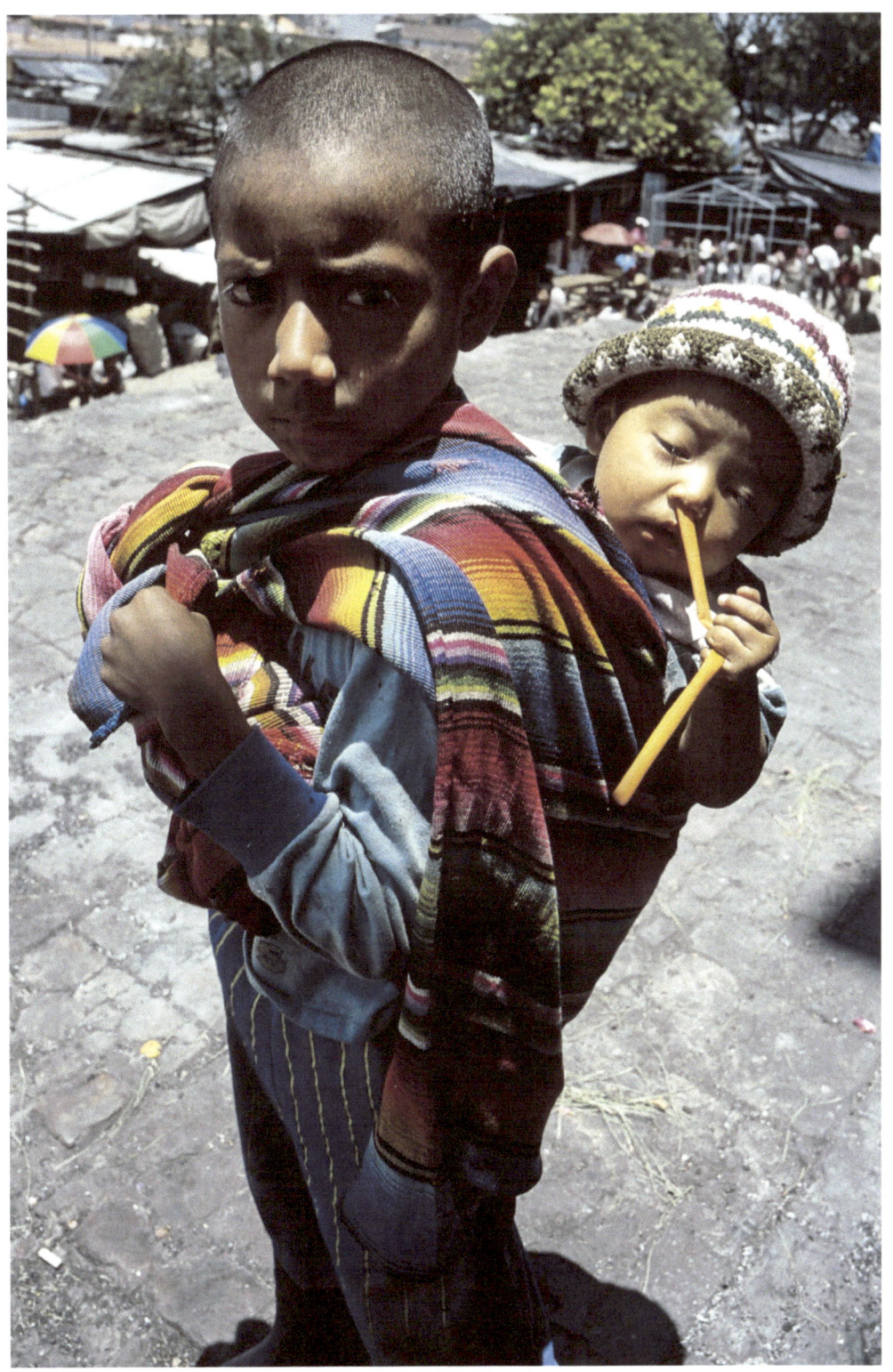

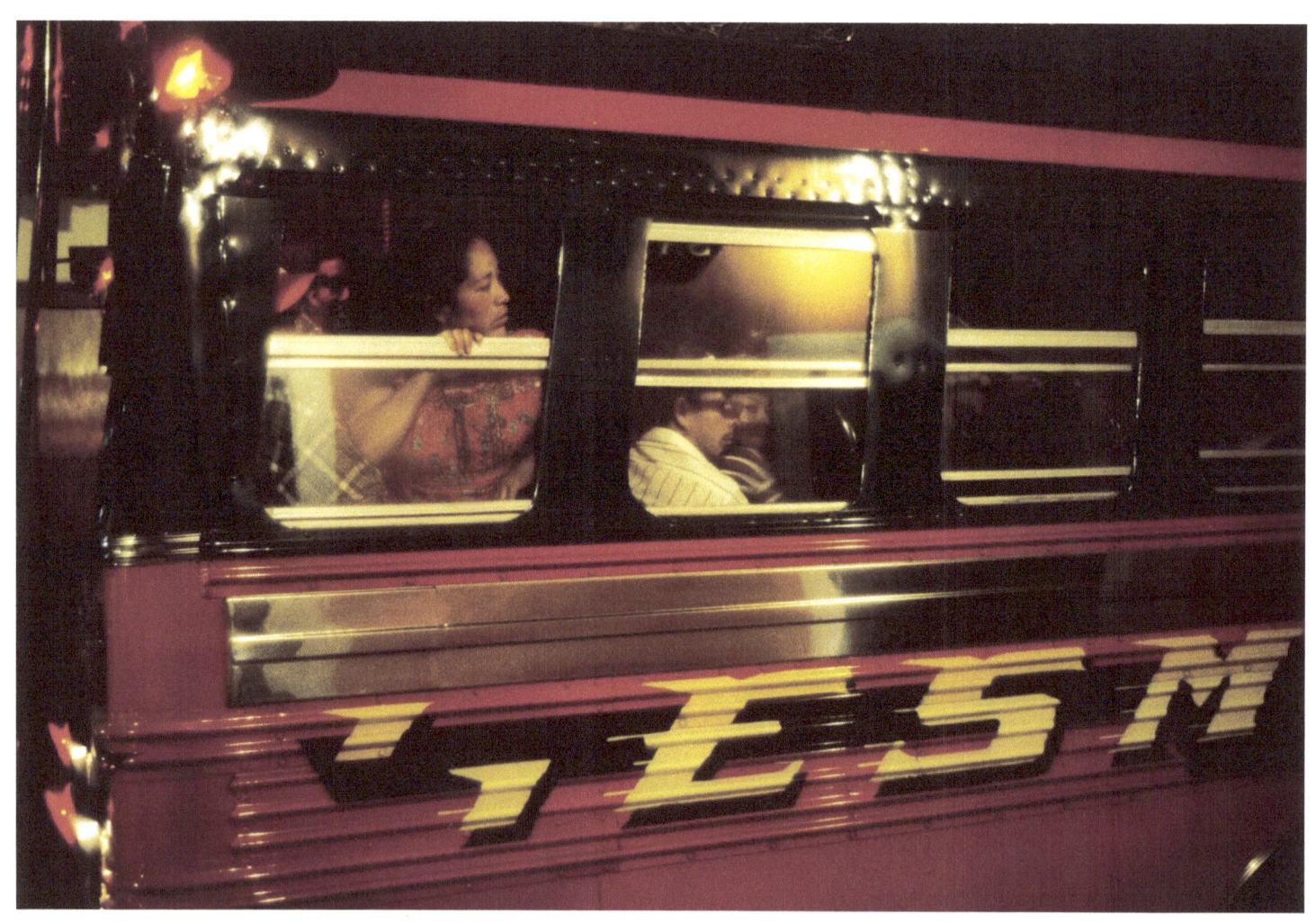

Guatemala, on the road to Mexico

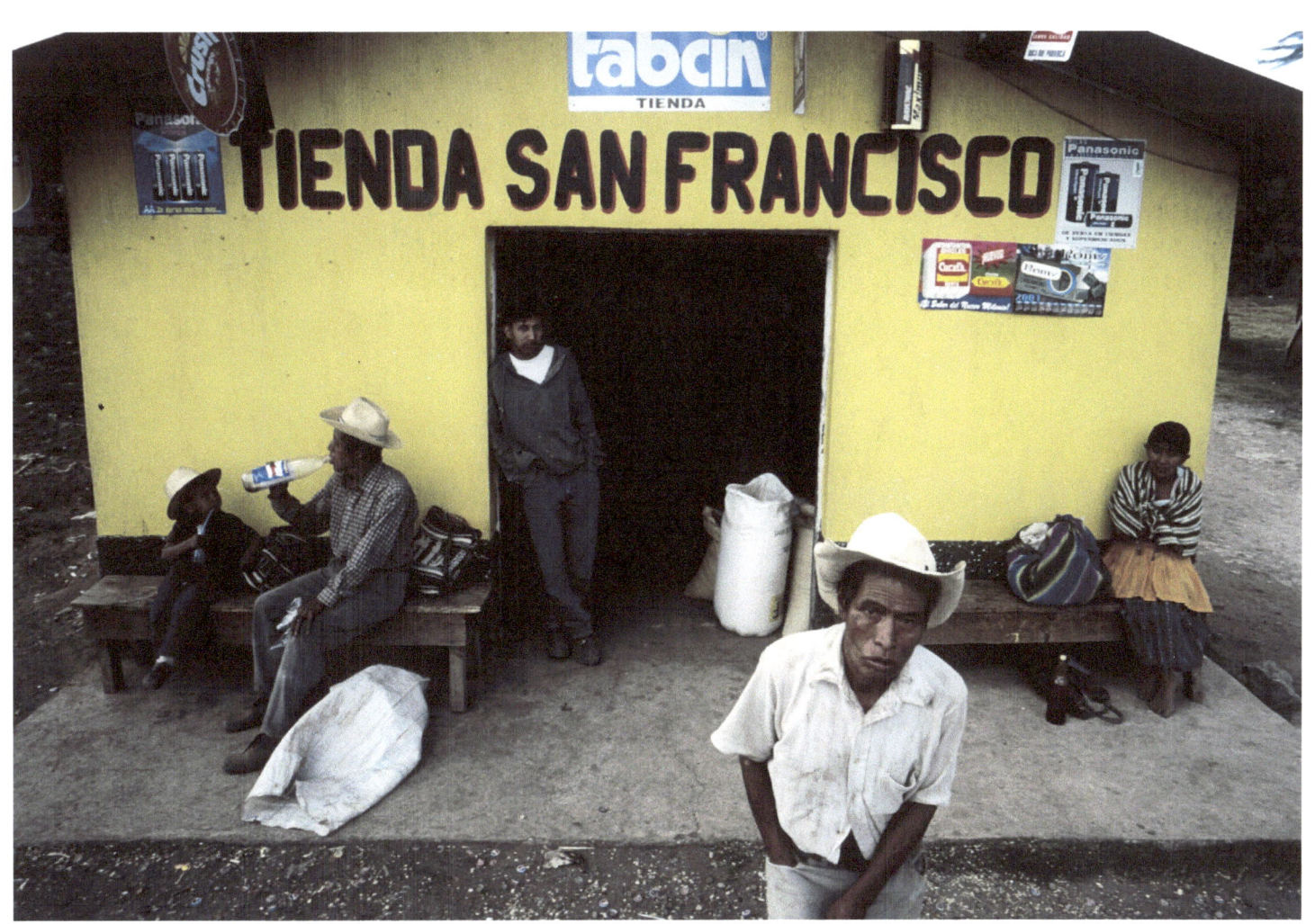

Guatemala, on the road to Mexico

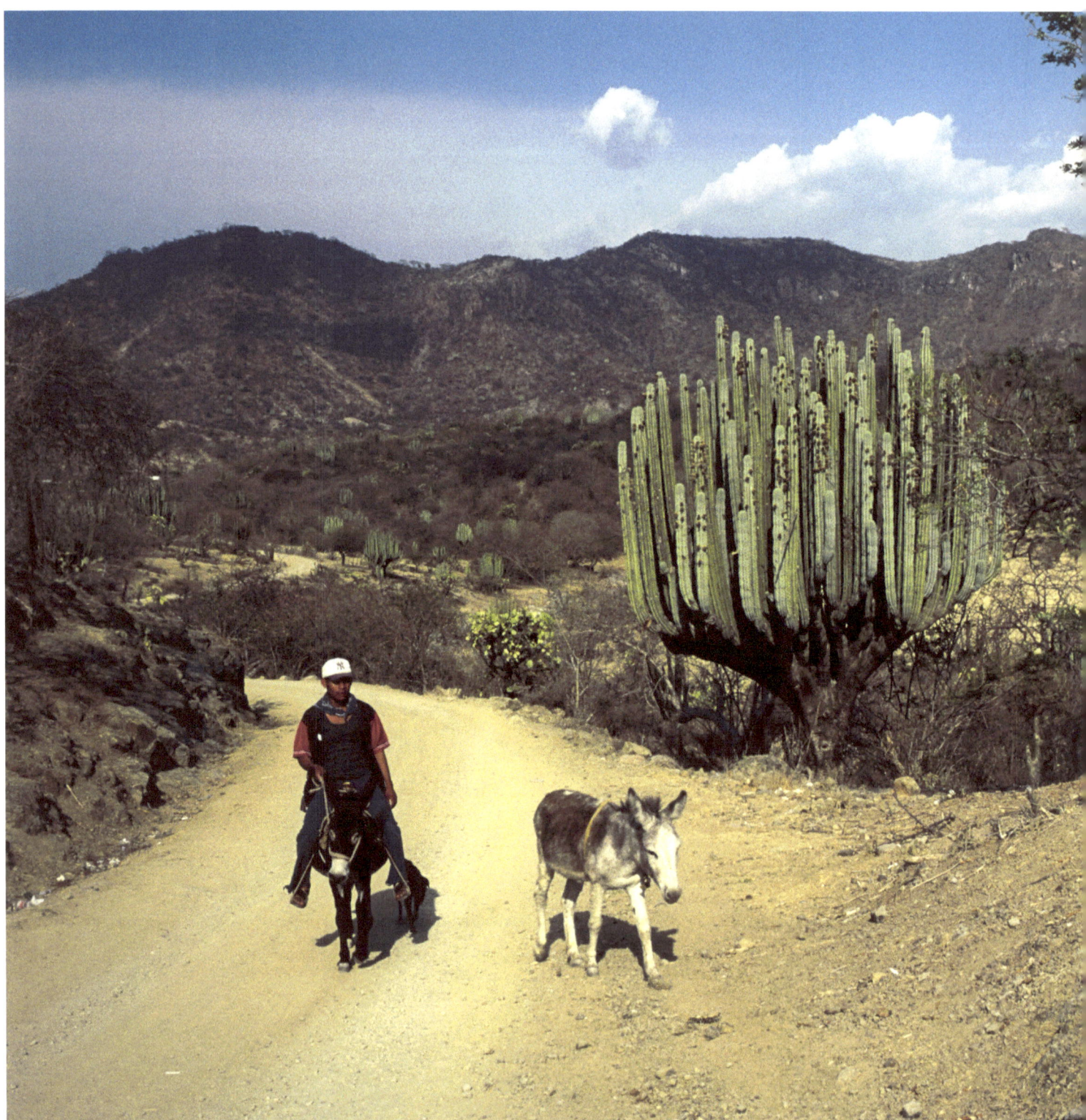

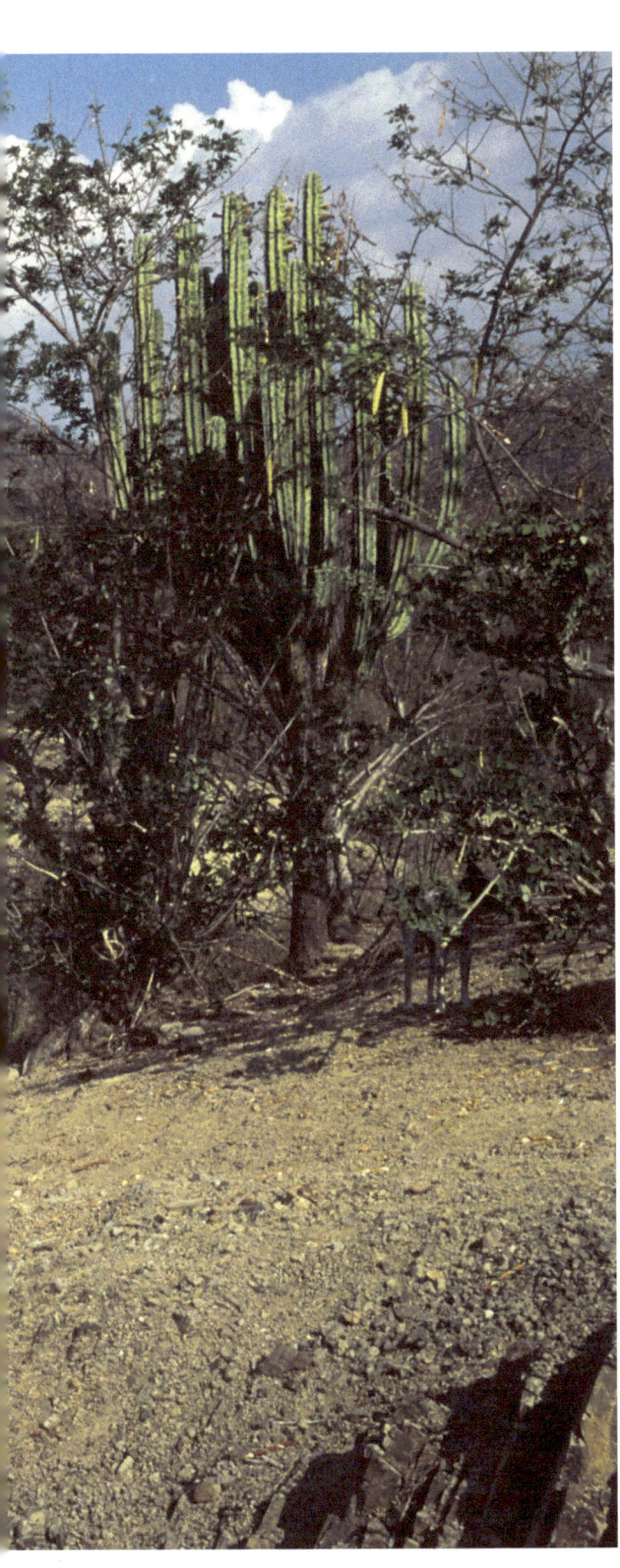

Mexico

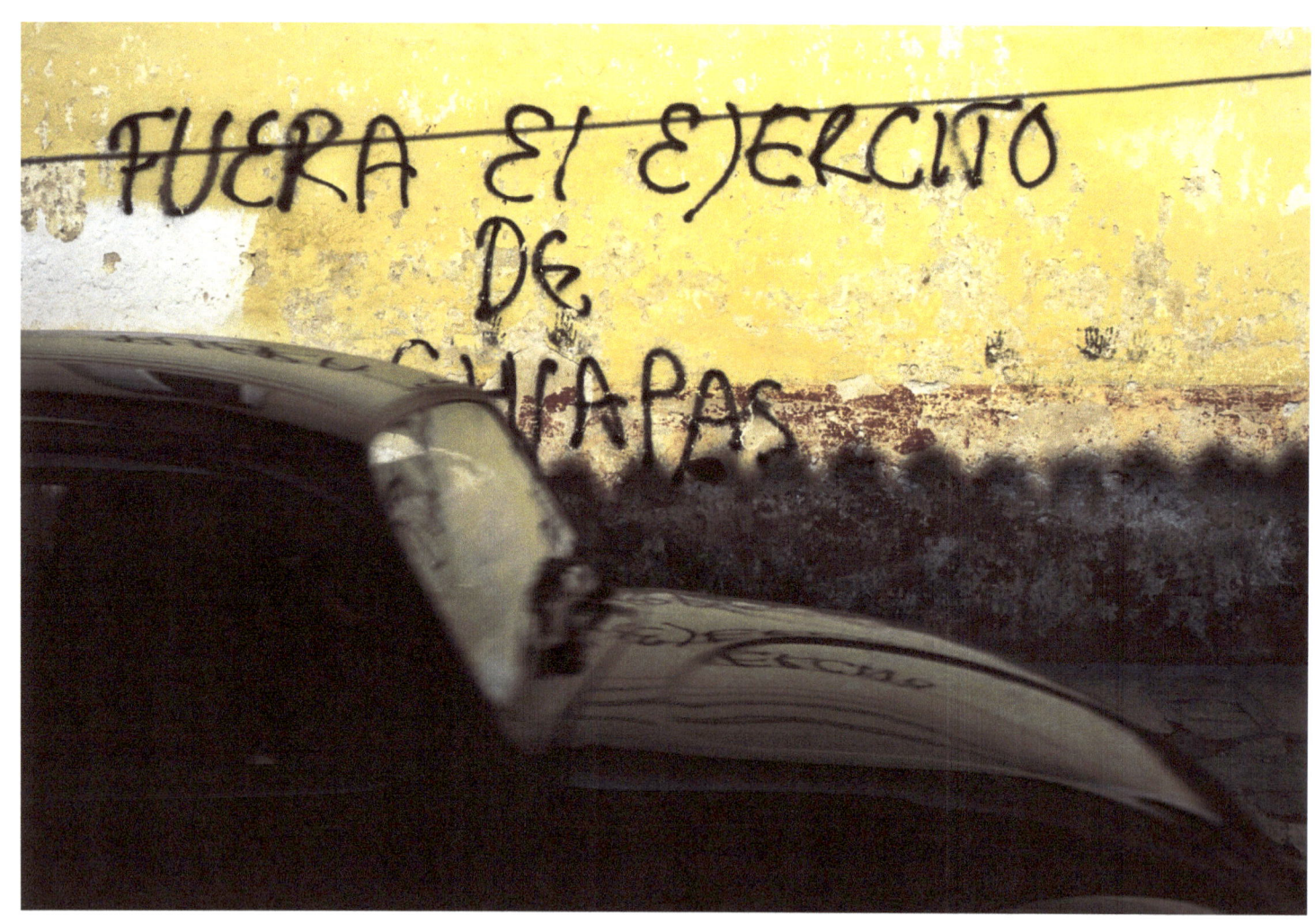

Latin Americans consider Mexico a Northern American country; Americans, well, we know...
Mexico is probably a mosaic of realities that only Mexicans can define.

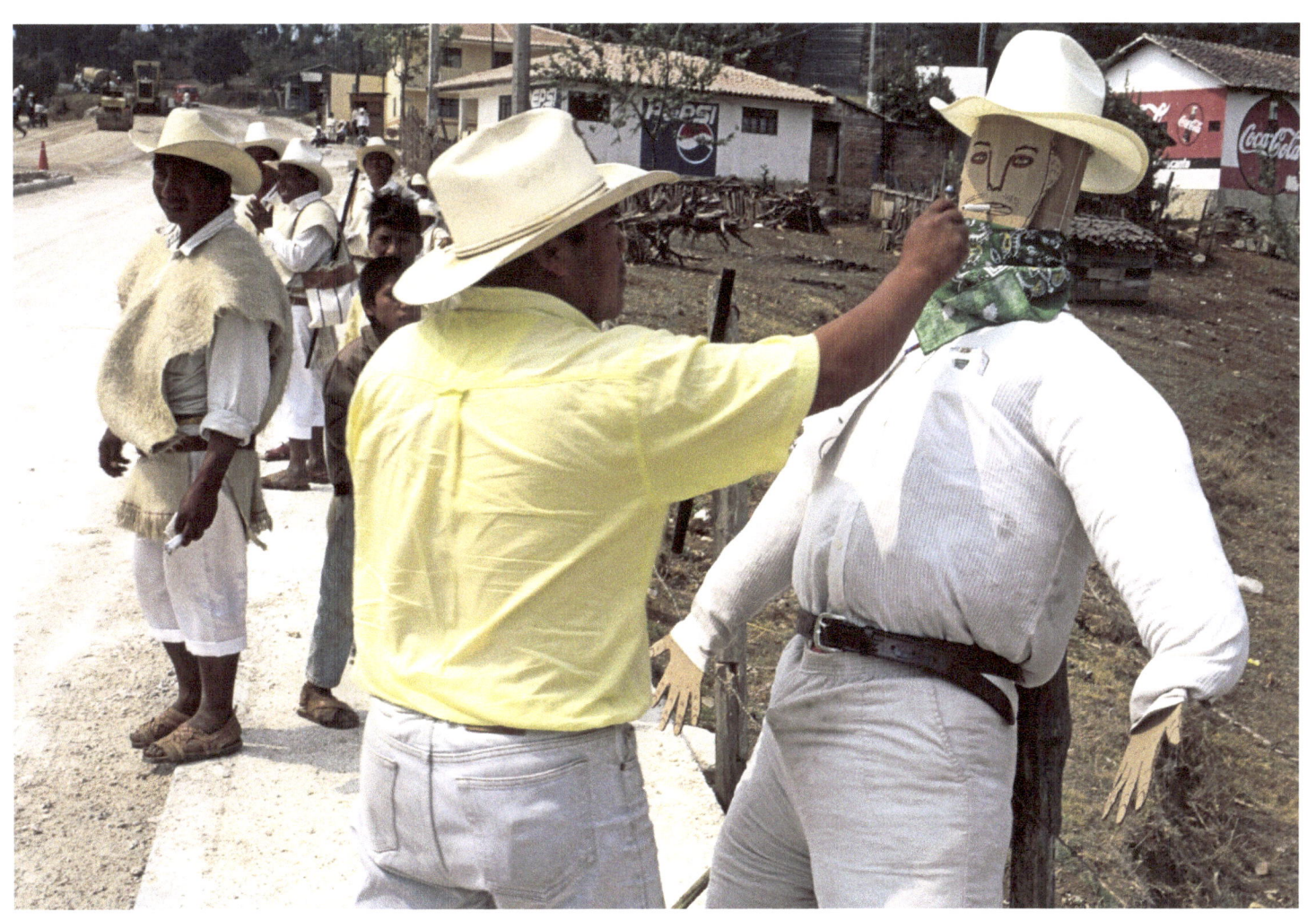

Chiapas was like a different country, a Maya nation under a Latin hat

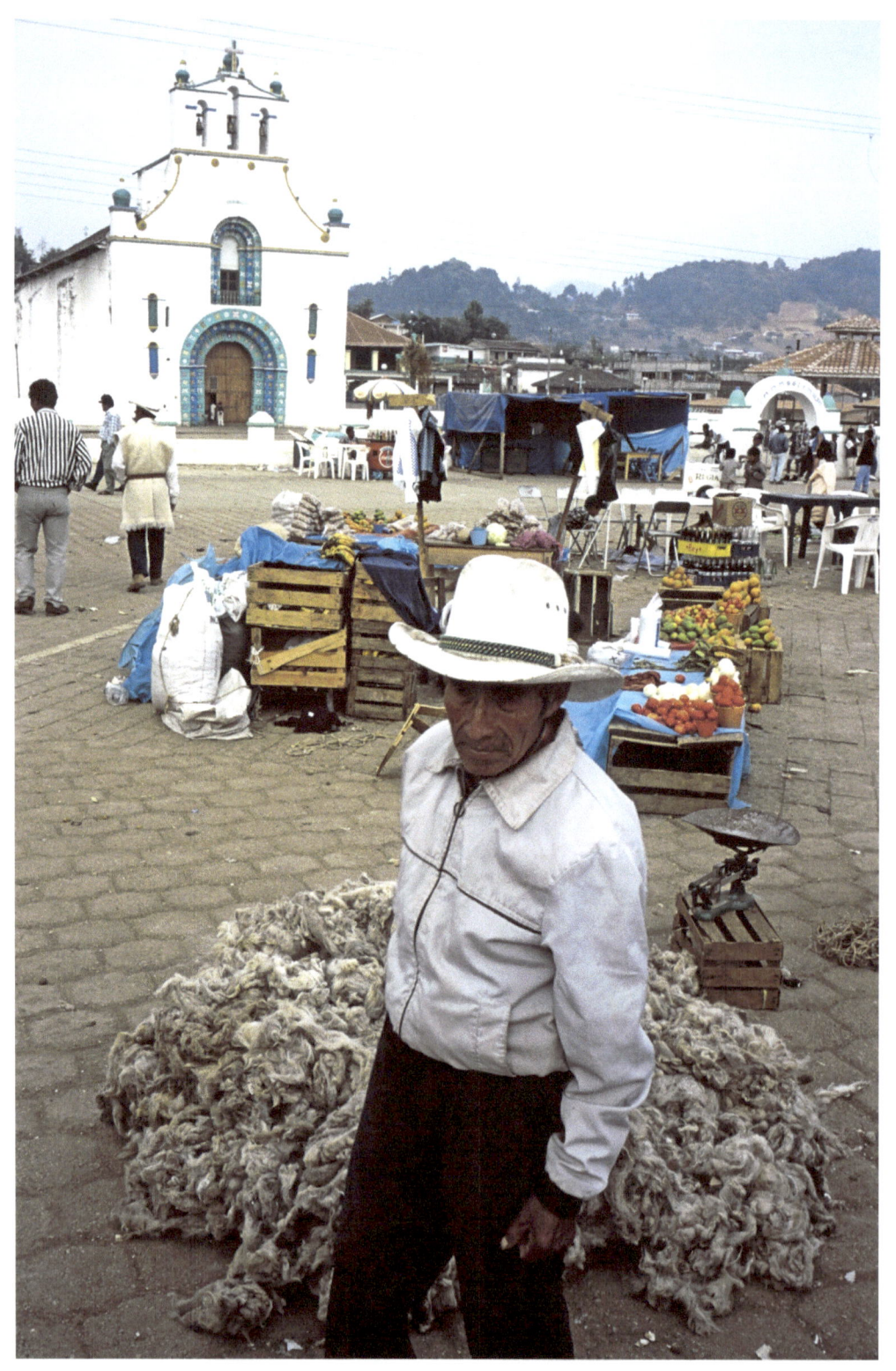

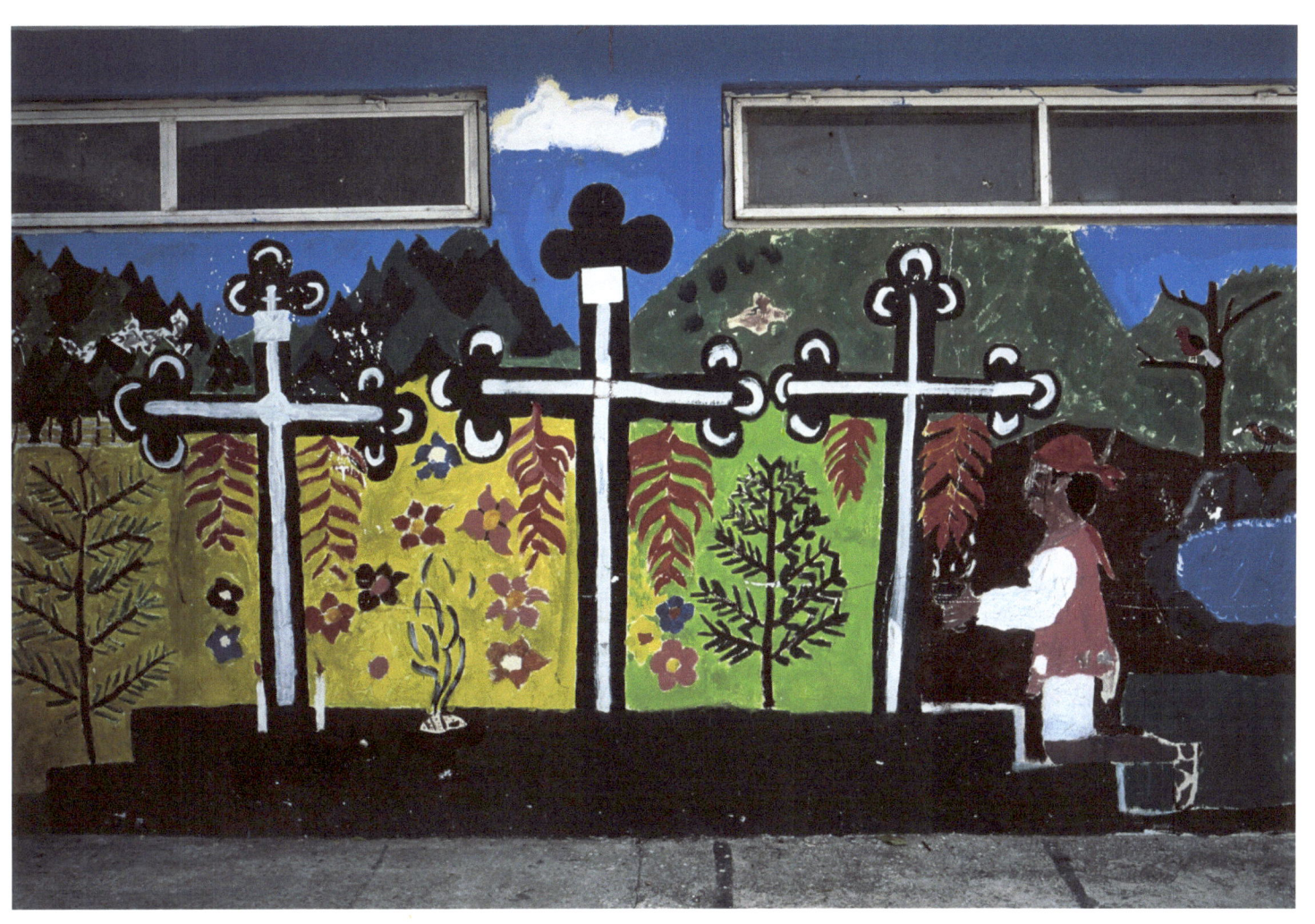

Chiapas might have been different in many ways, but poverty was familiar

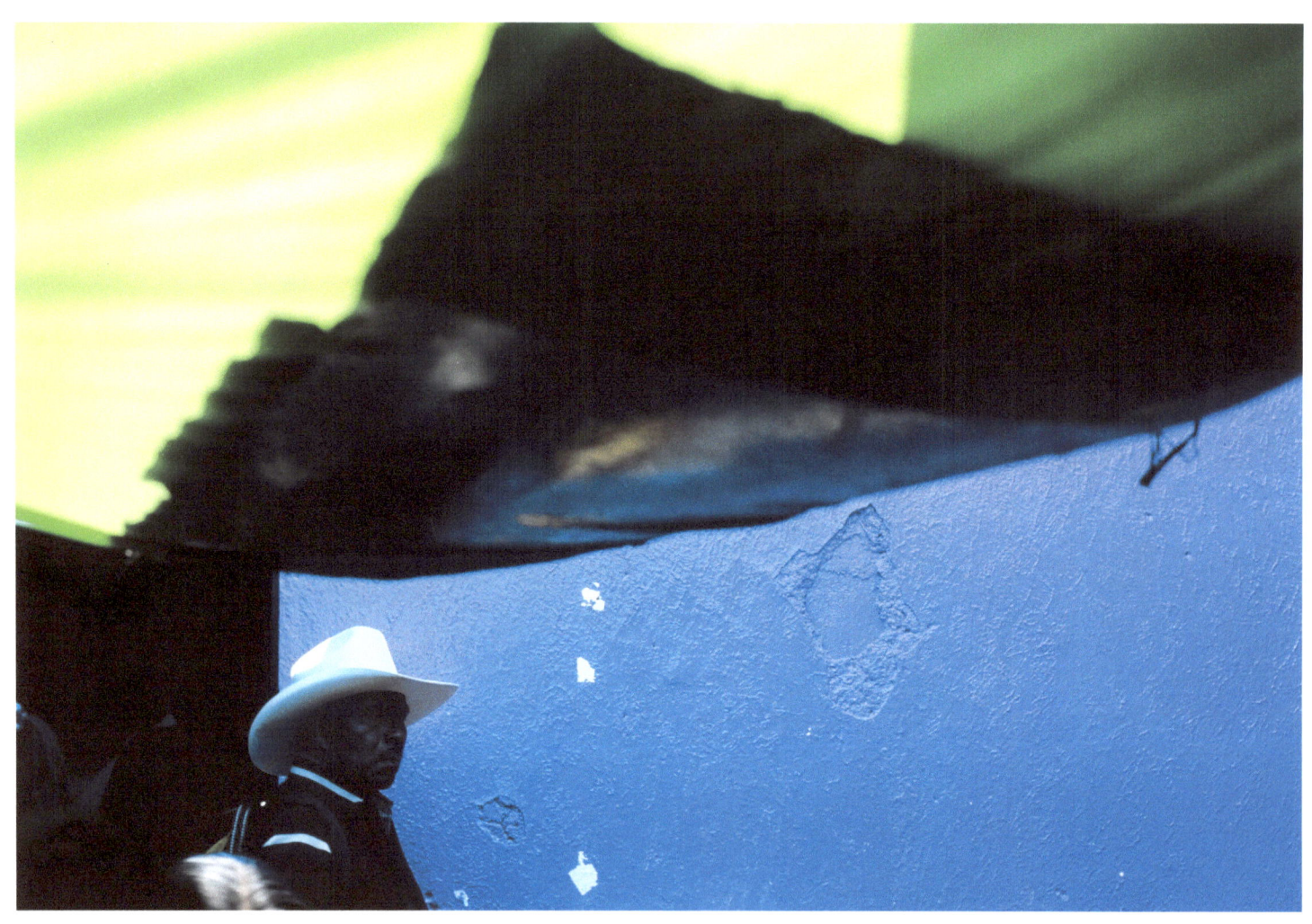

Market in San Cristobal de Las Casas, Chiapas

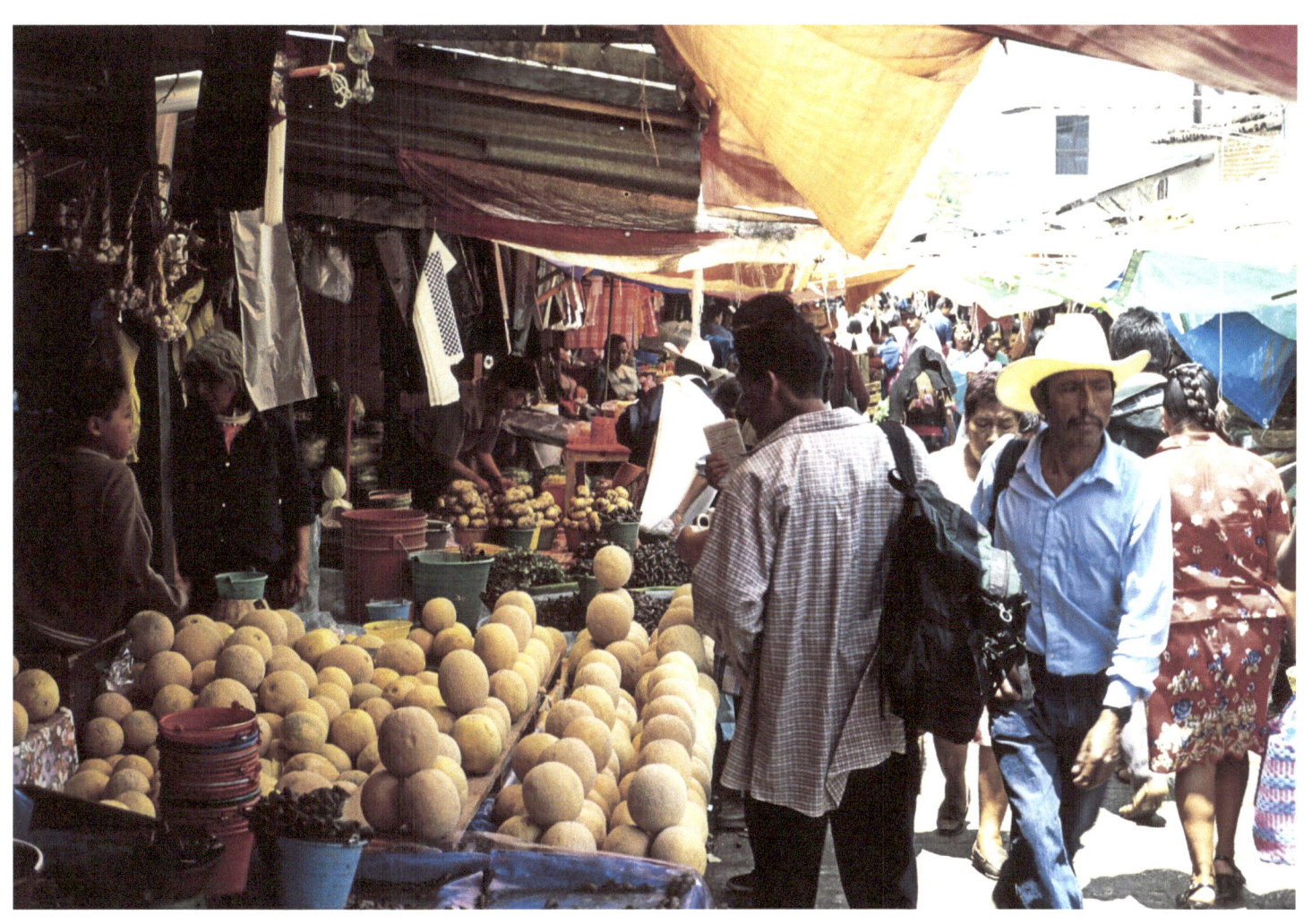

Market in San Cristobal de Las Casas, Chiapas

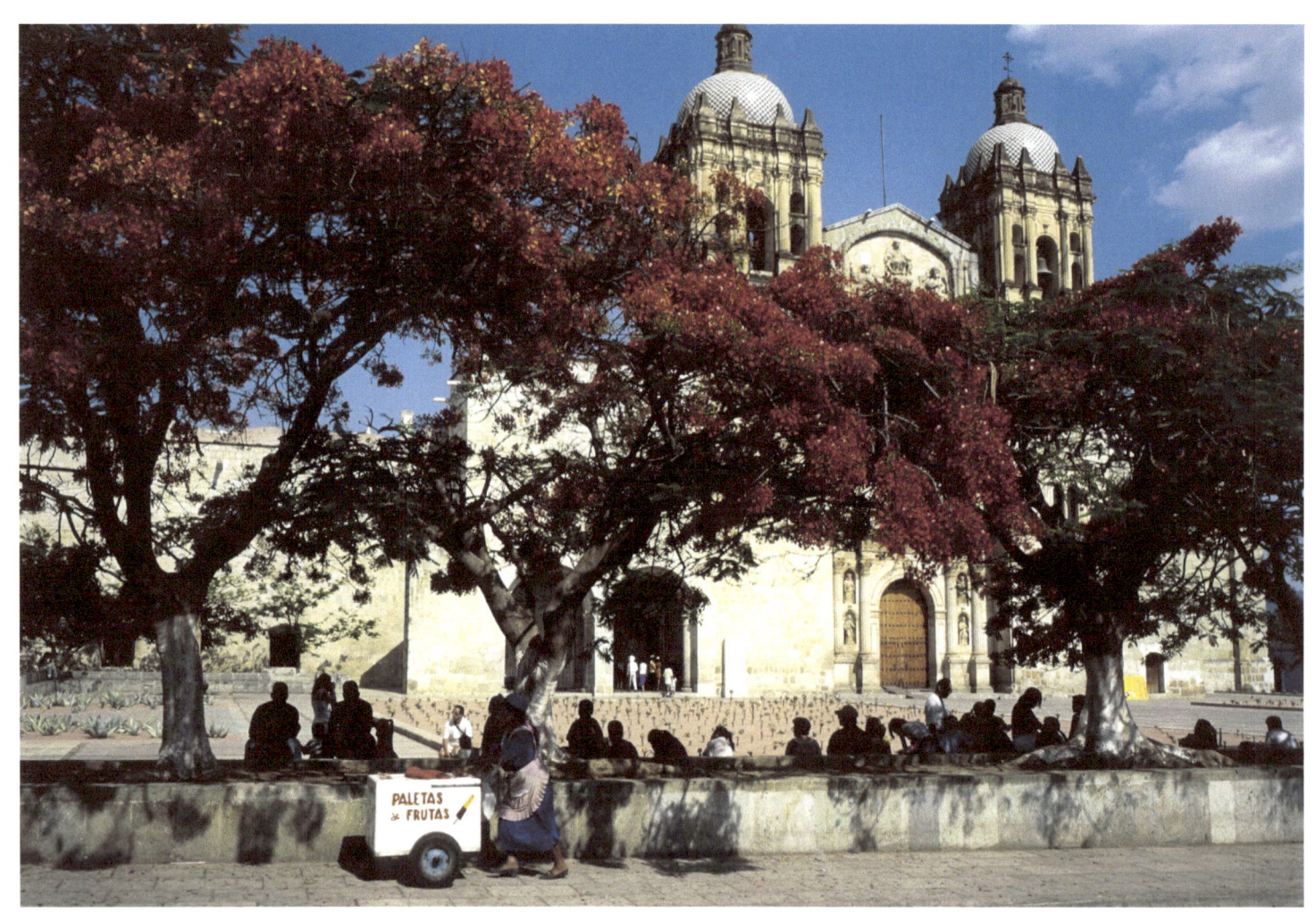

Oaxaca, the Cathedral

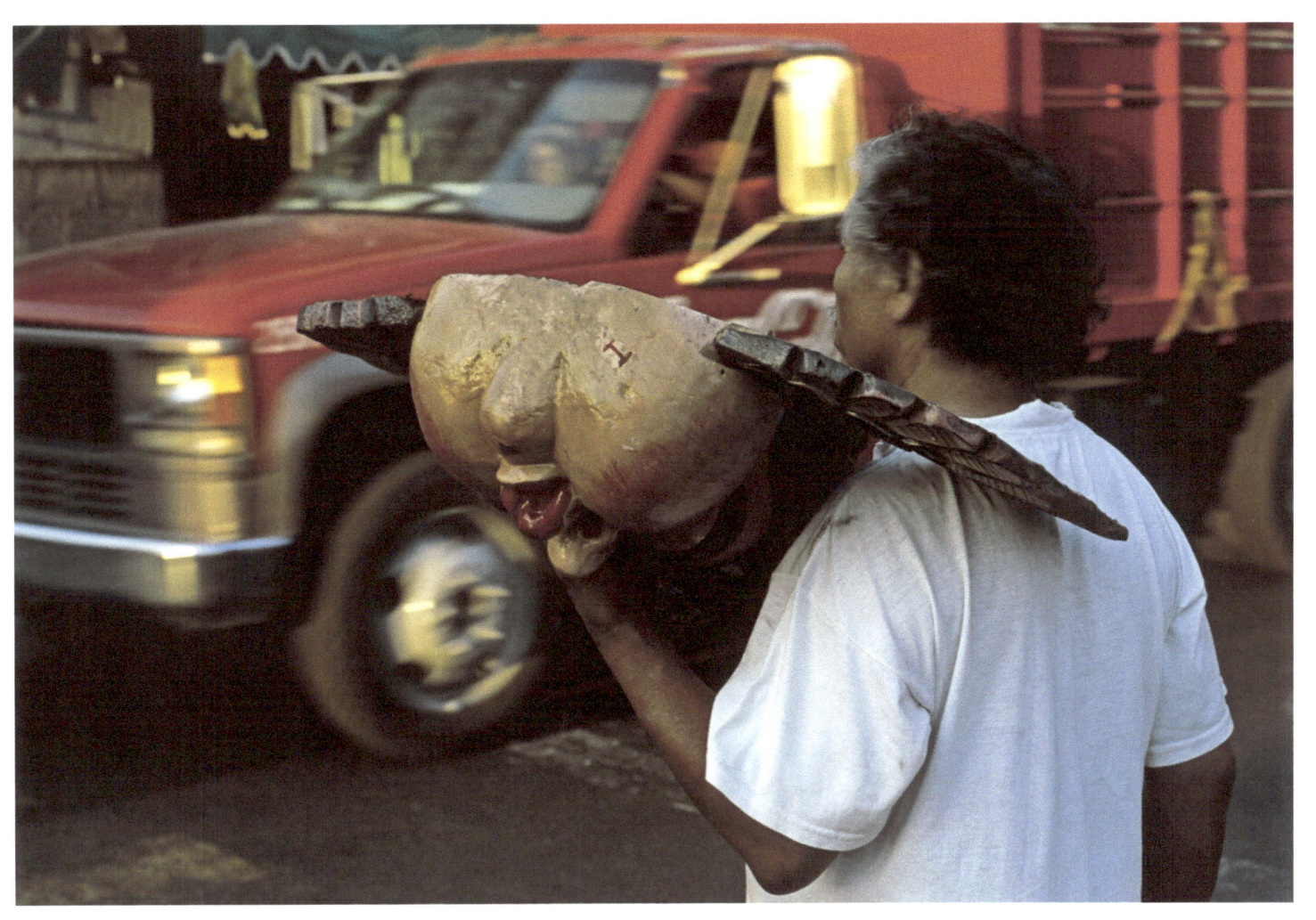

Oaxaca, is a city of culture and intense spirituality..

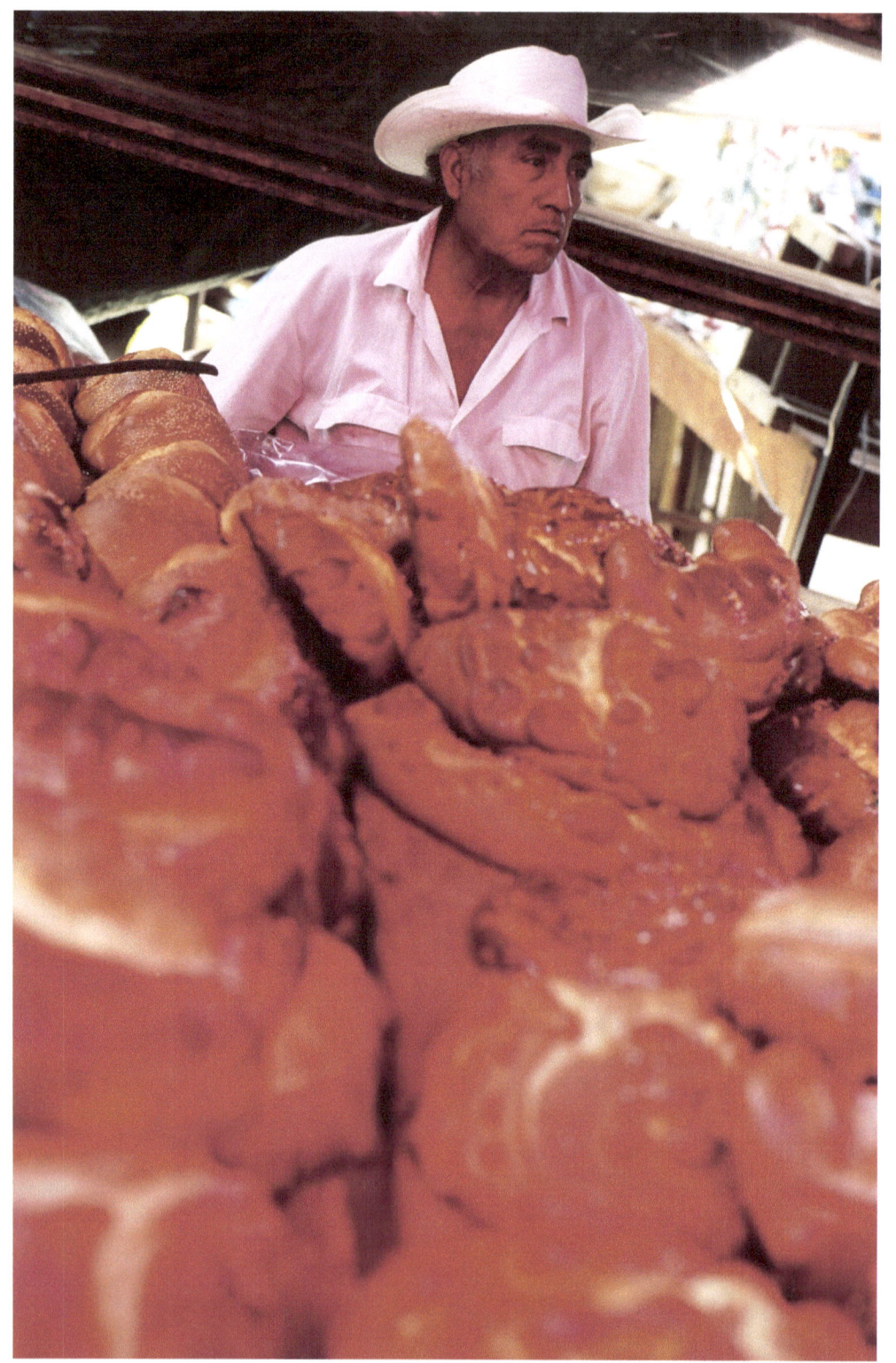

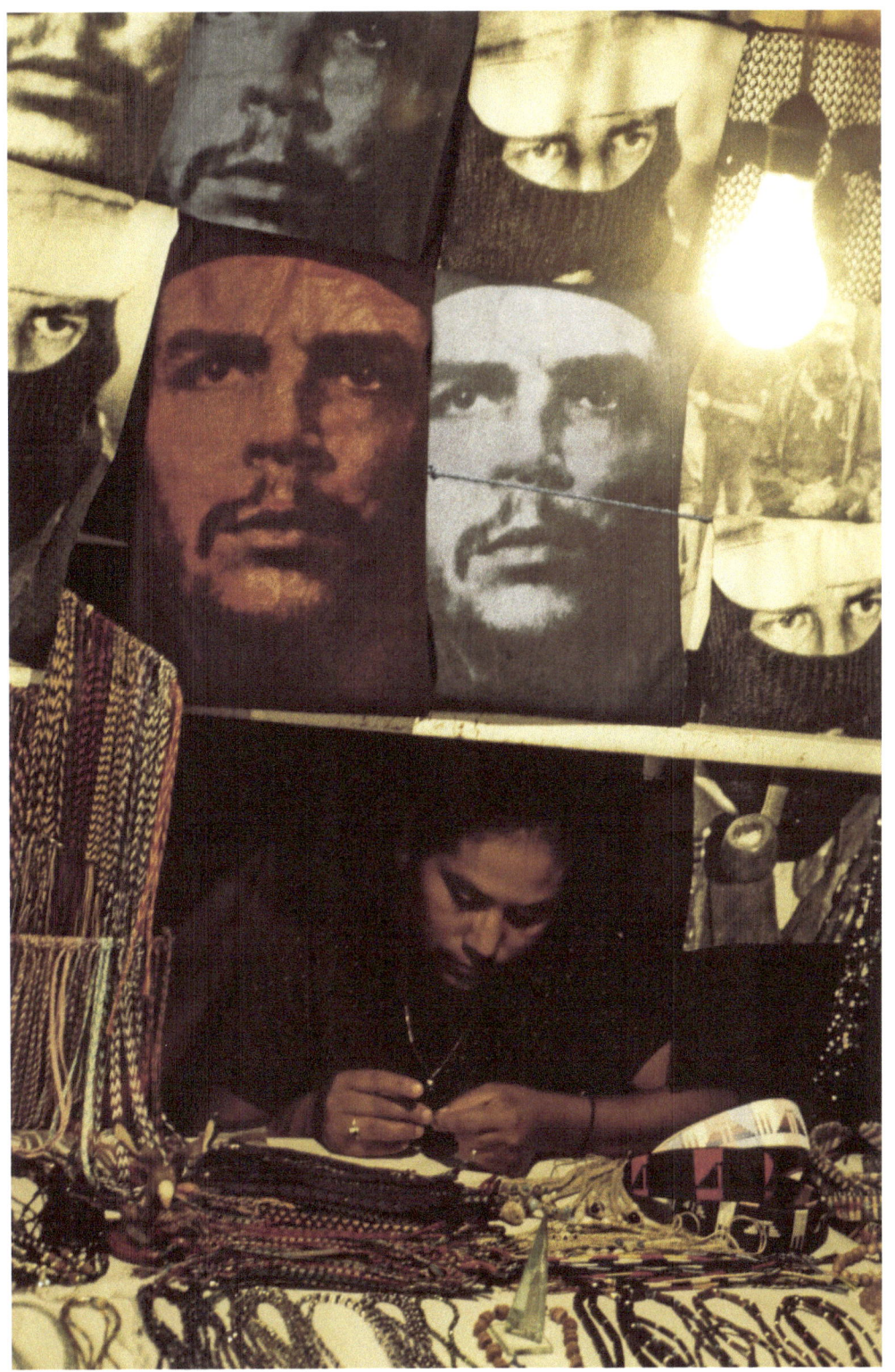

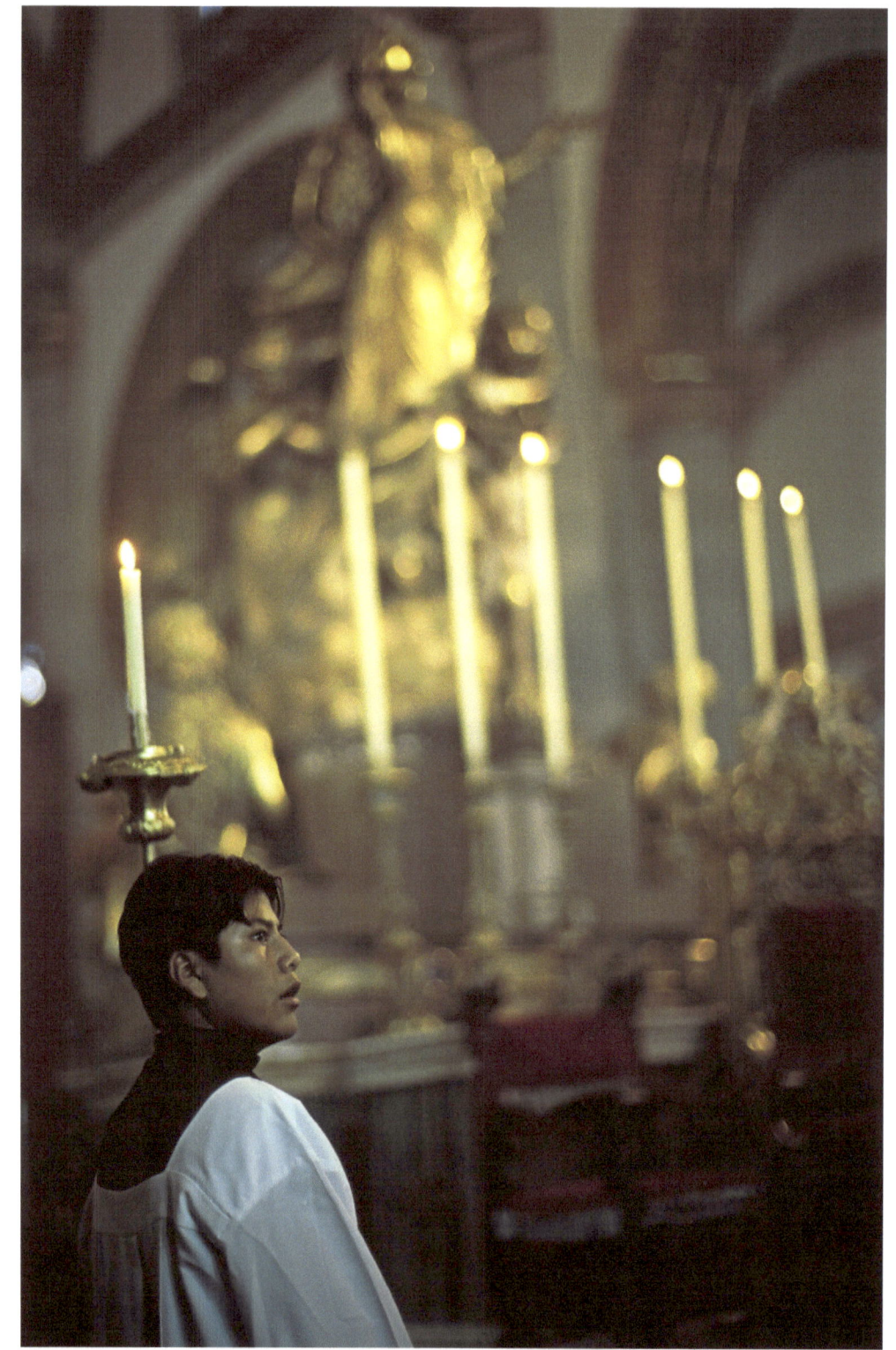

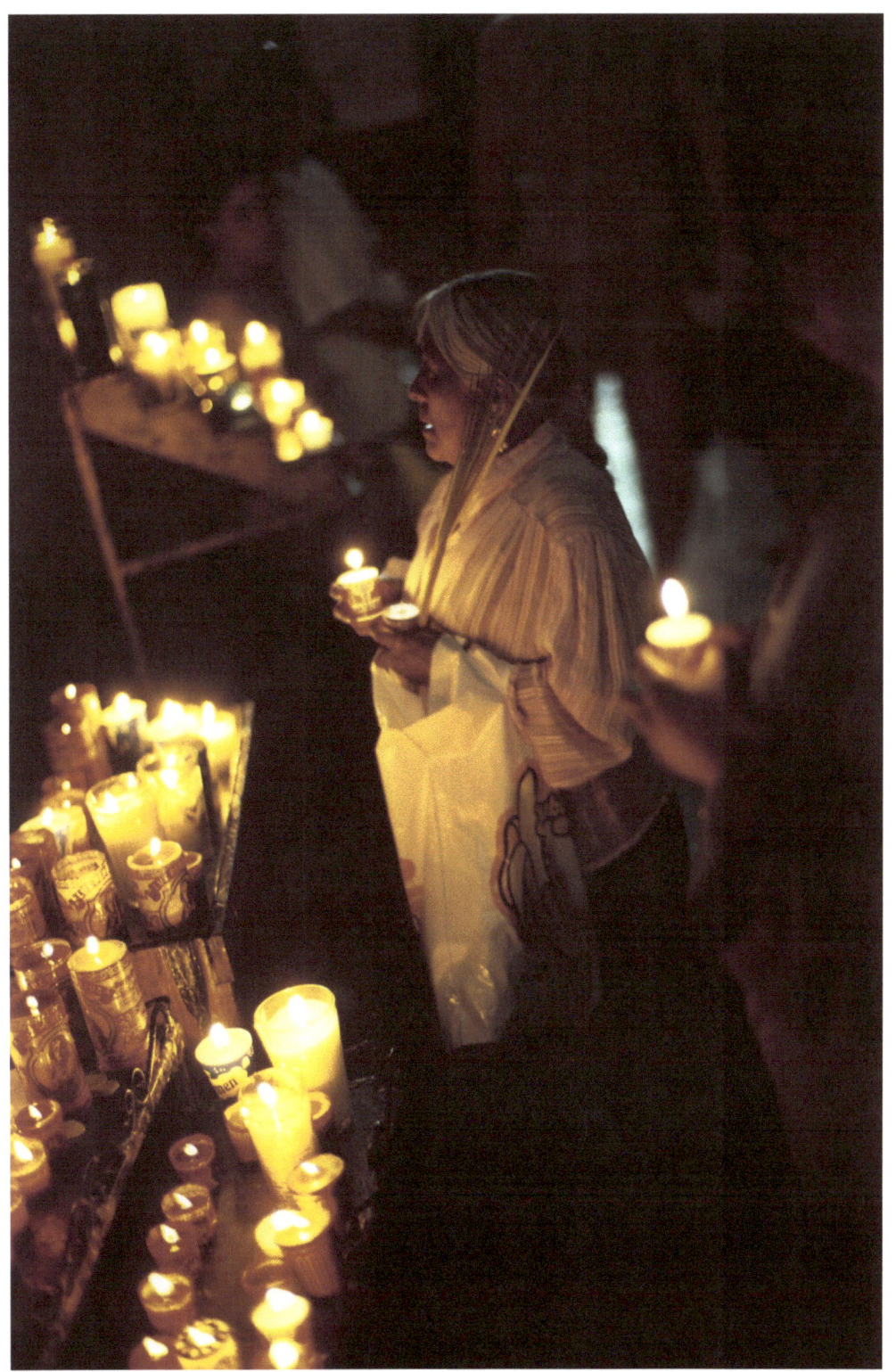

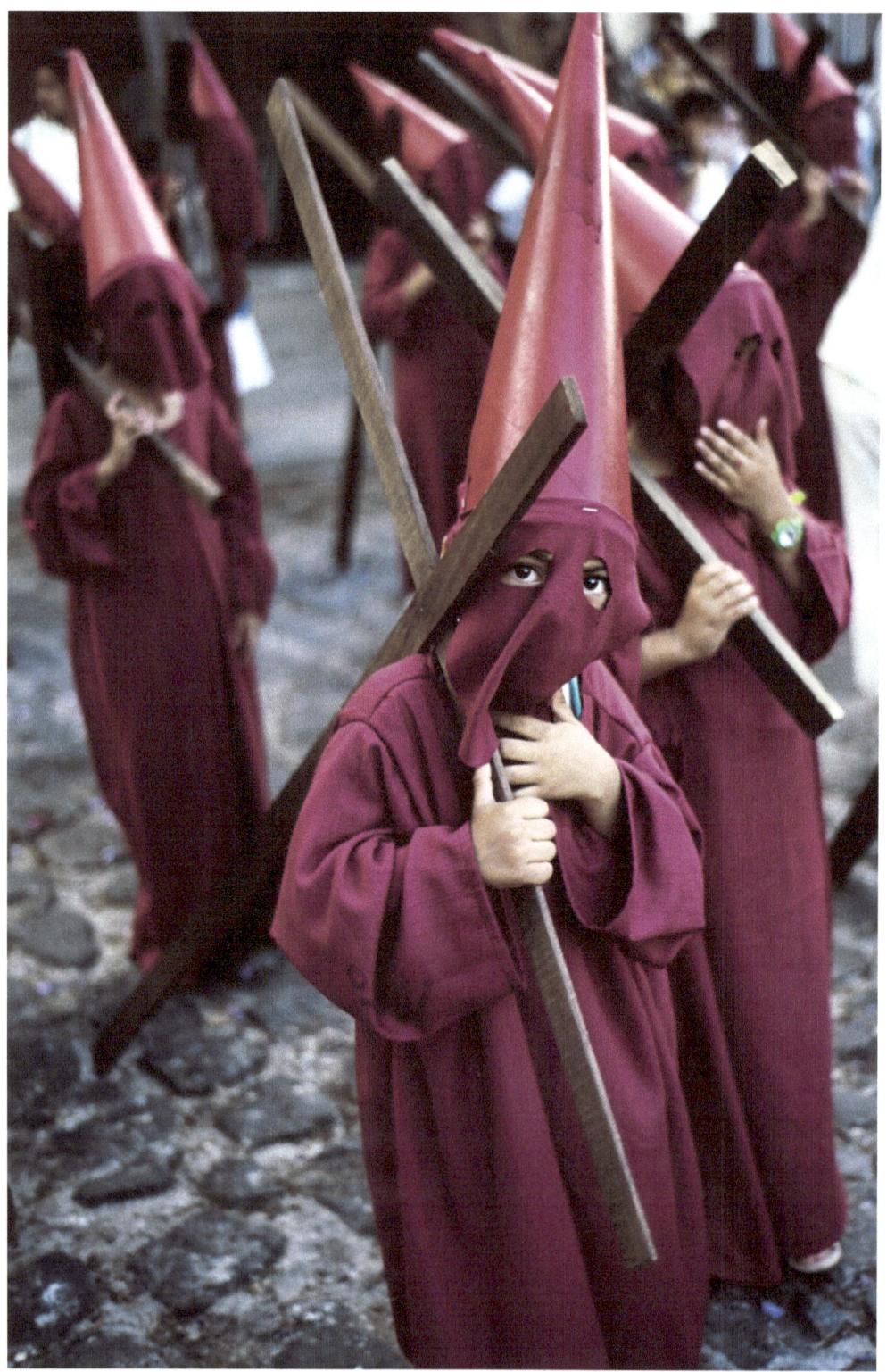

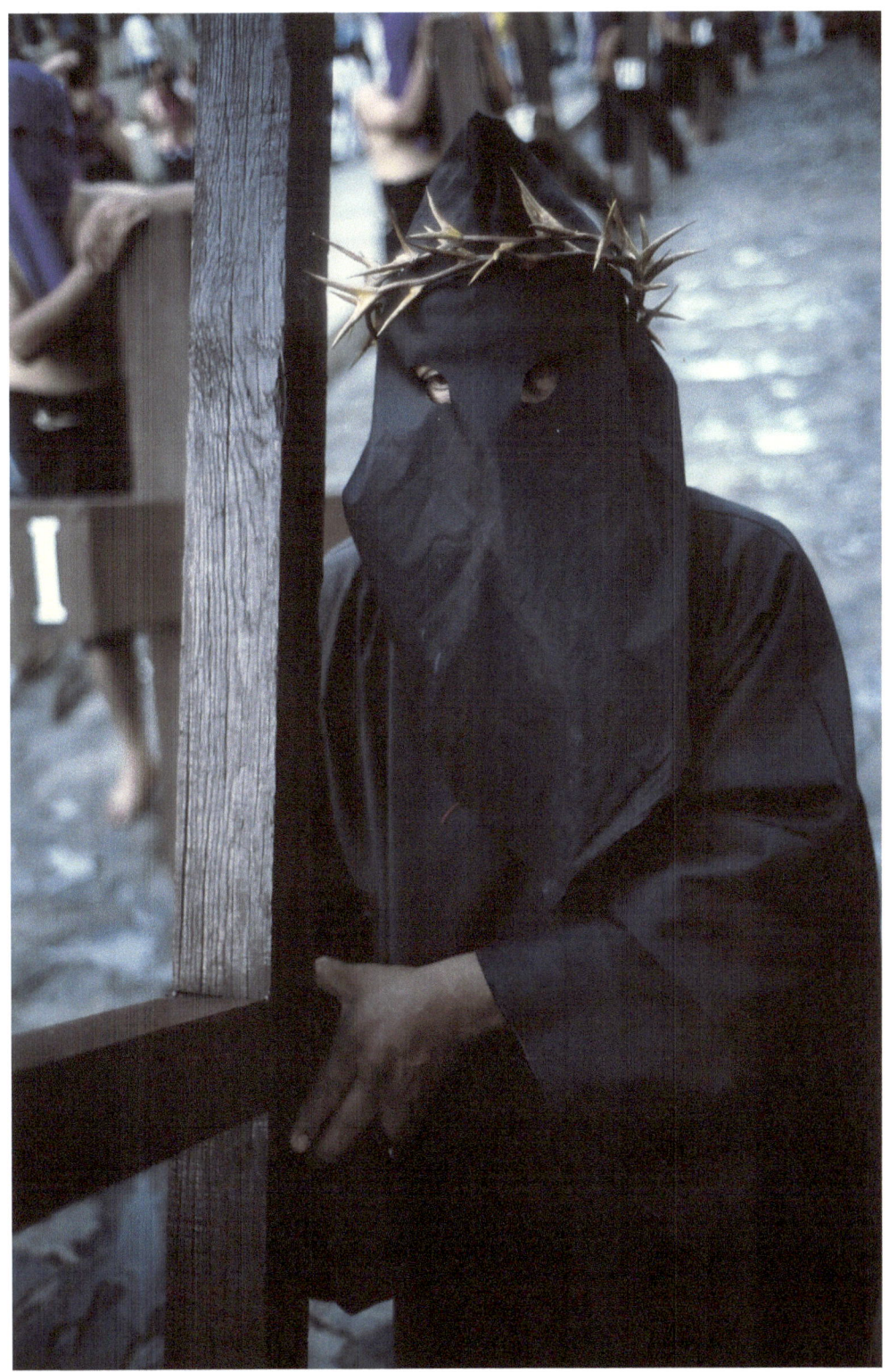

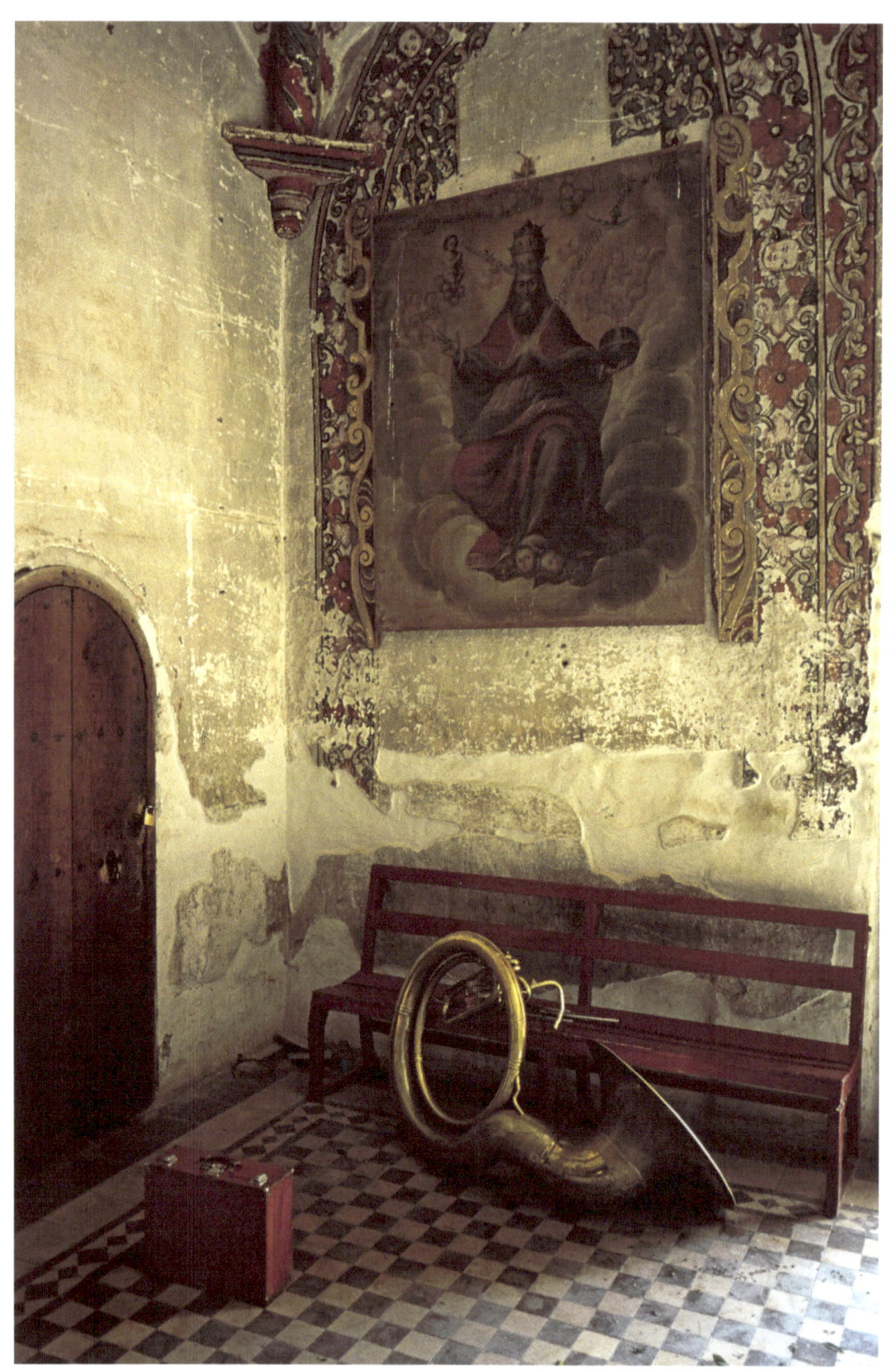

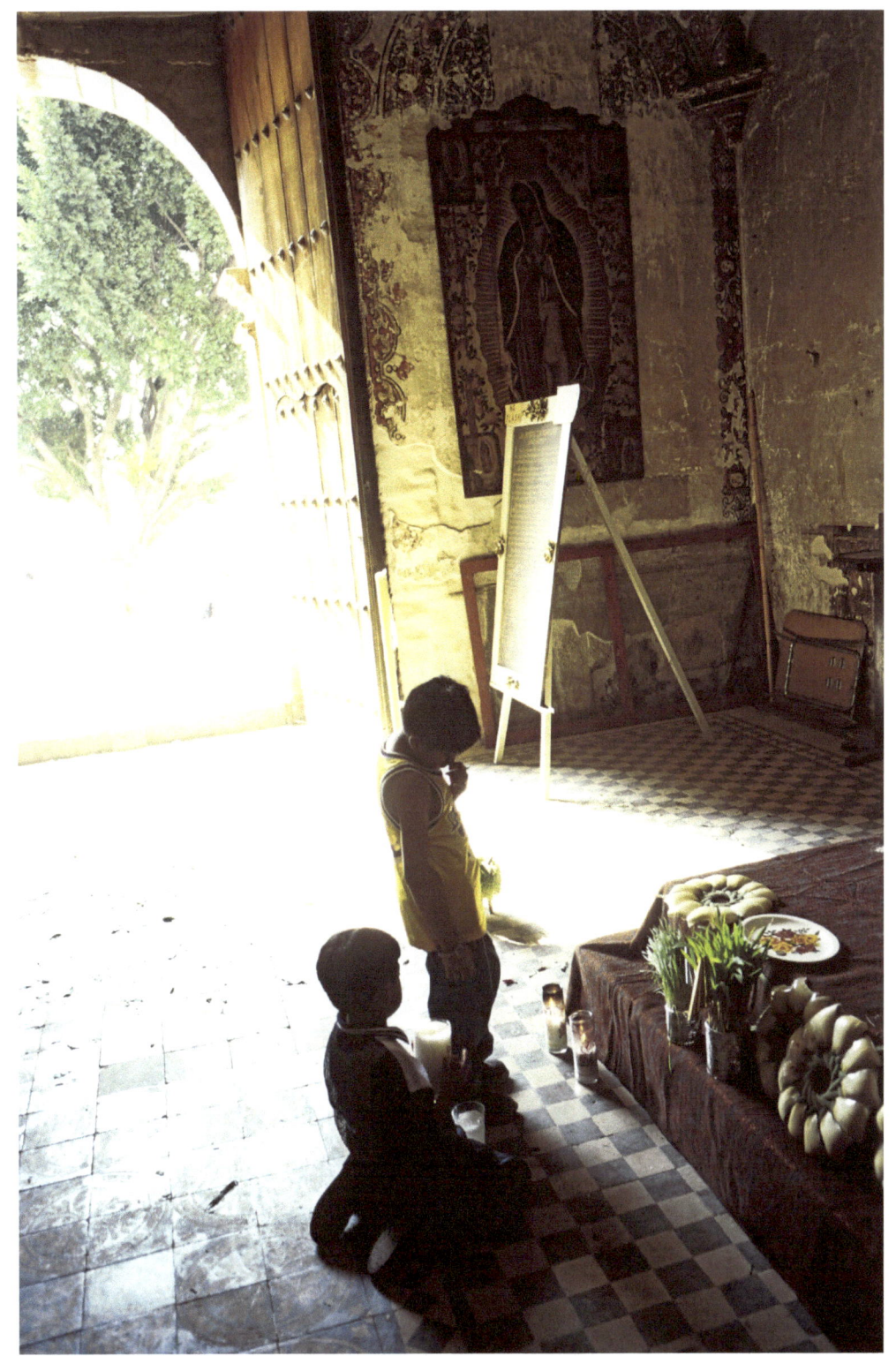

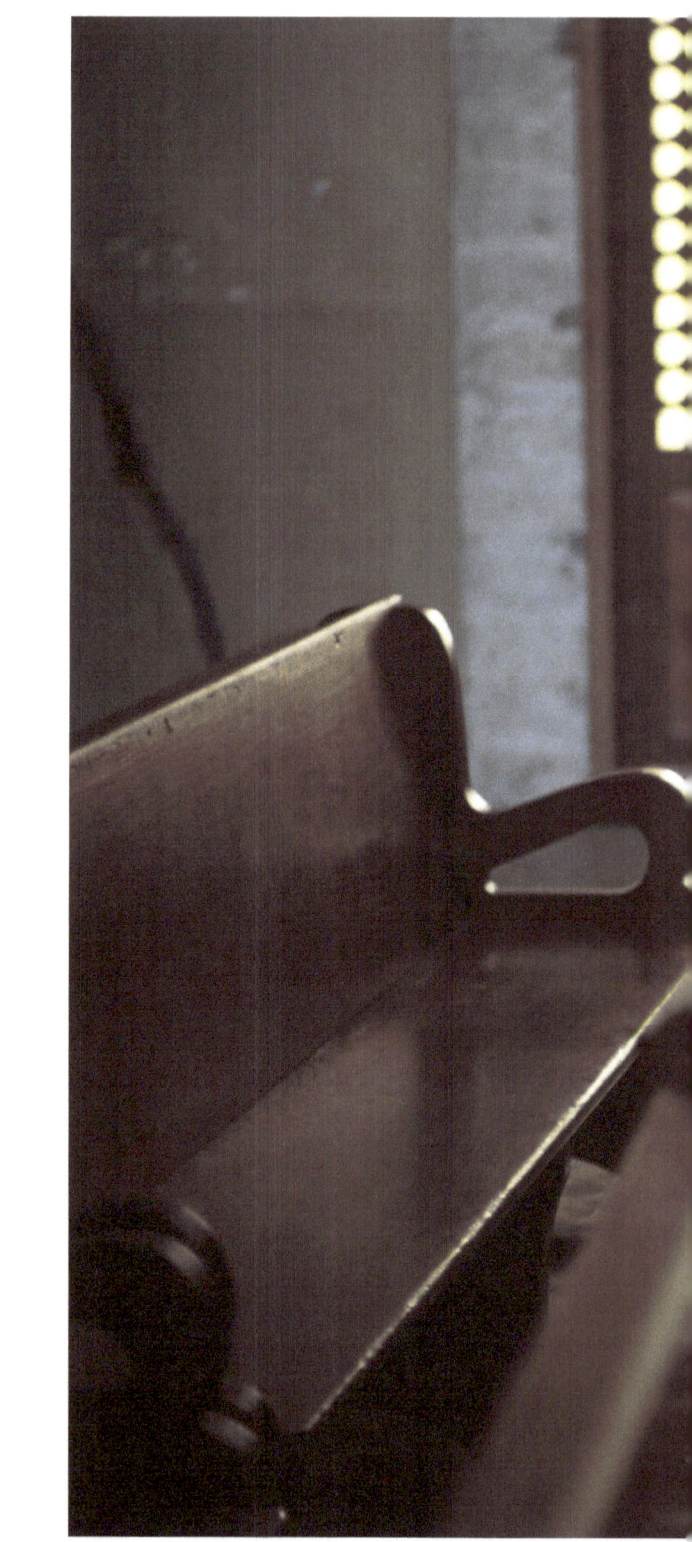

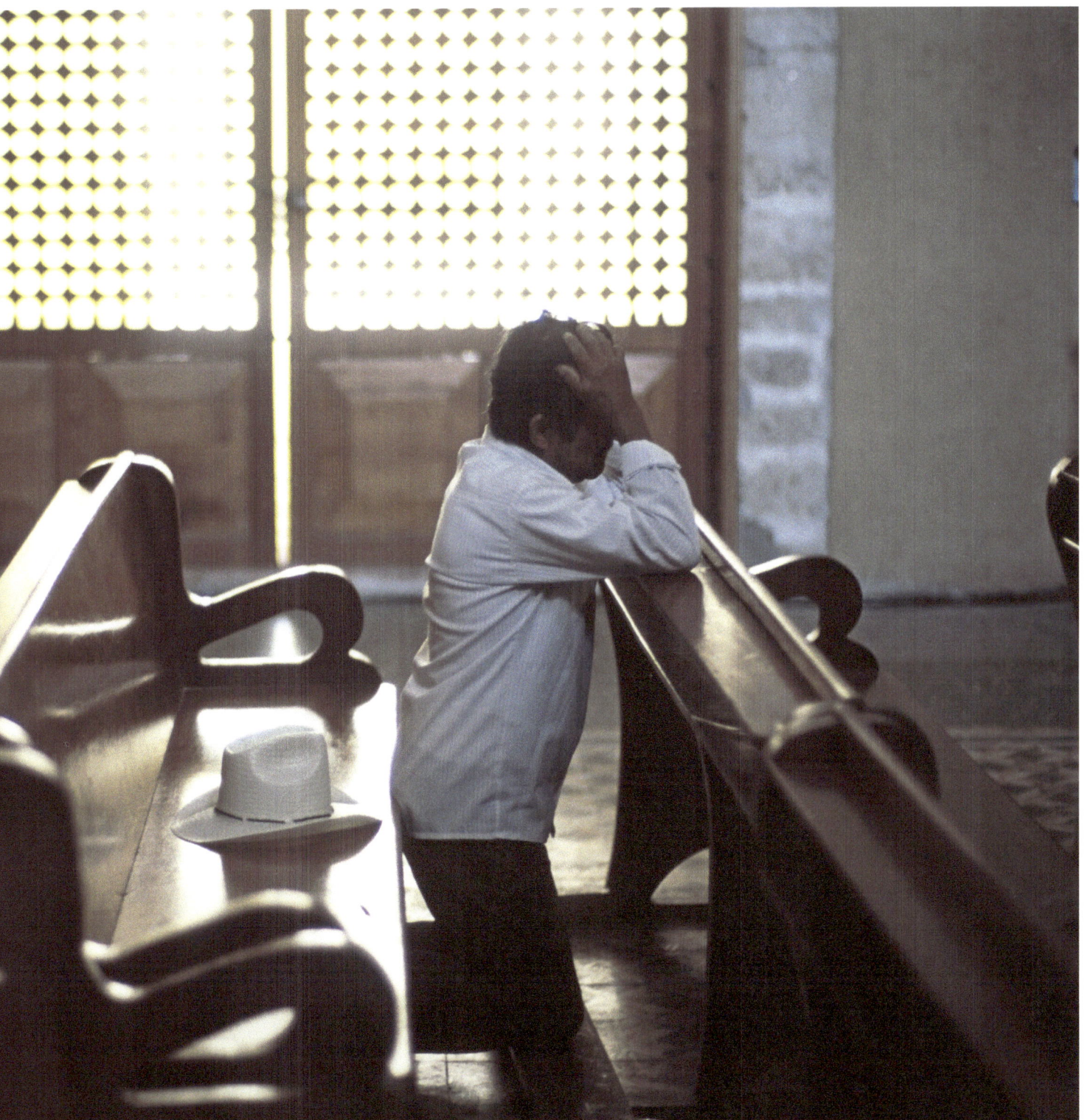

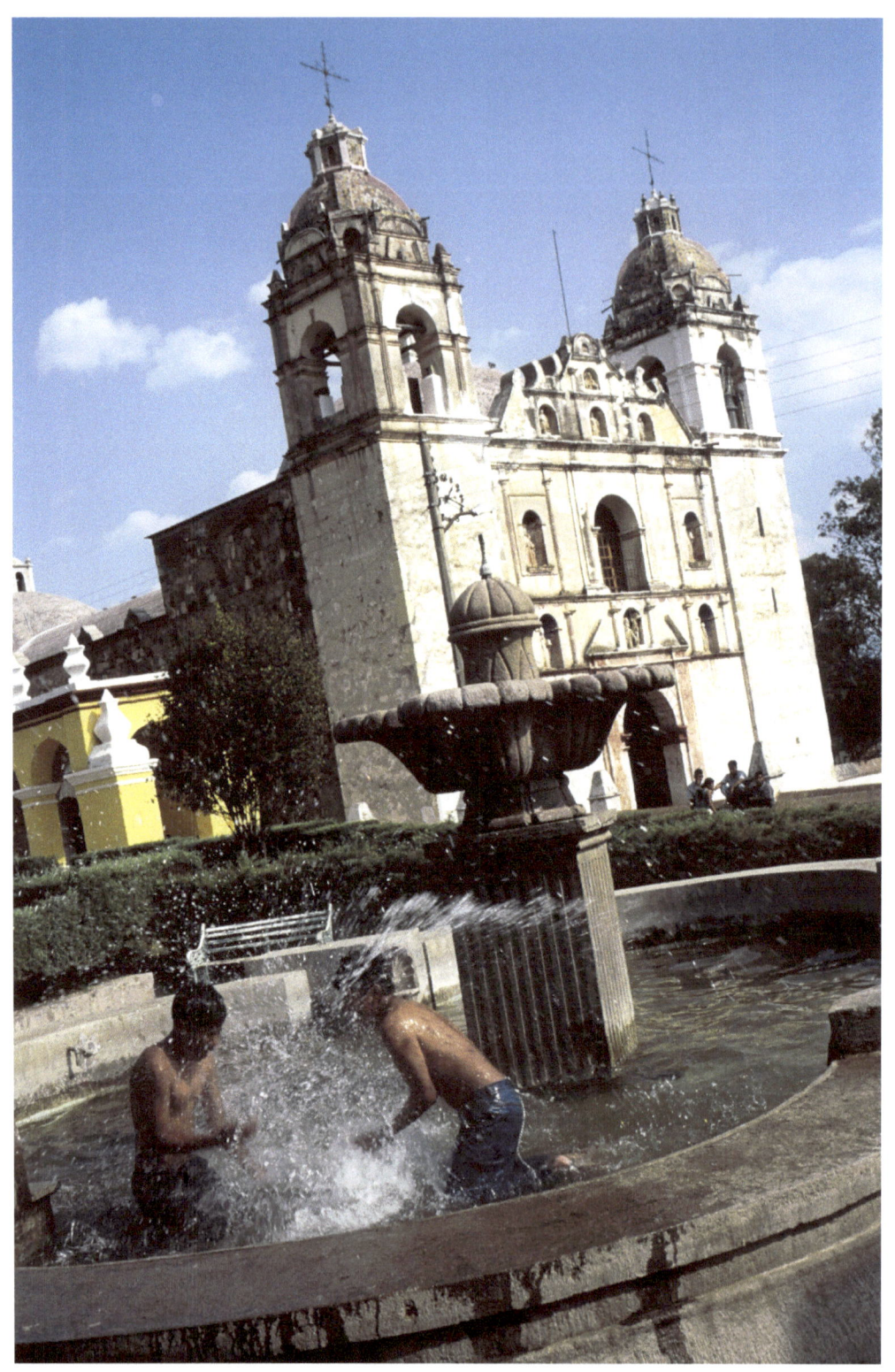

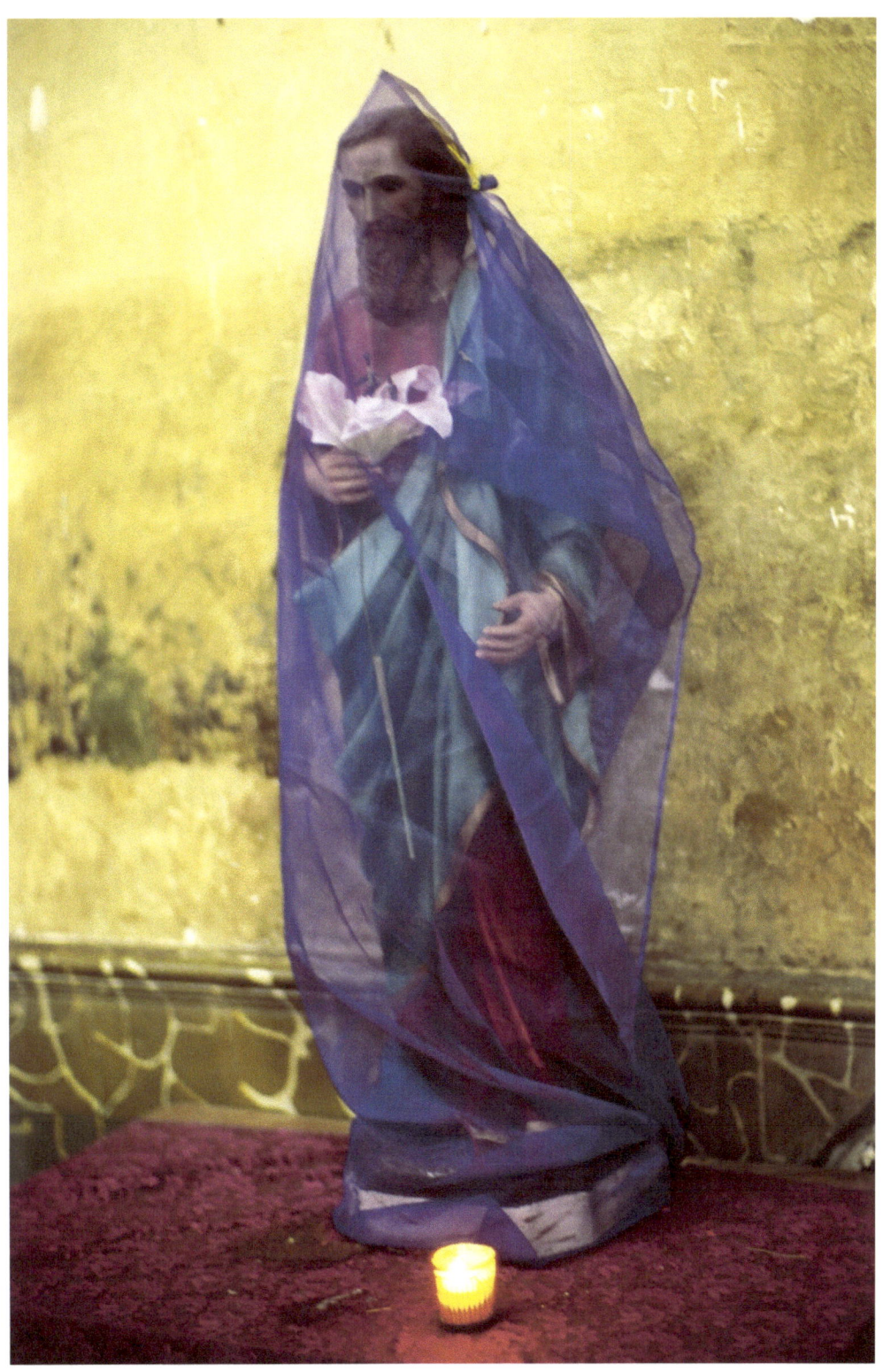

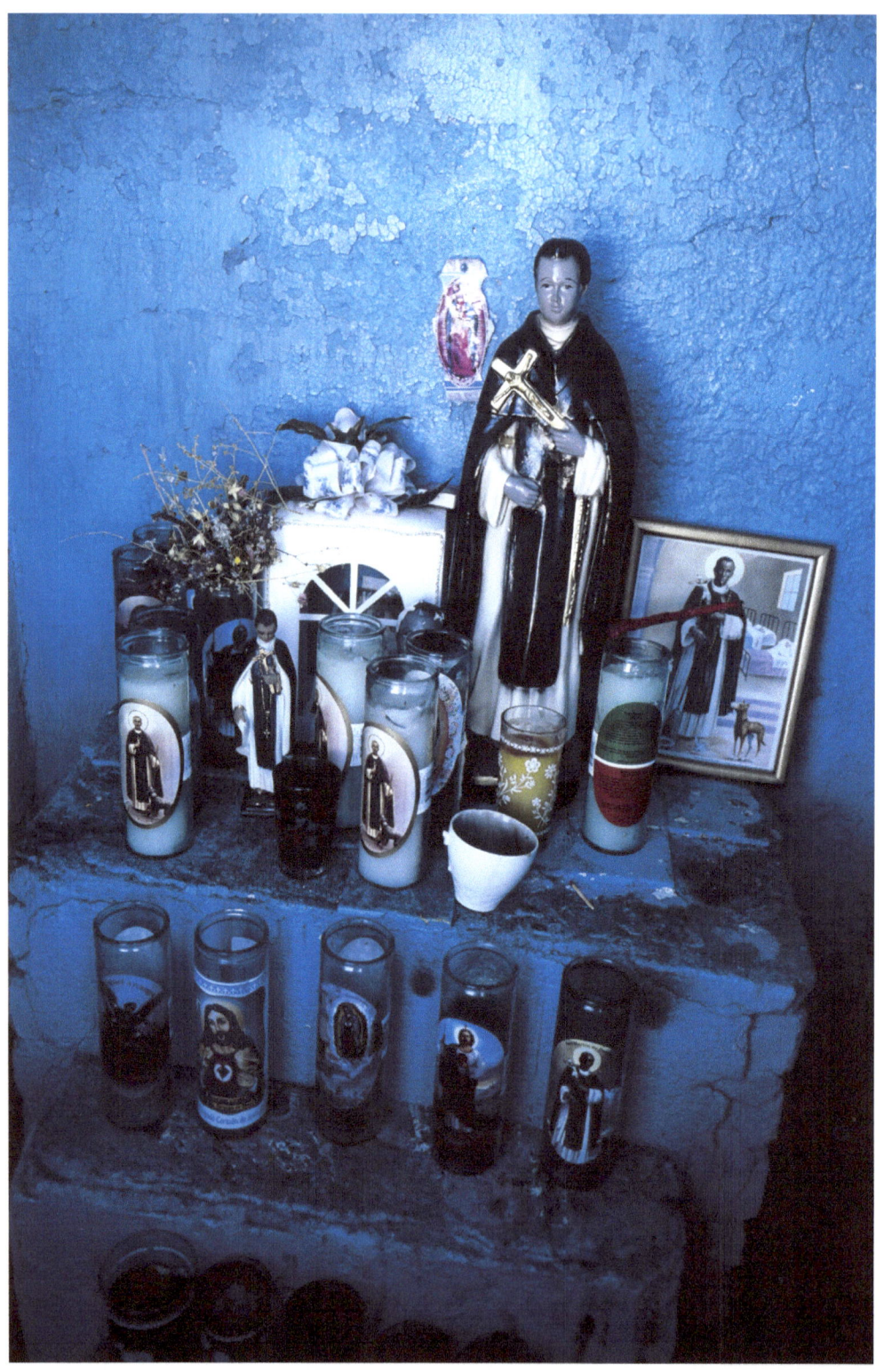

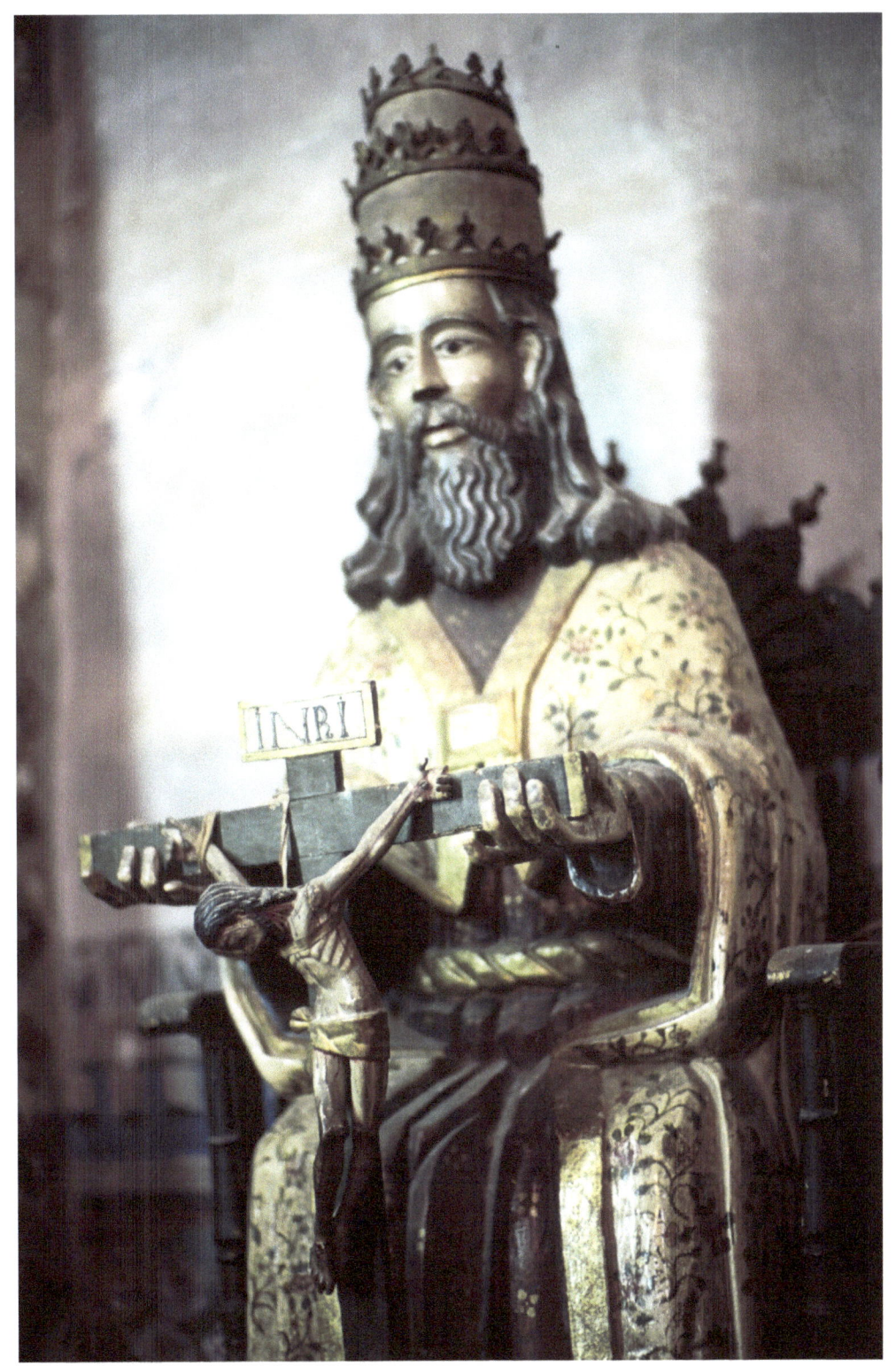

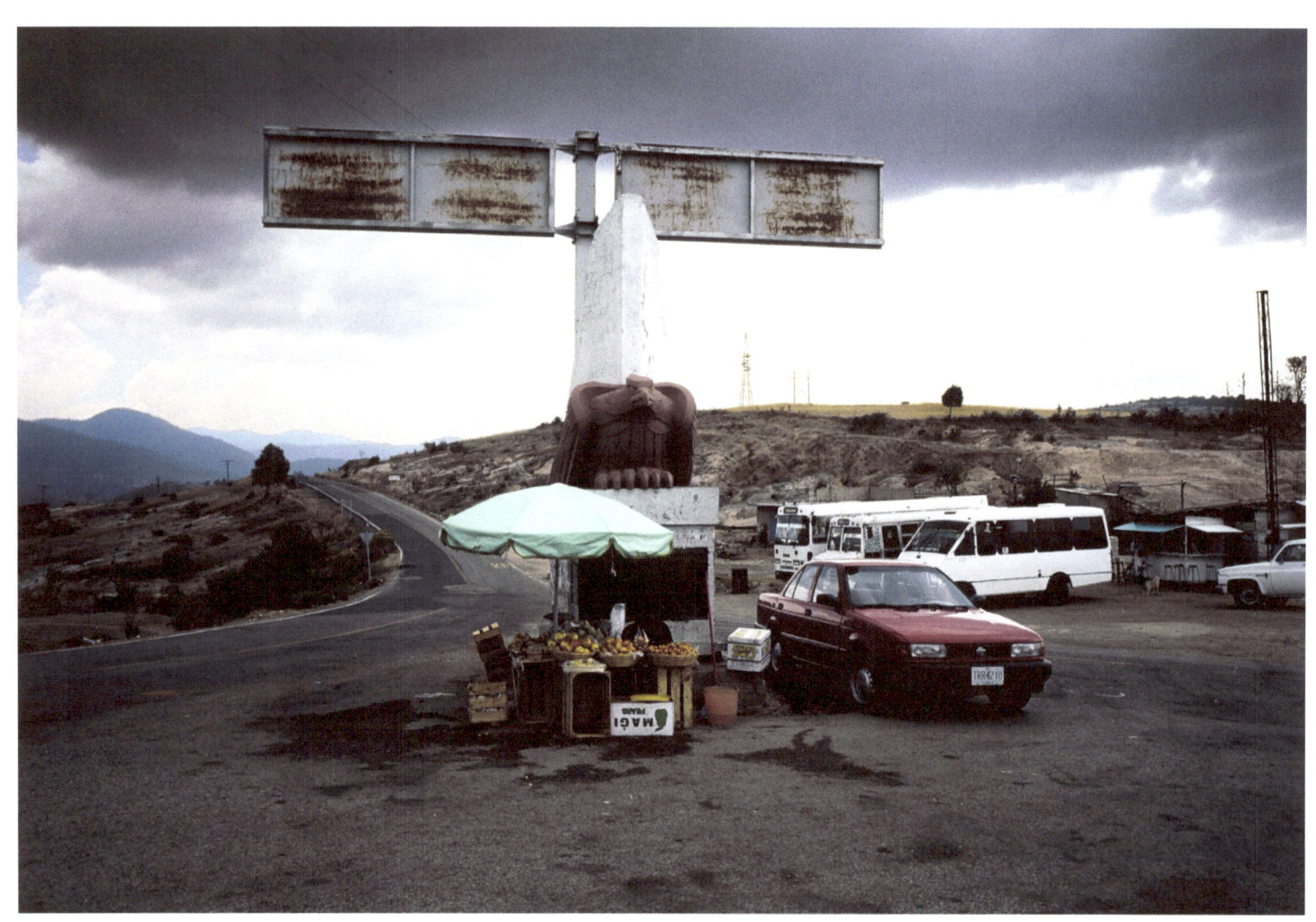
On the road to Mexico City

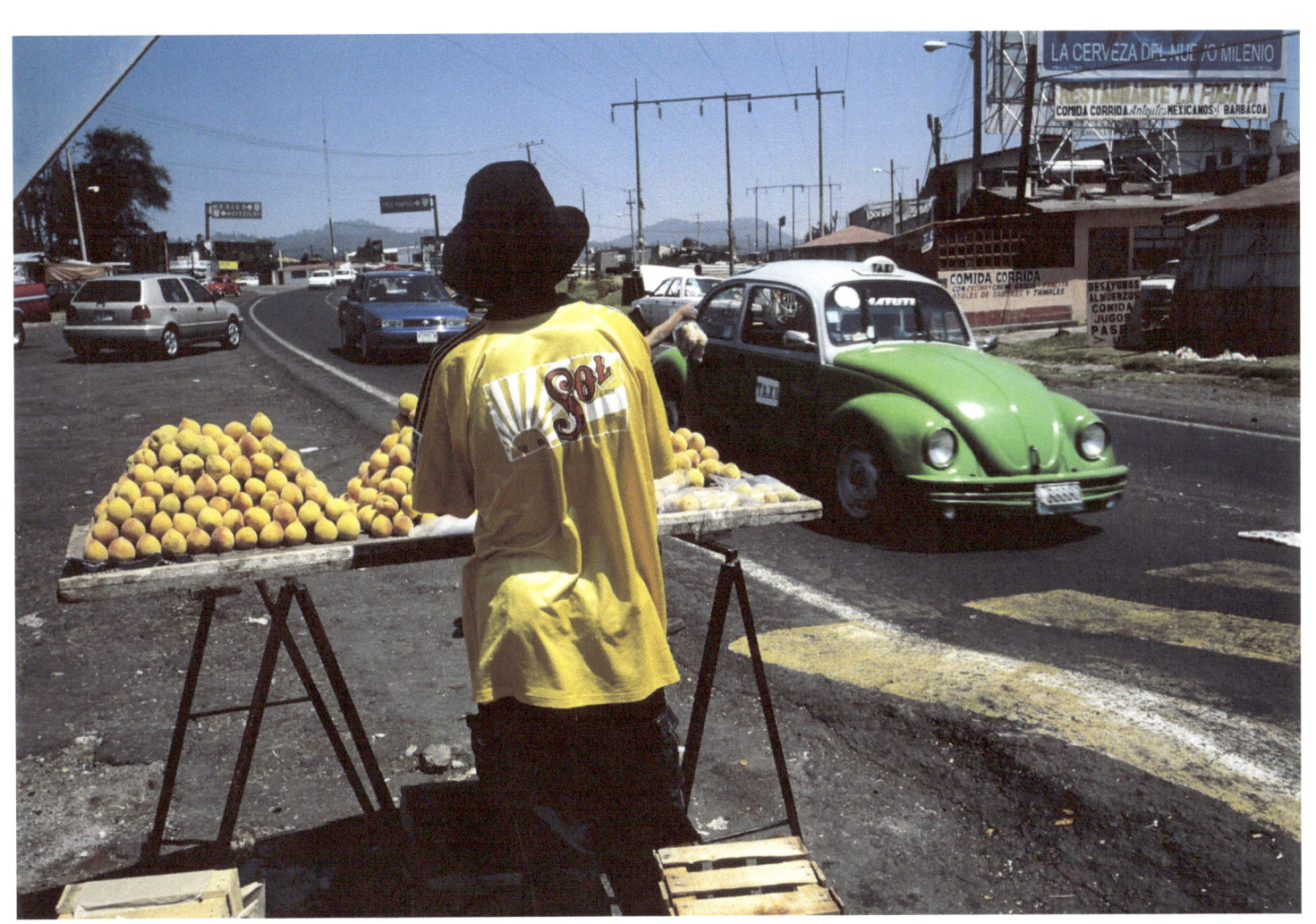

On the road to Mexico City

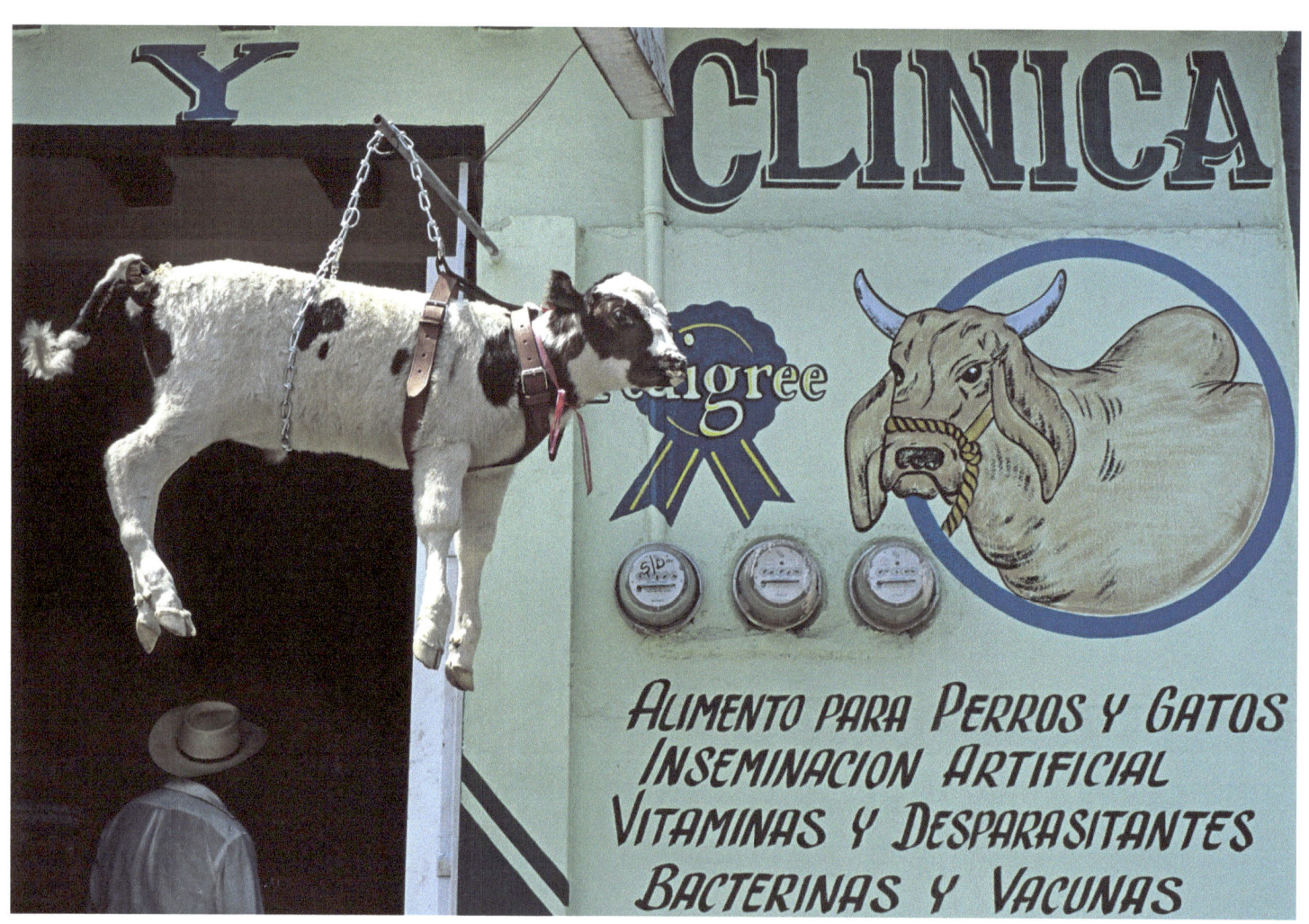

On the road to Mexico City

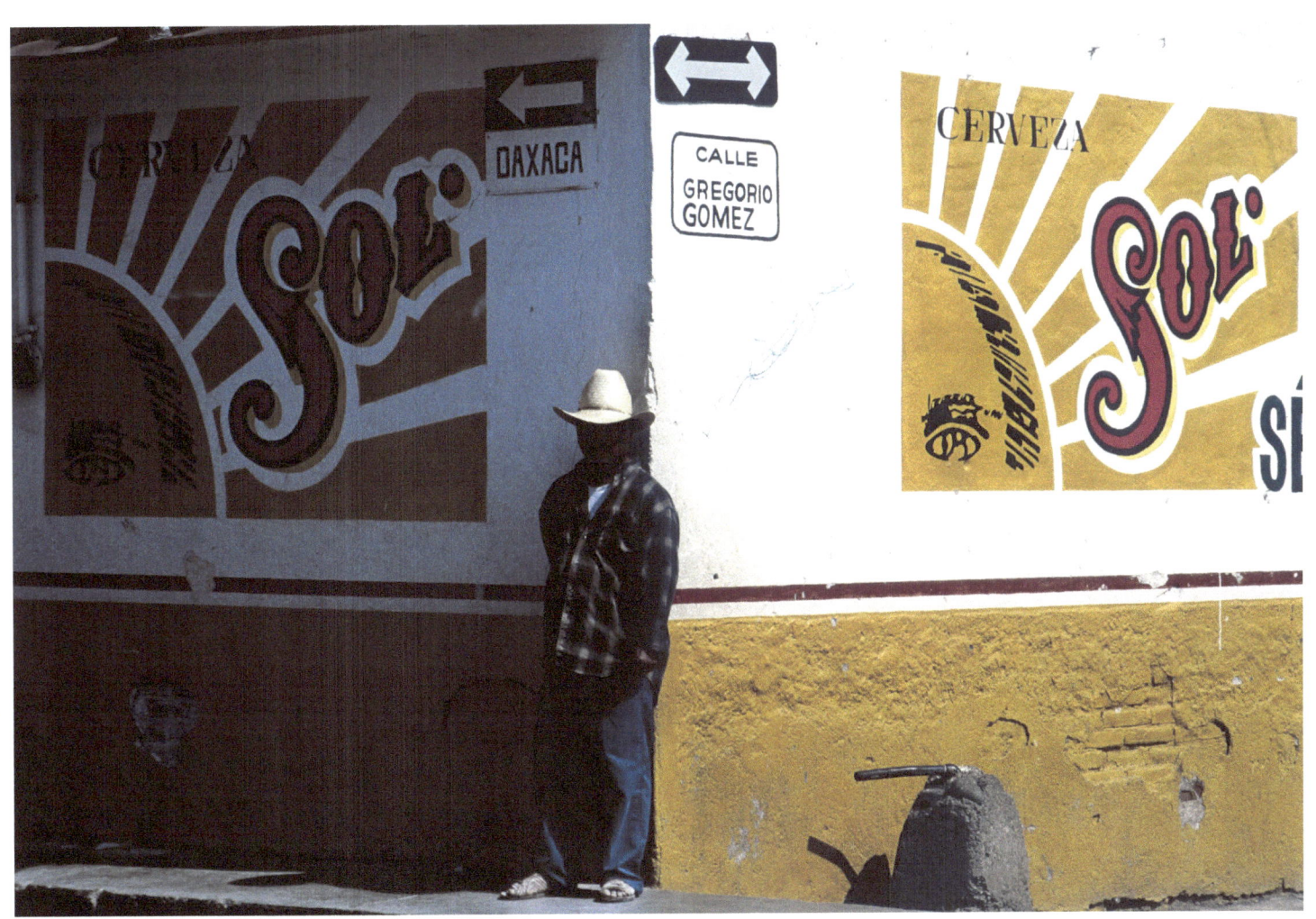
On the road to Mexico City

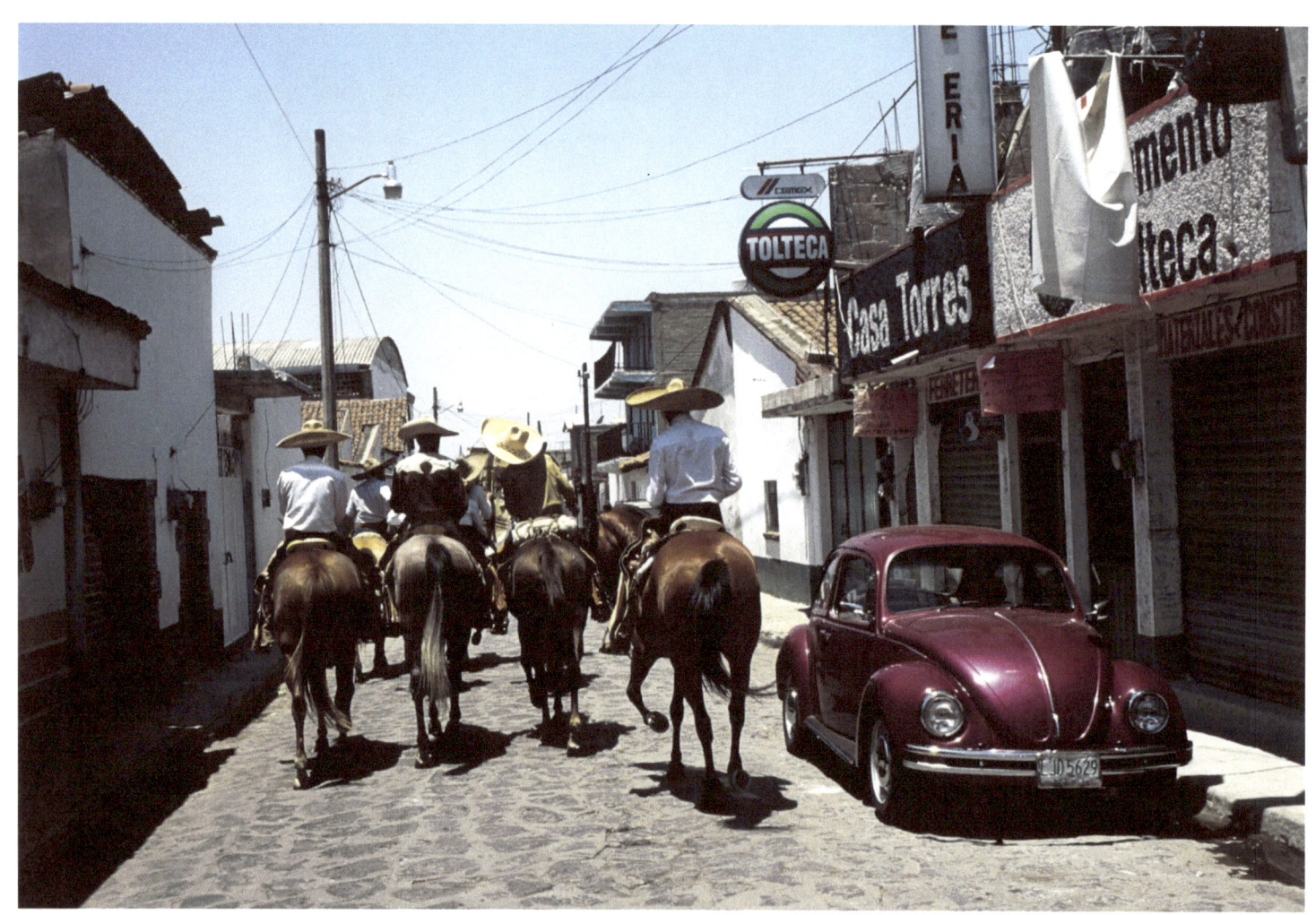

On the road to Mexico City

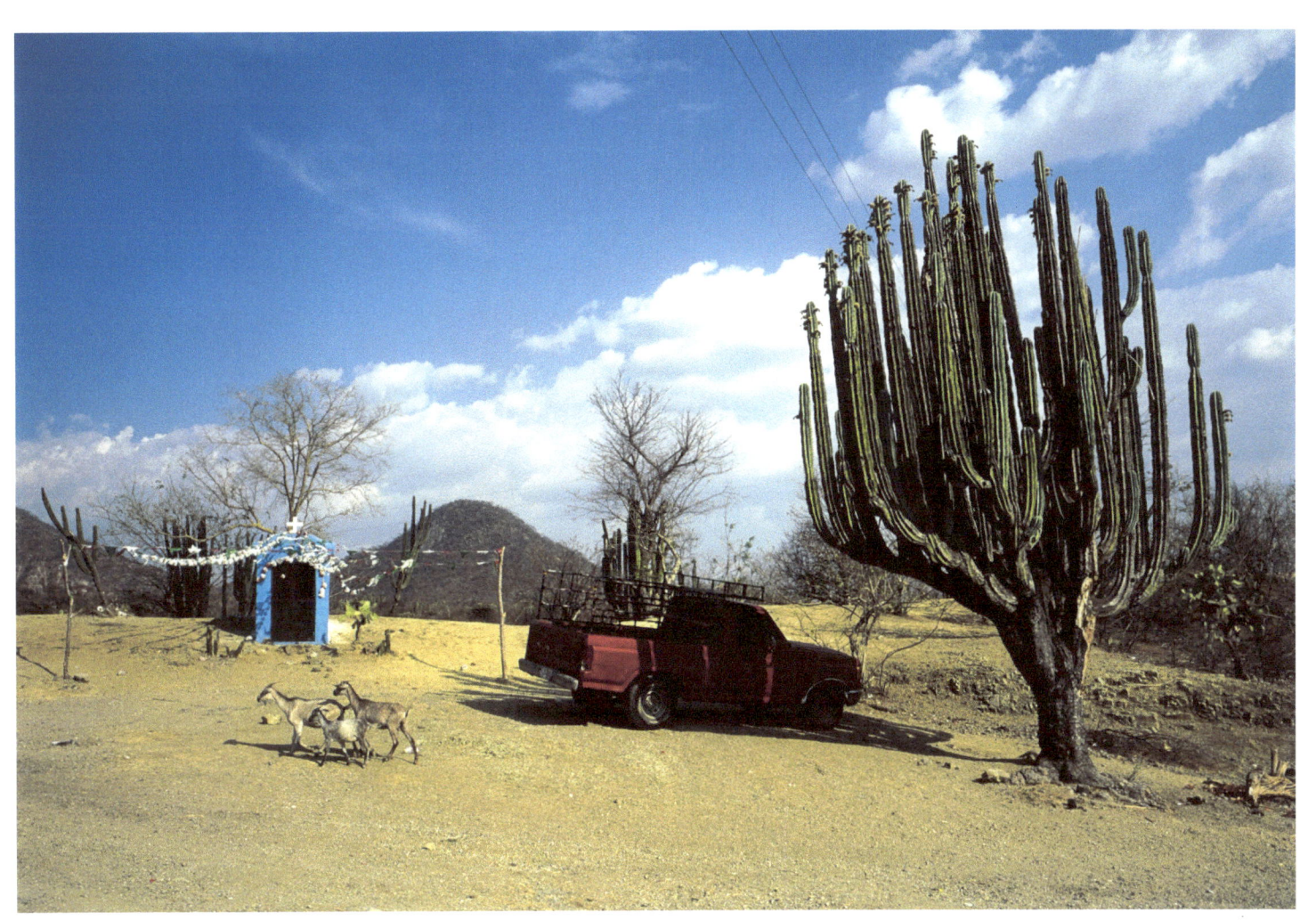

On the road to Mexico City

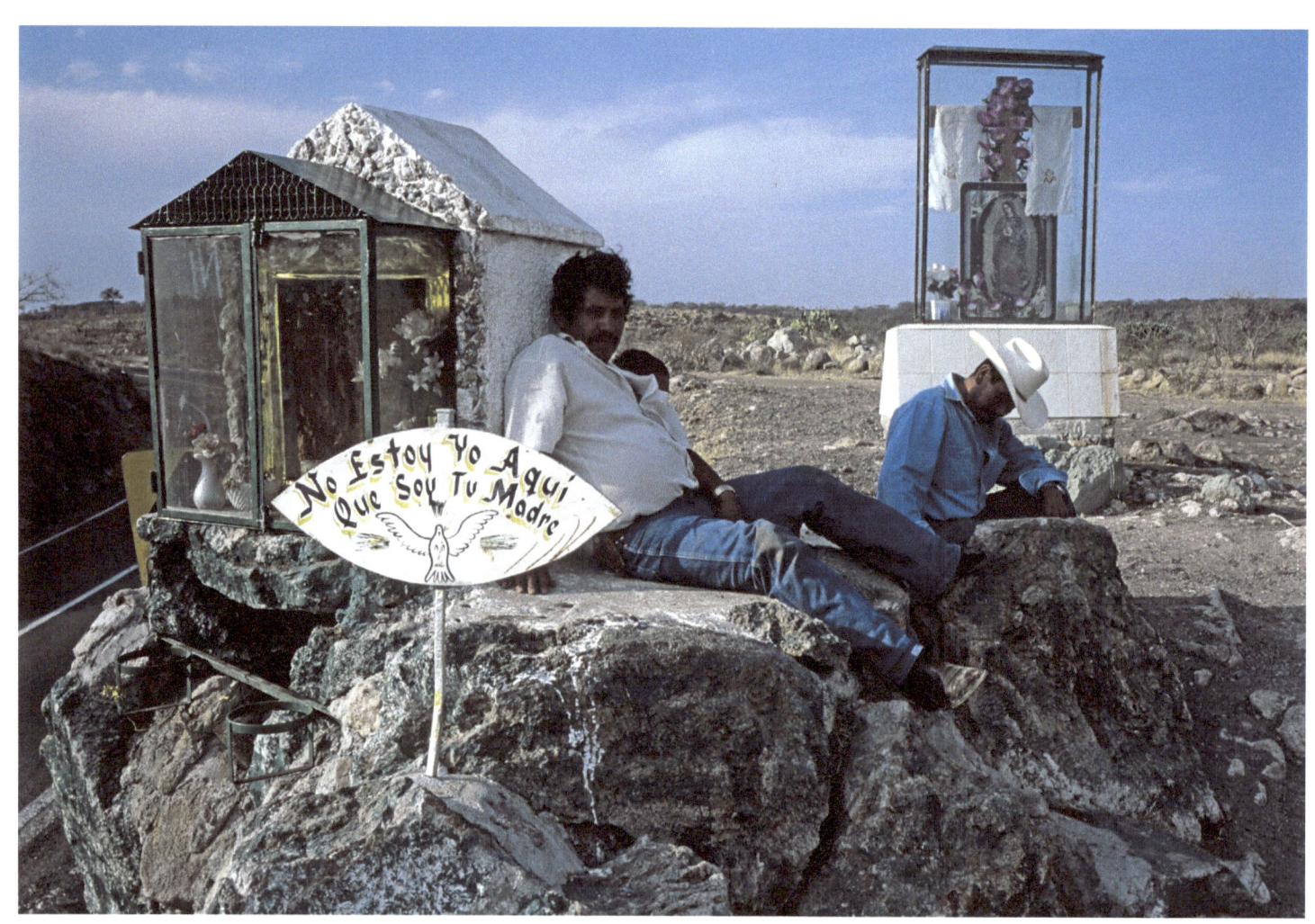

On the road to Mexico City

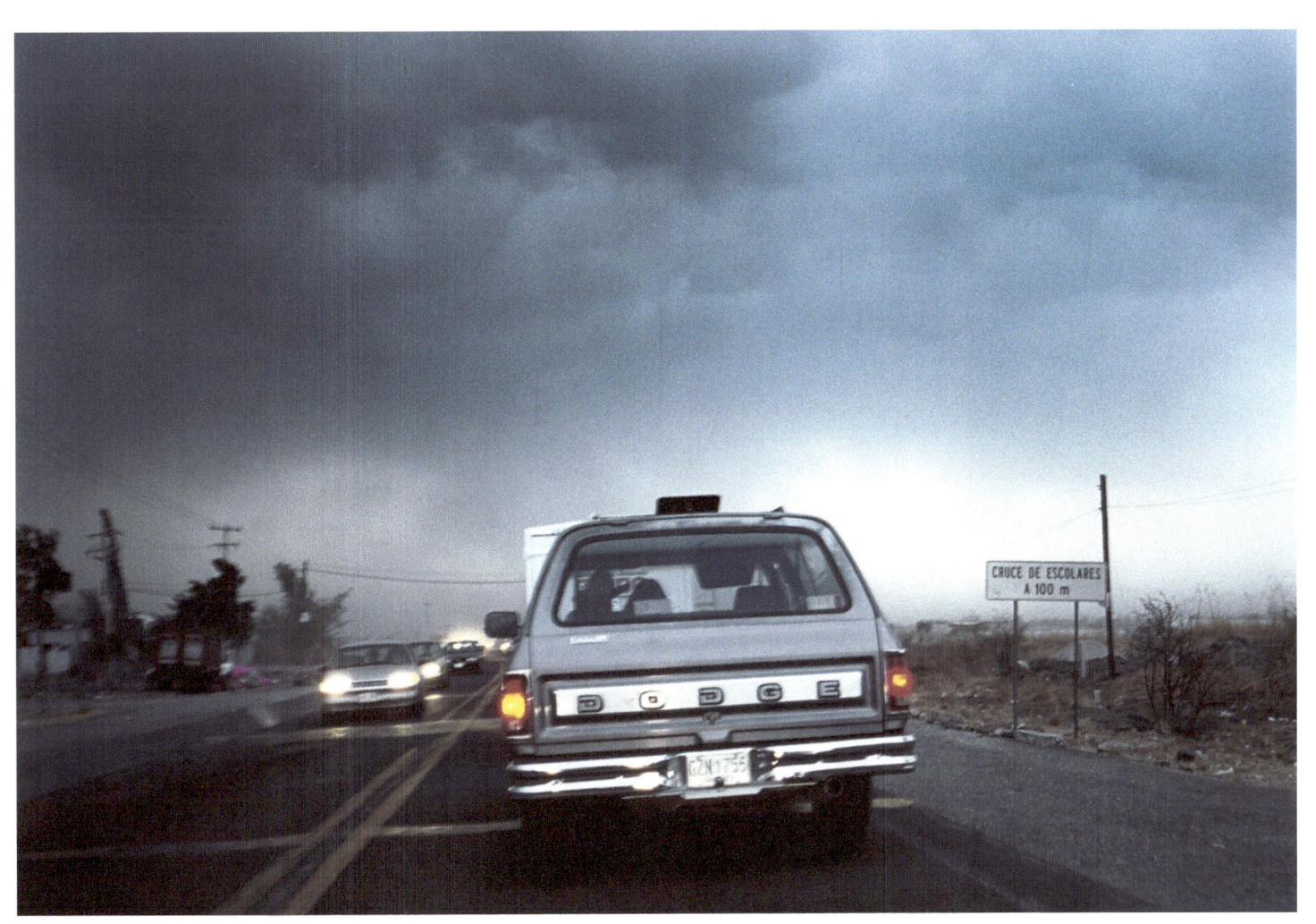

On the road to Mexico City

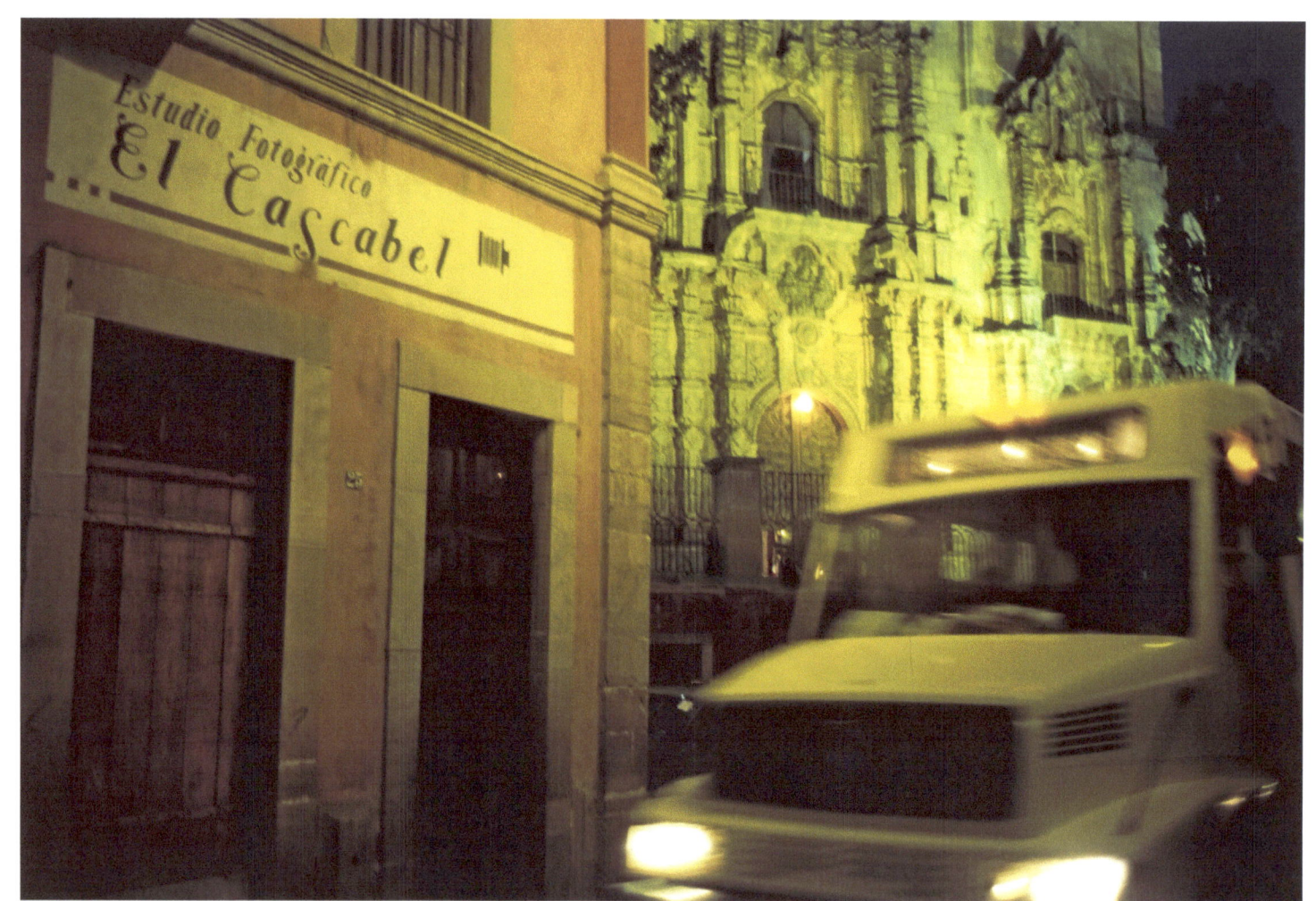

Guanajuato

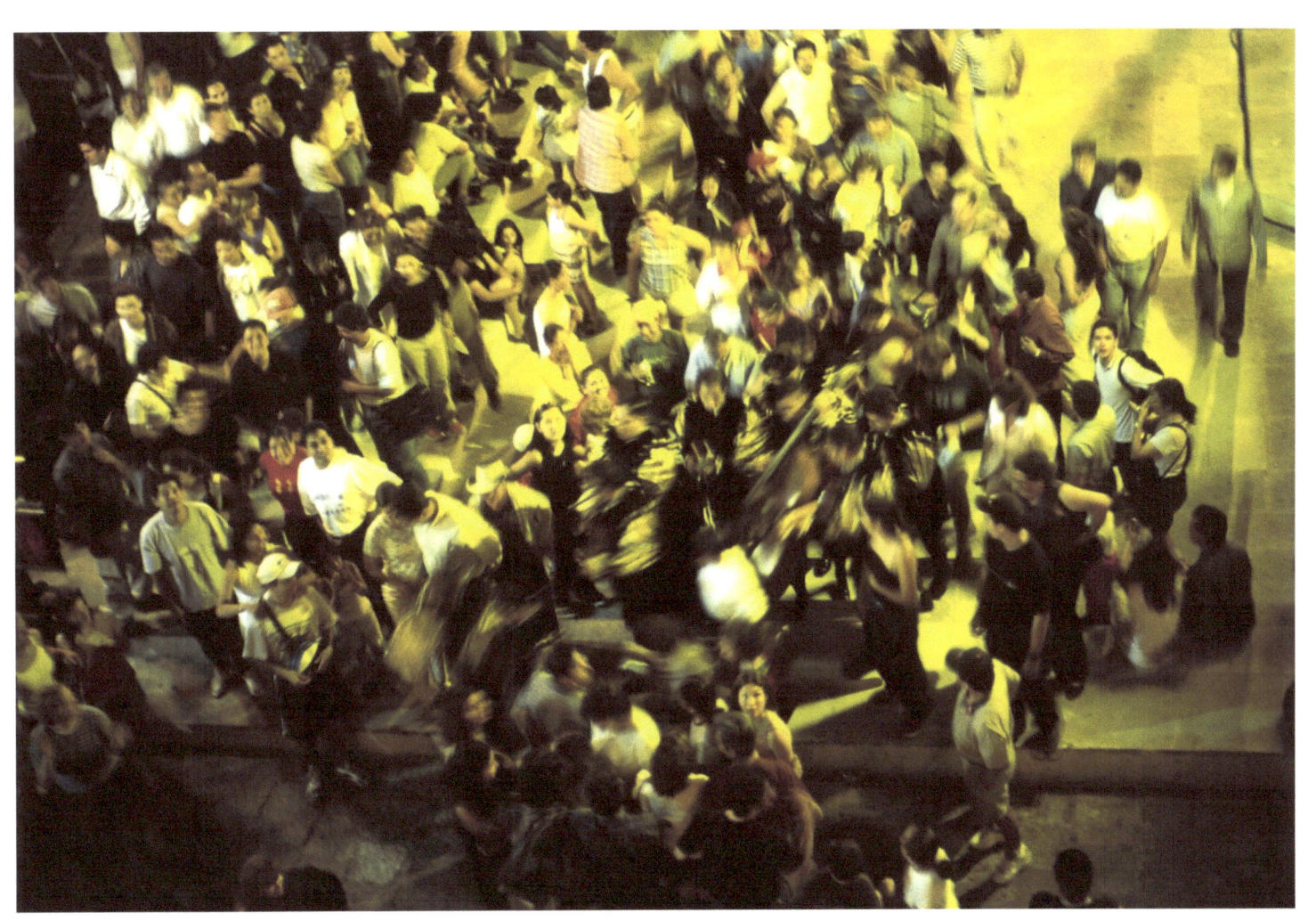

Guanajuato, dancing in the streets at night

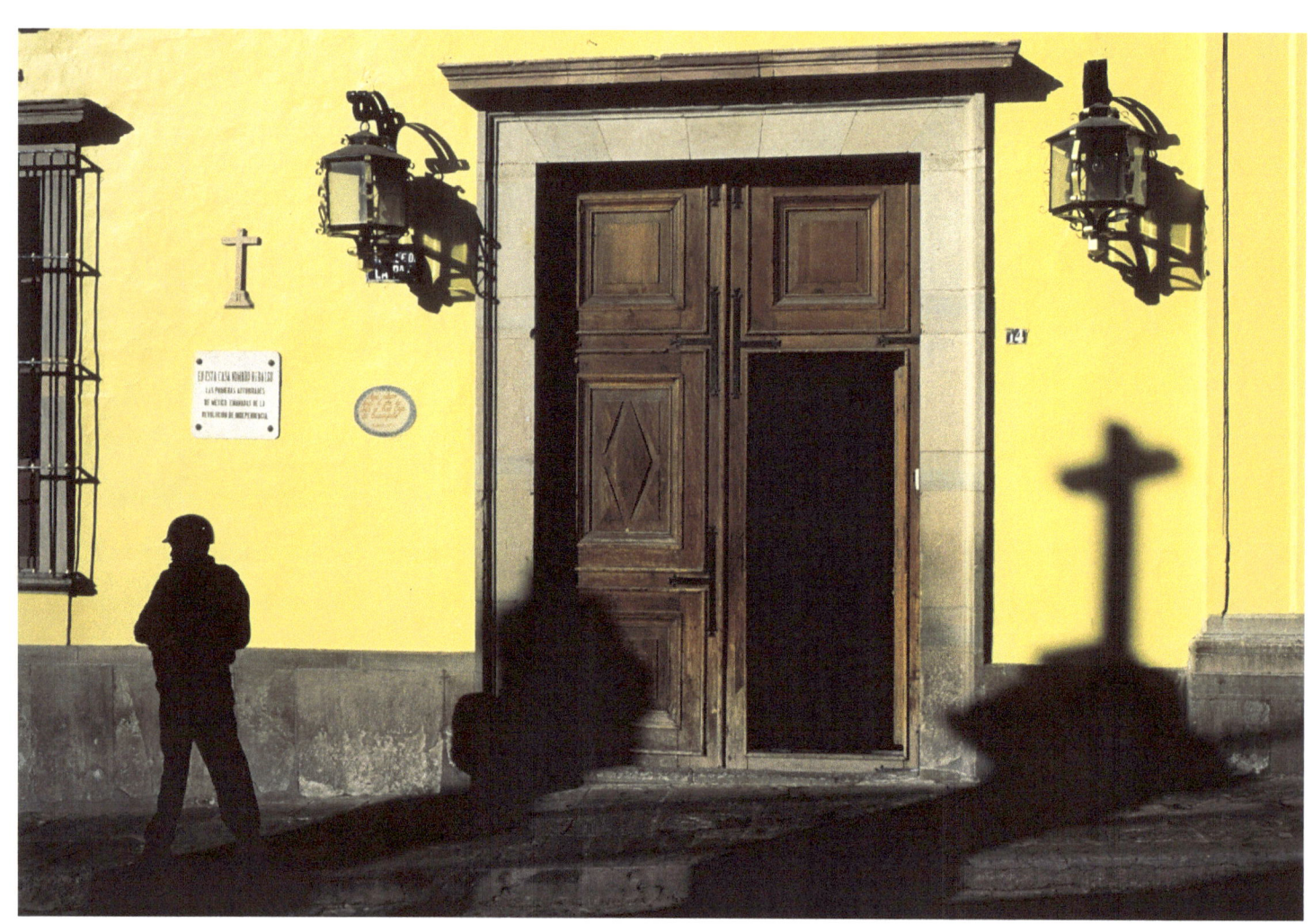

Guanajuato

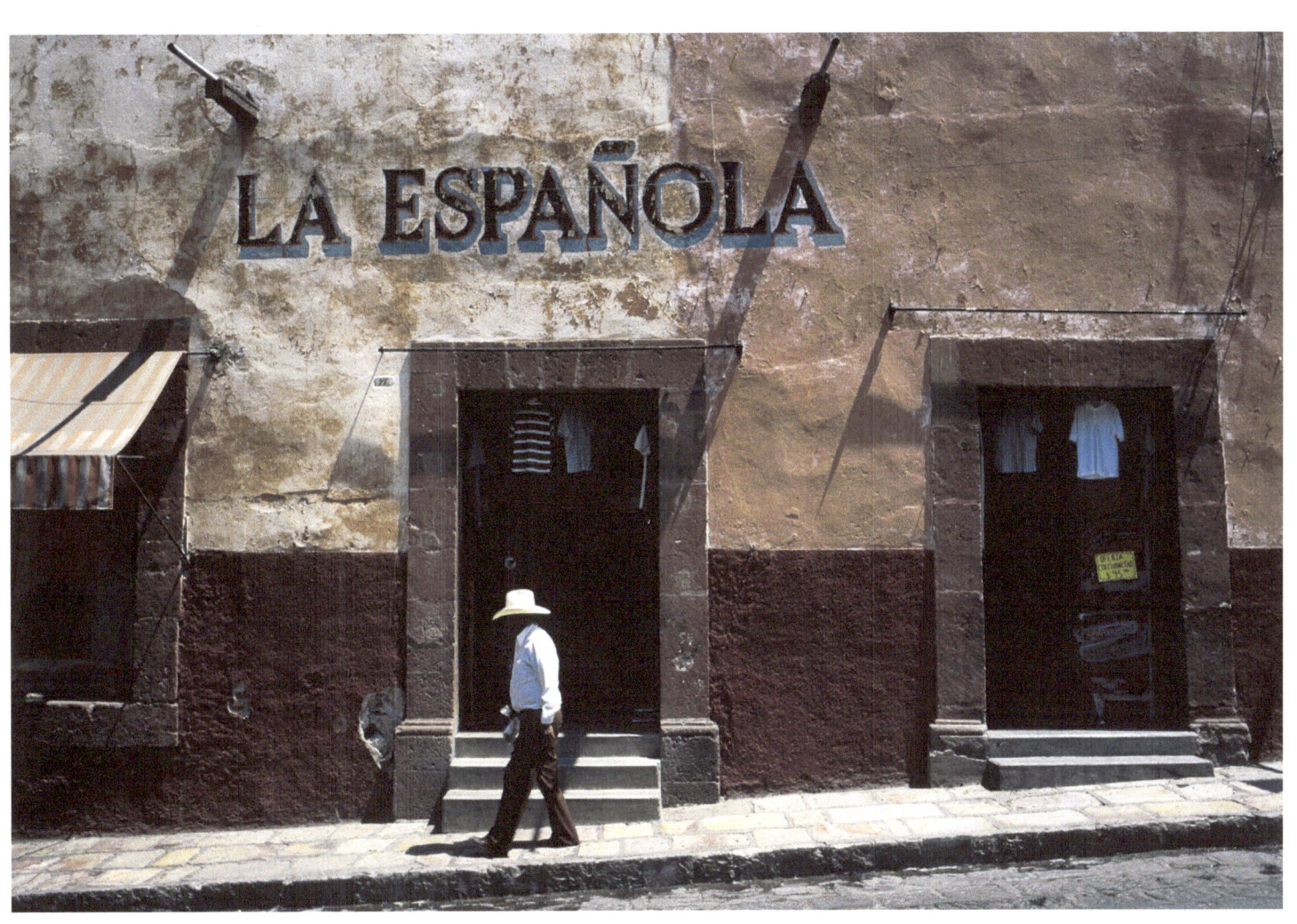

San Miguel de Allende

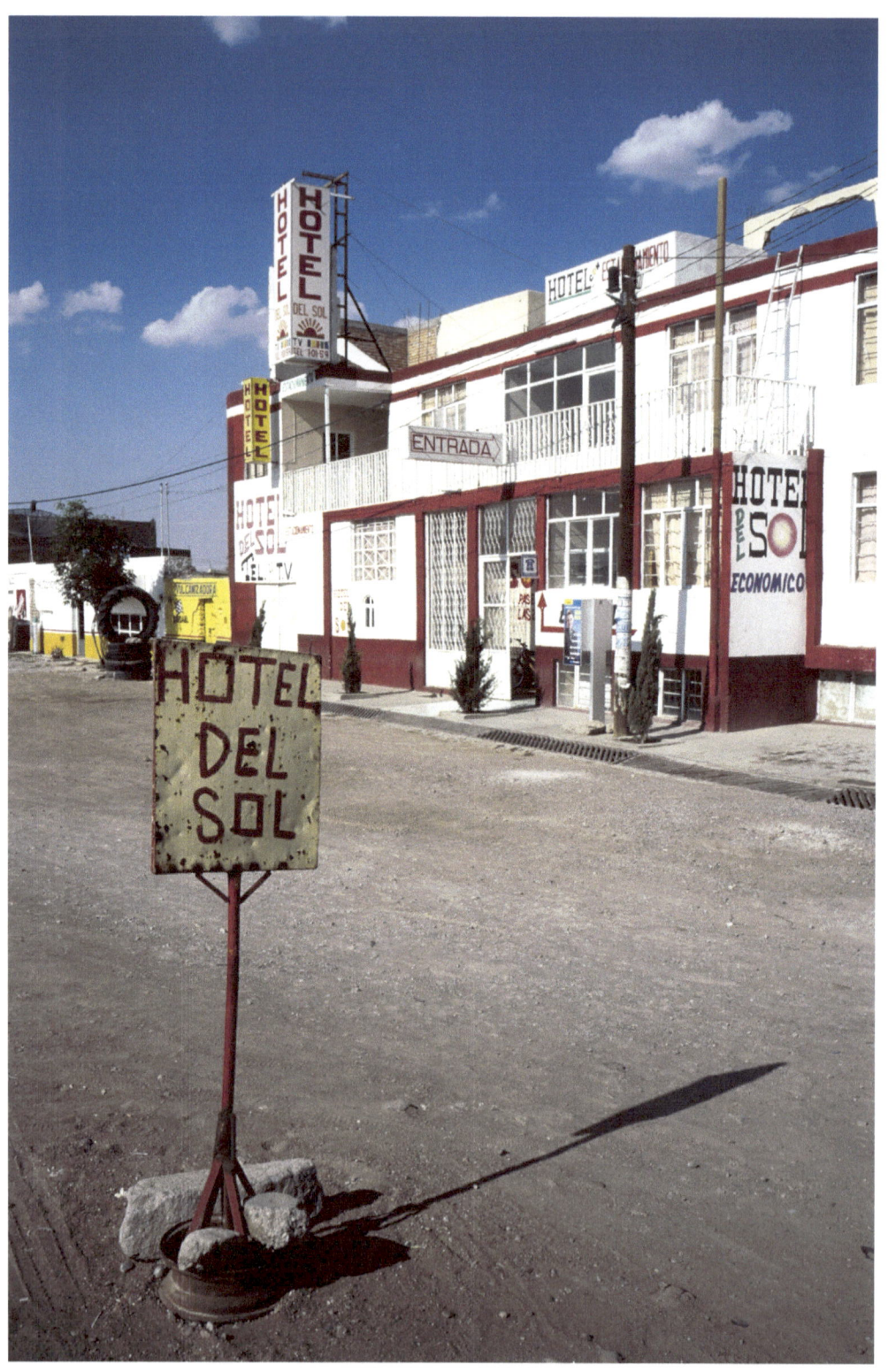

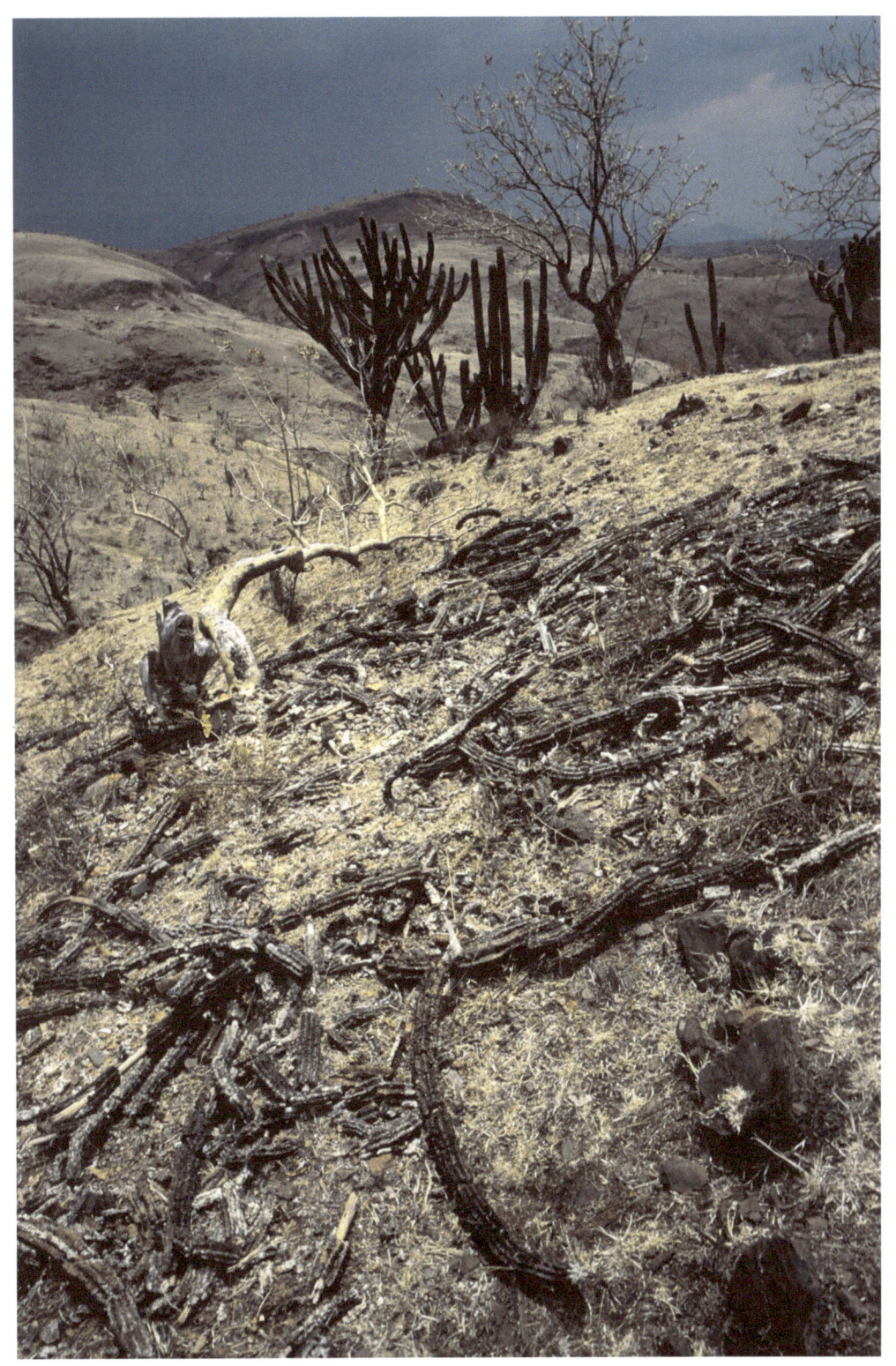

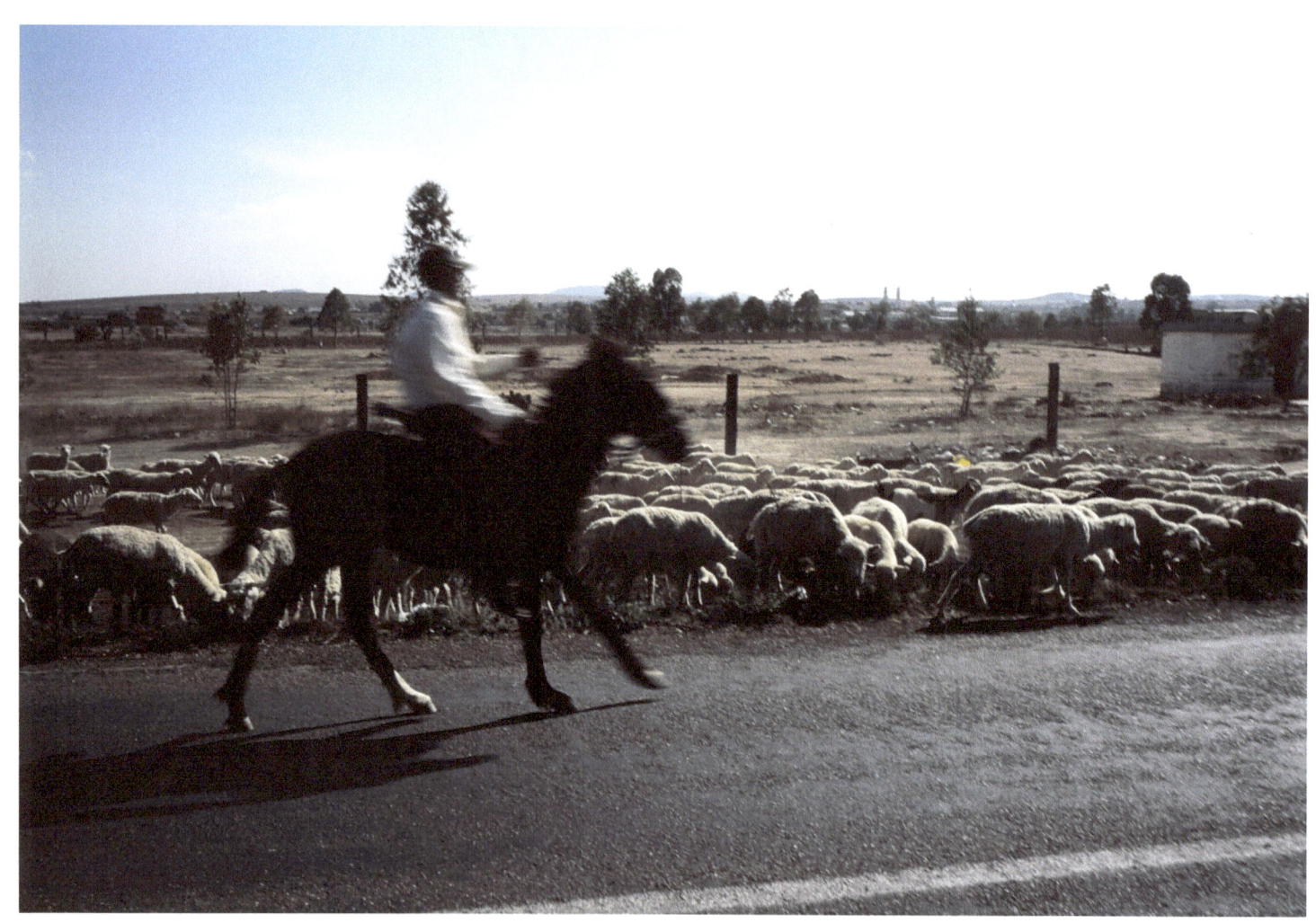

On the Road 15, going north

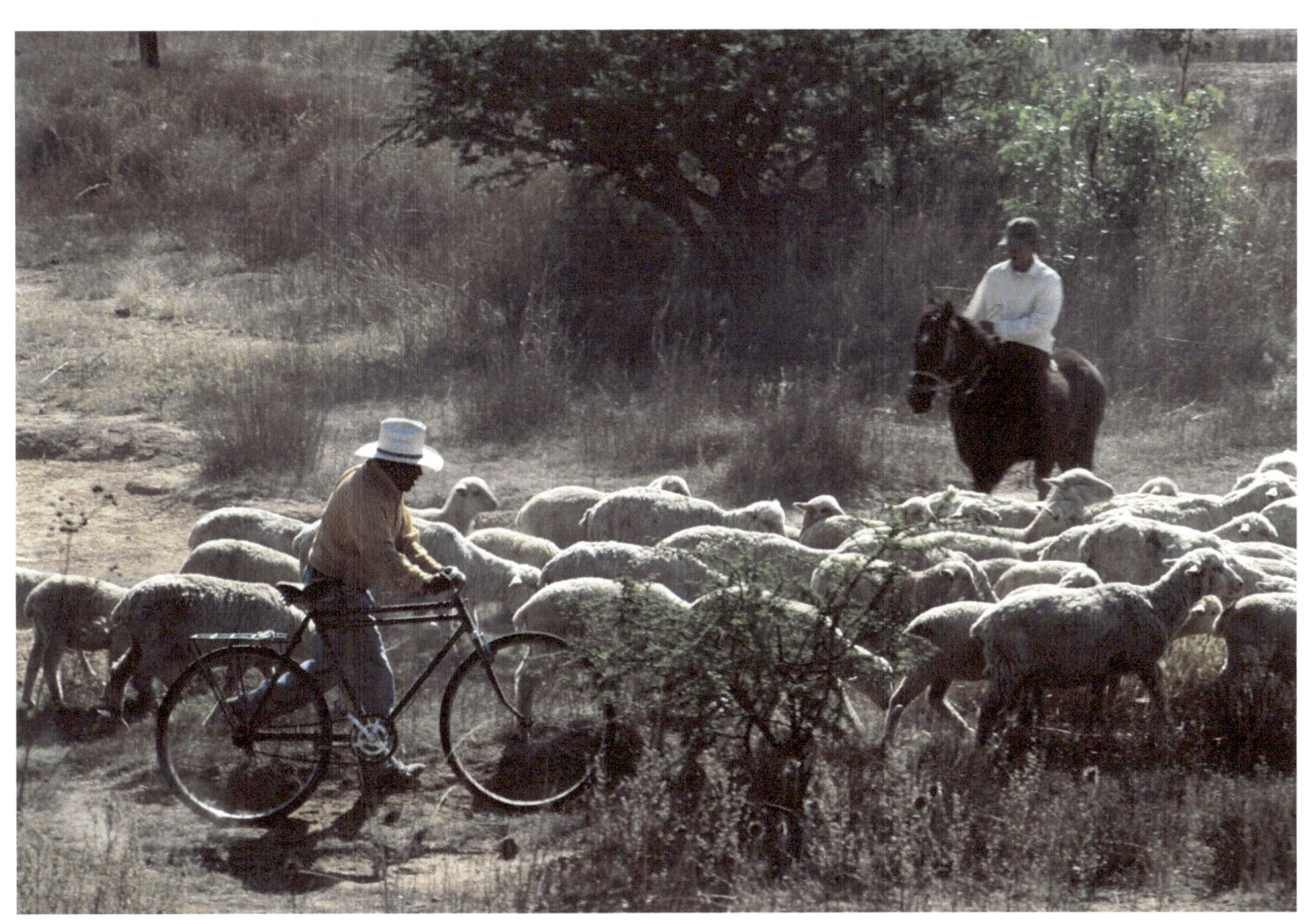

On the Road 15, going north

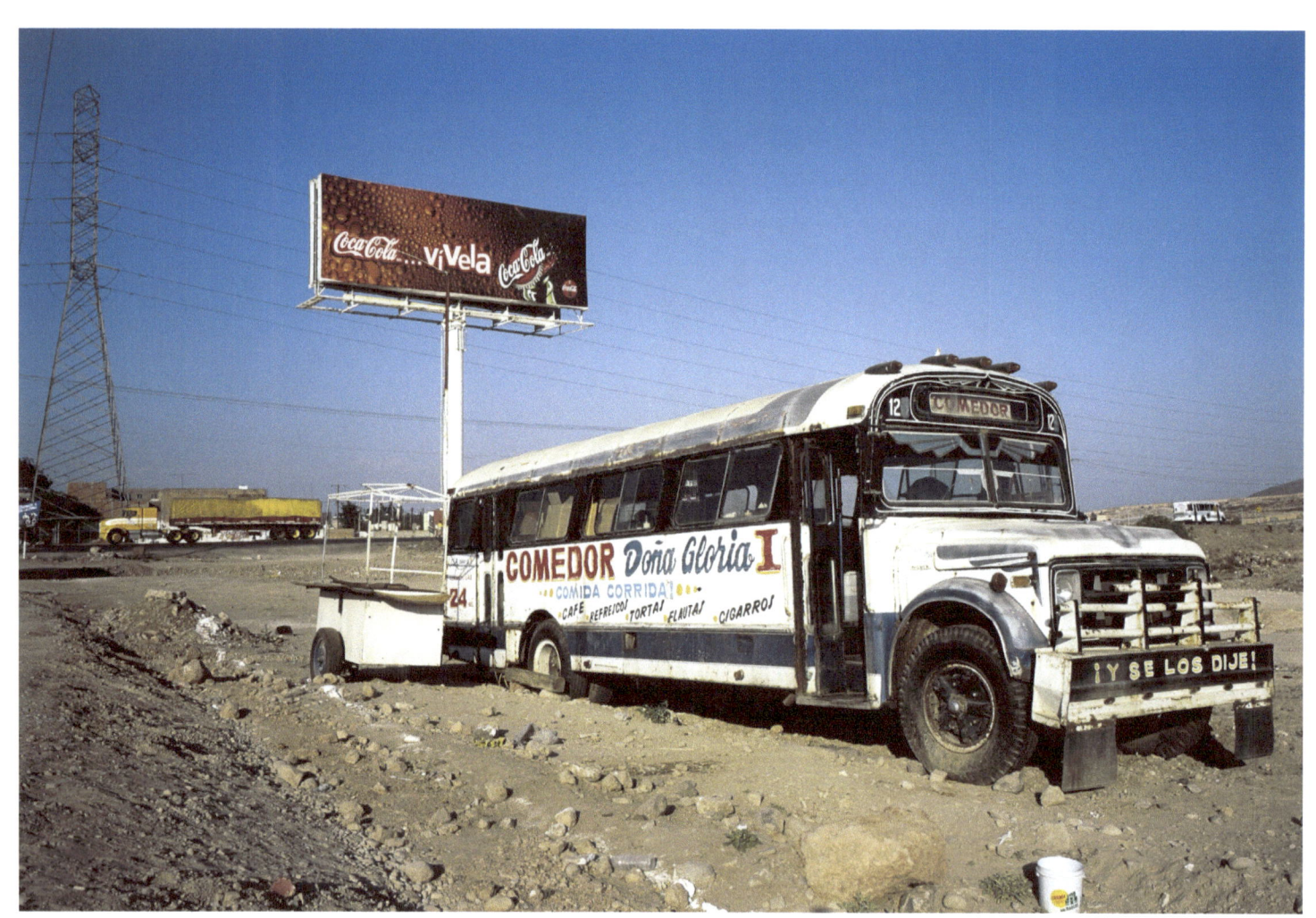

On the Road 15, going north

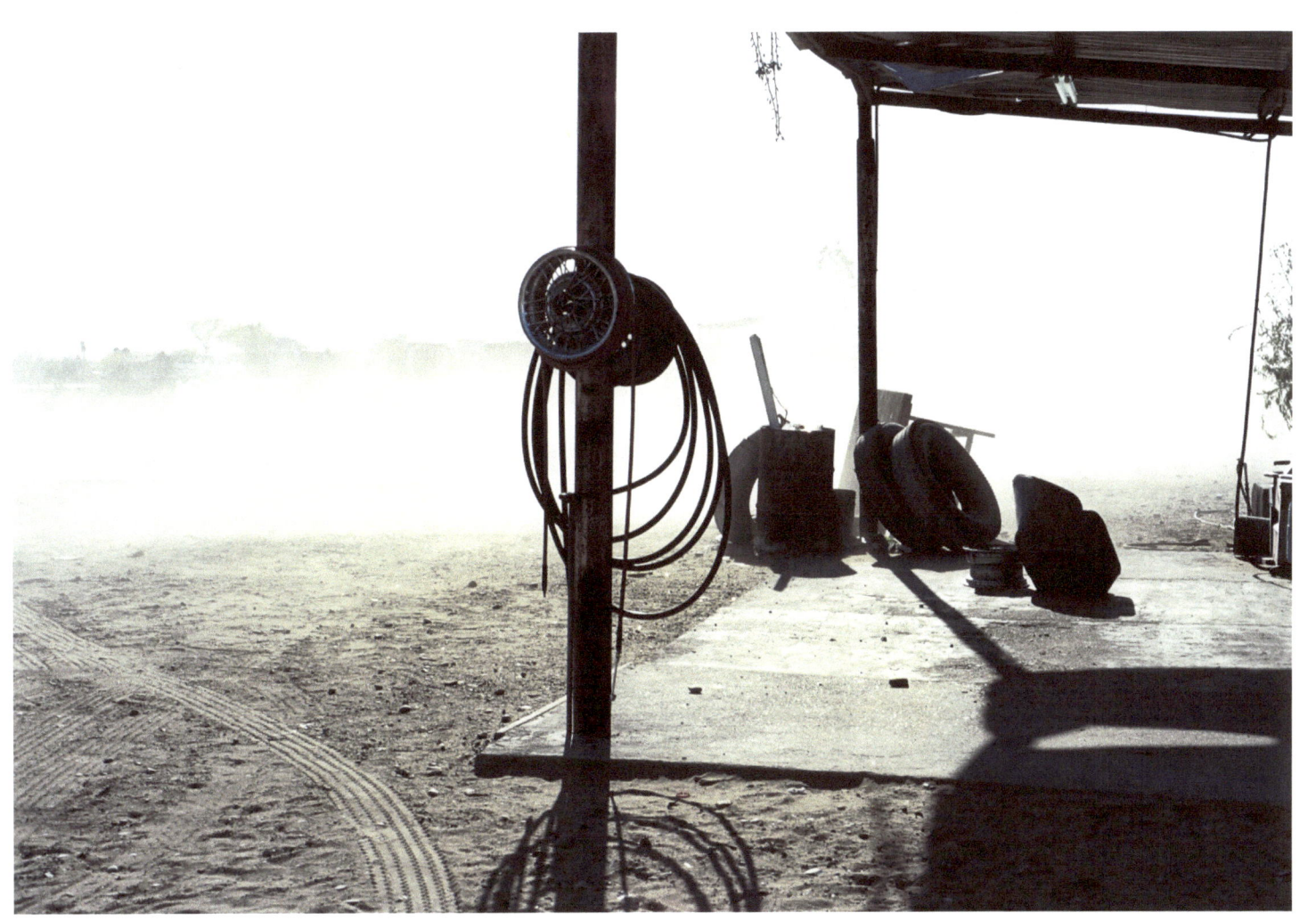

On the Road 15, going north

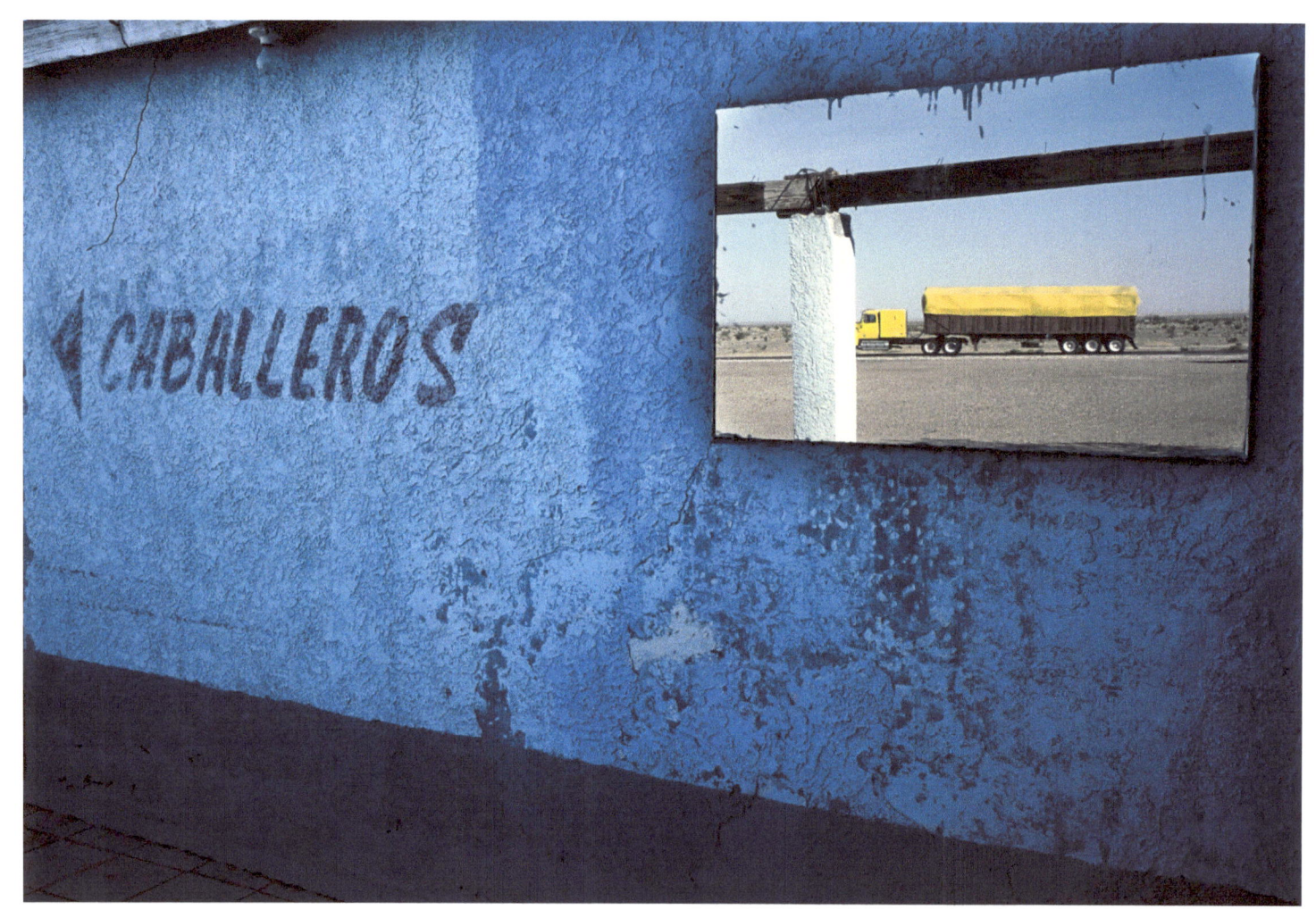

On the Road 2, going north-west

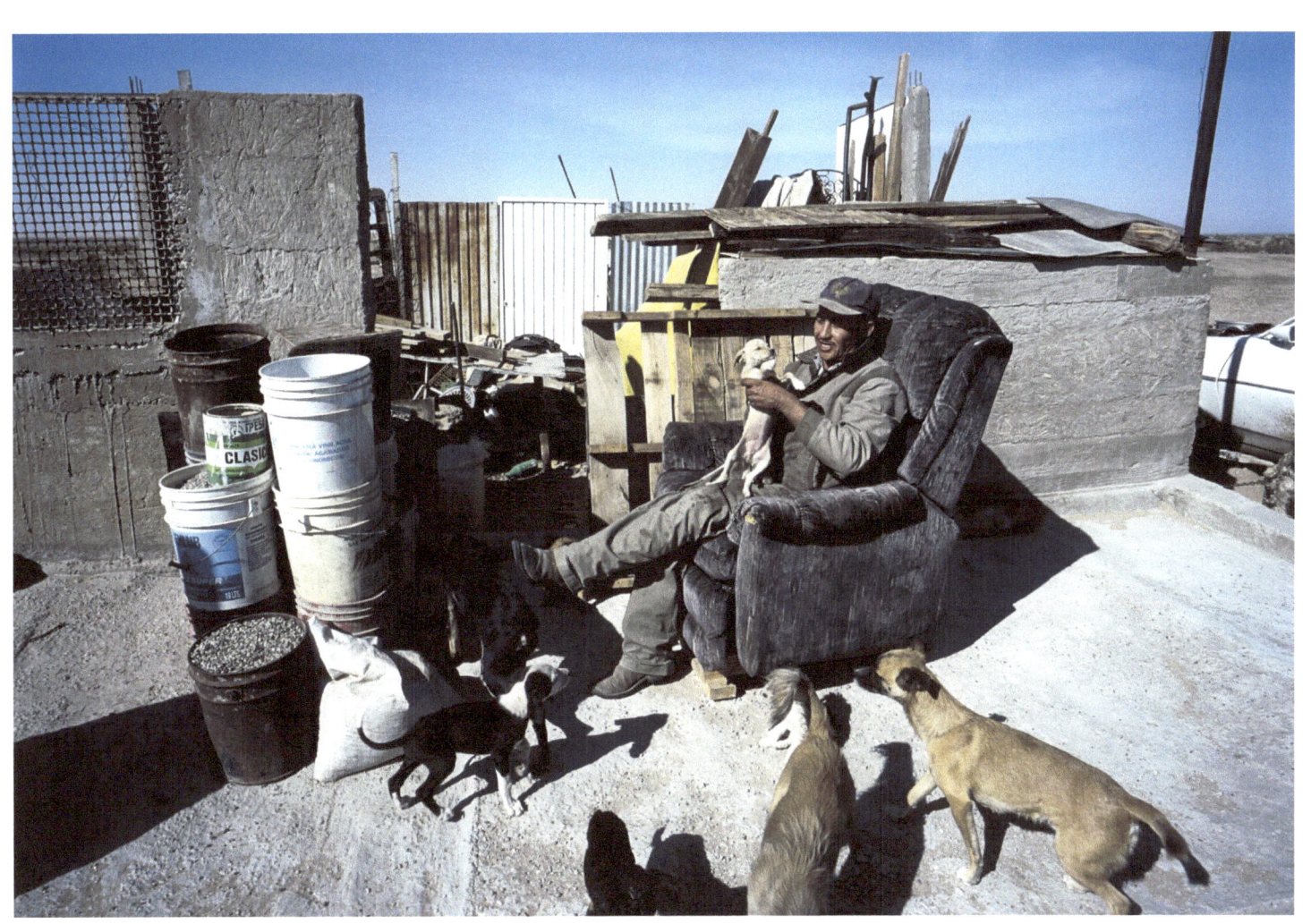

Living on the roadside, with many dogs but no roof

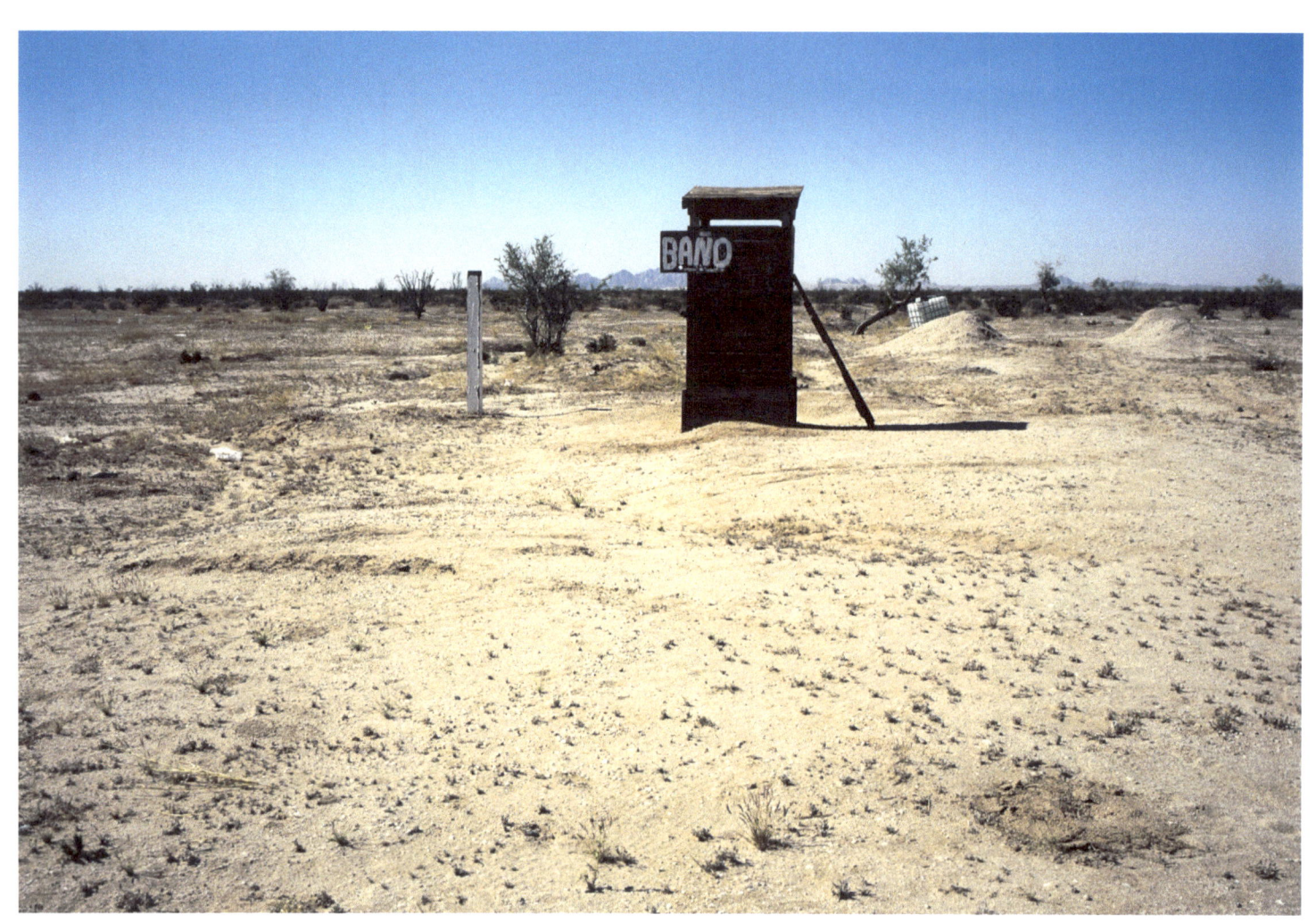

On the Road 2, going north-west

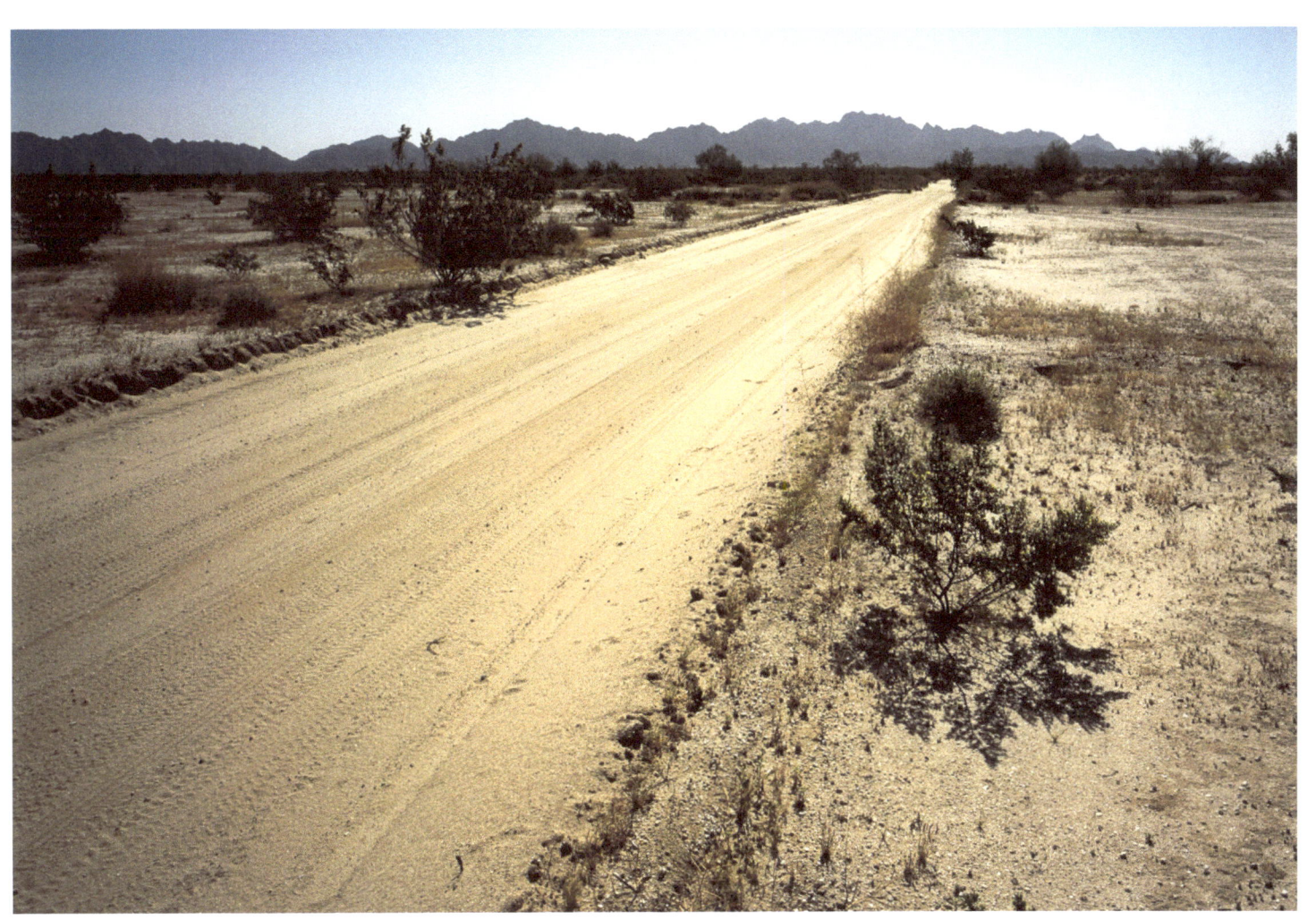
The Mexico-USA border was just this road, in the desert

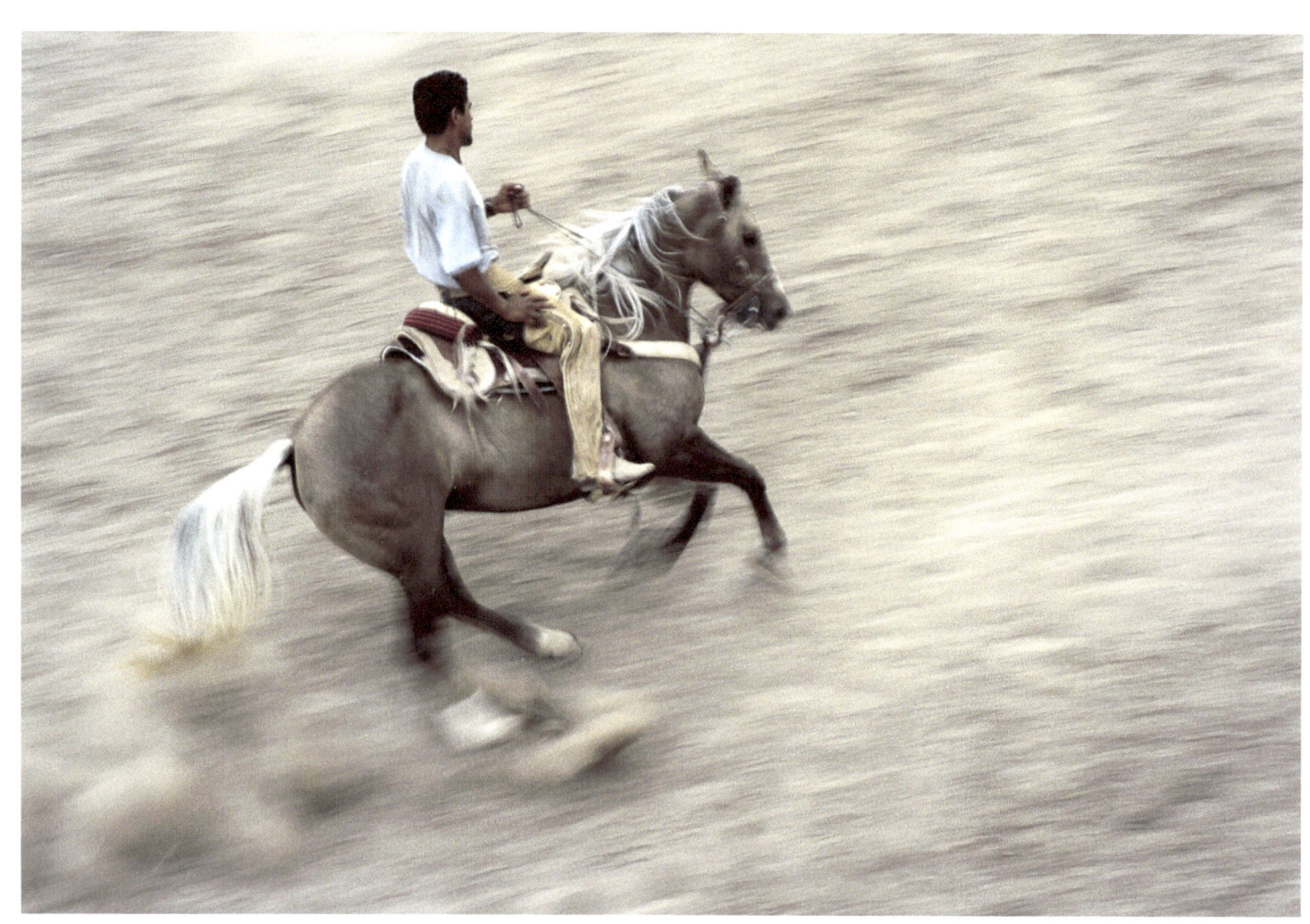

Ranch near Mexicali

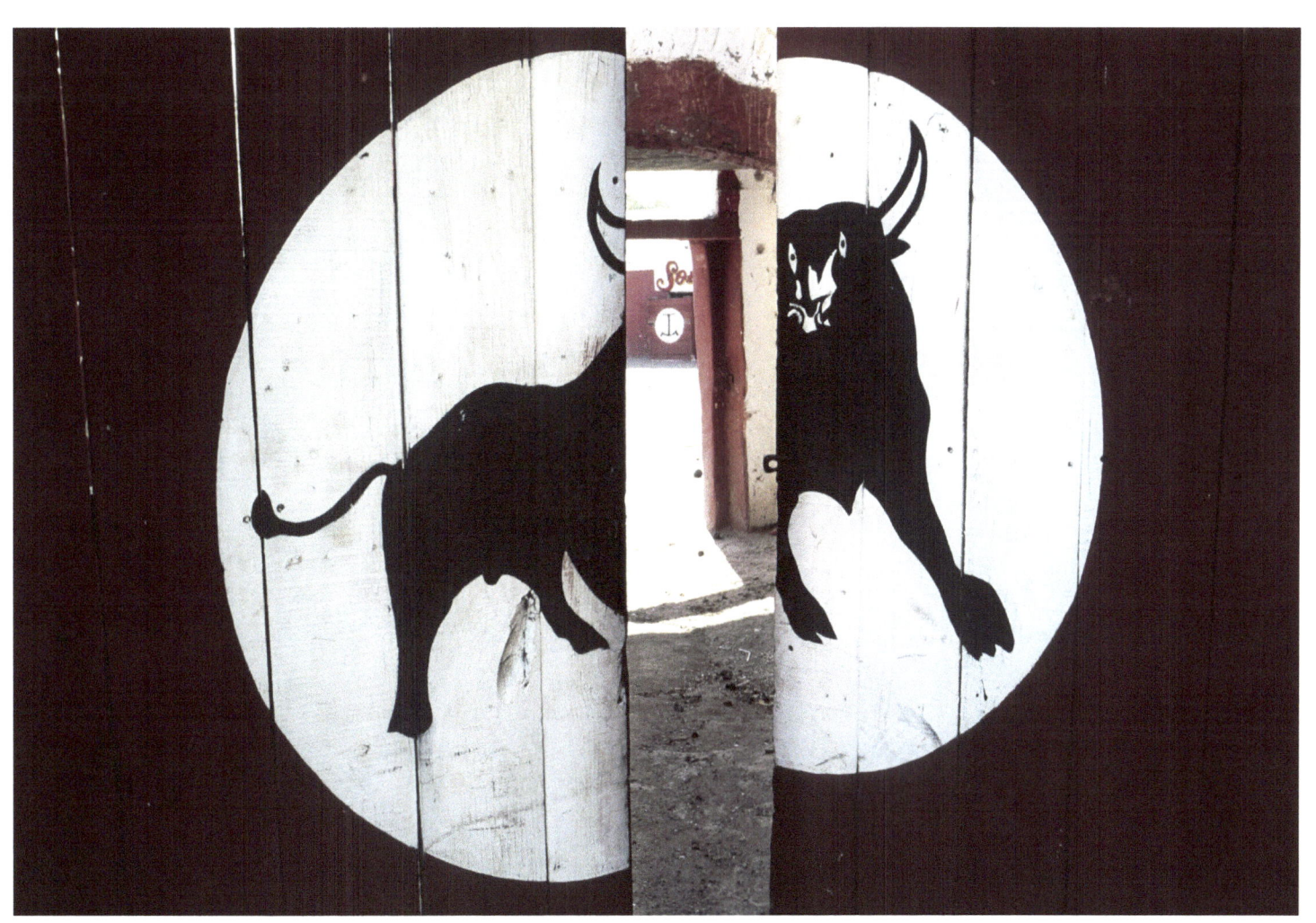

Plaza de Toros, near Mexicali

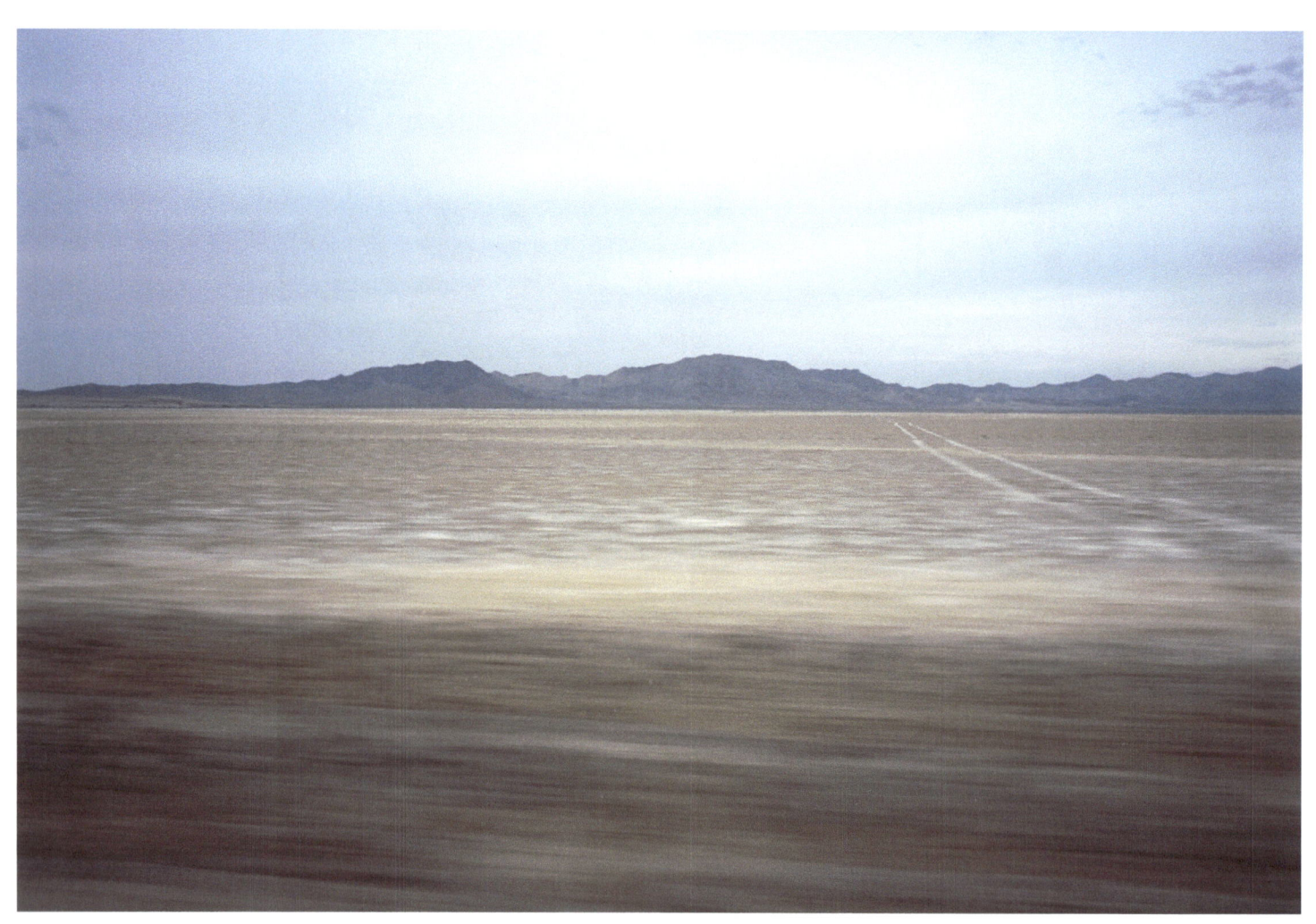

On the Road 2, to Mexicali

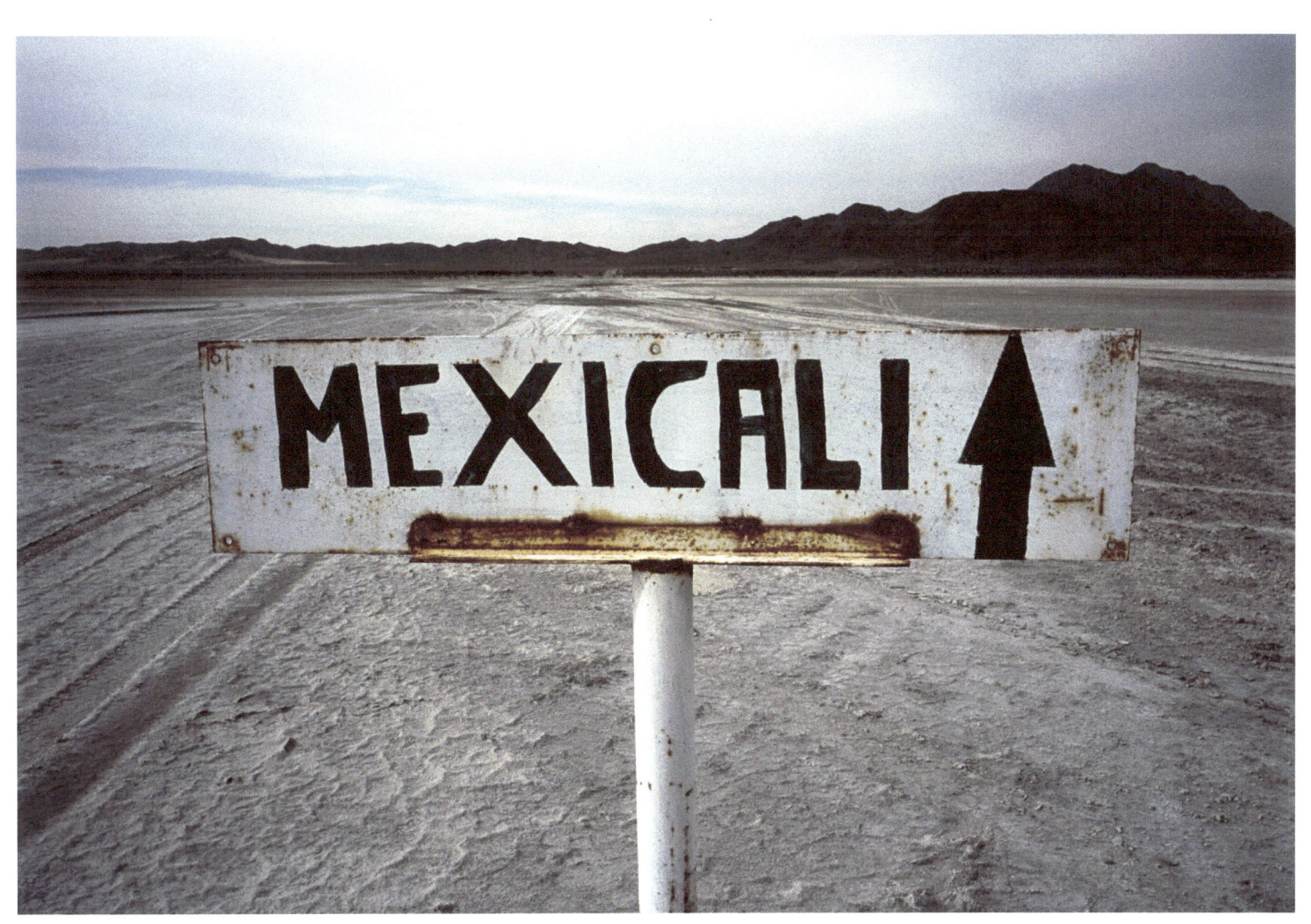

On the Road 2, to Mexicali

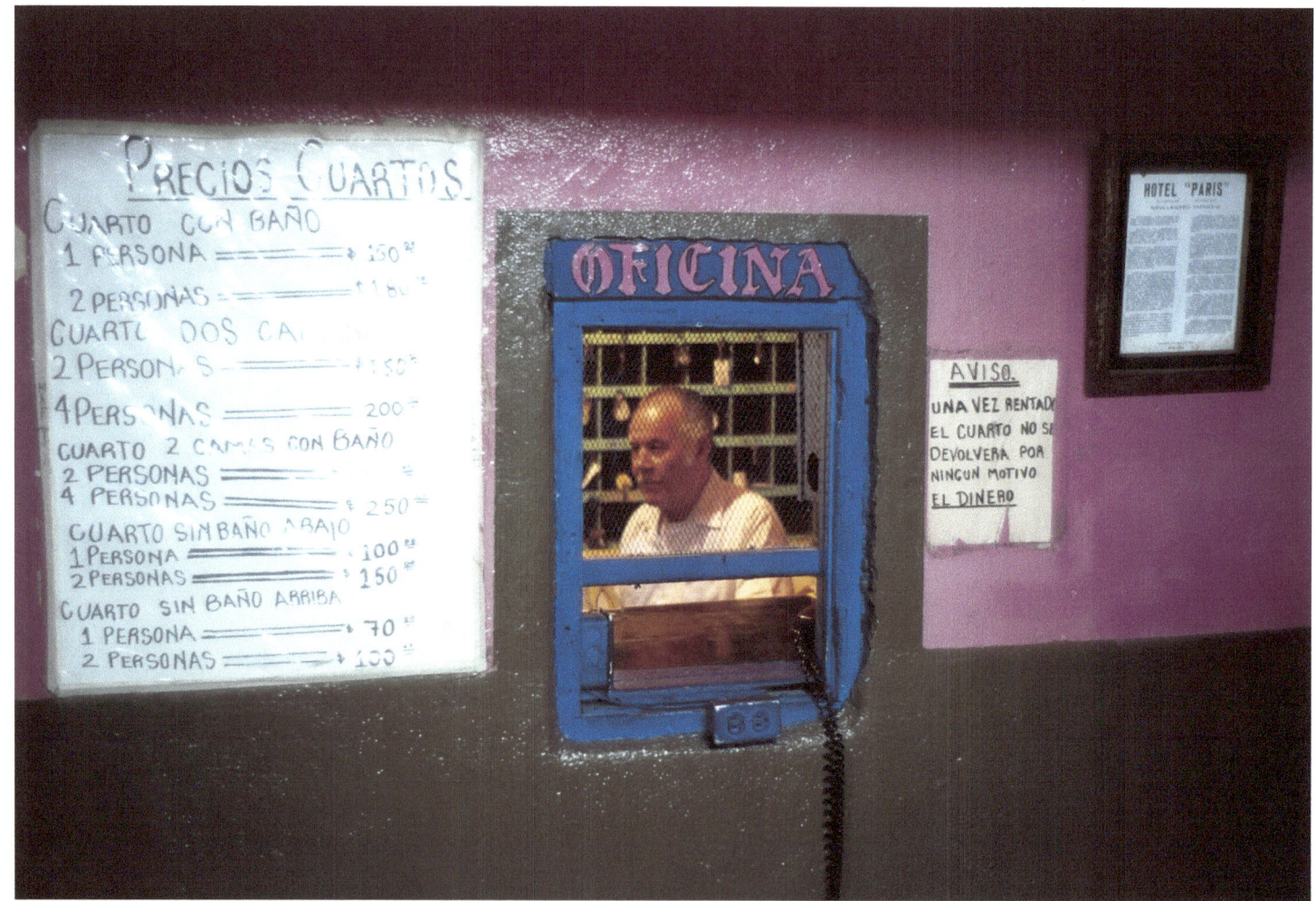

Mexicali, the hotel reception

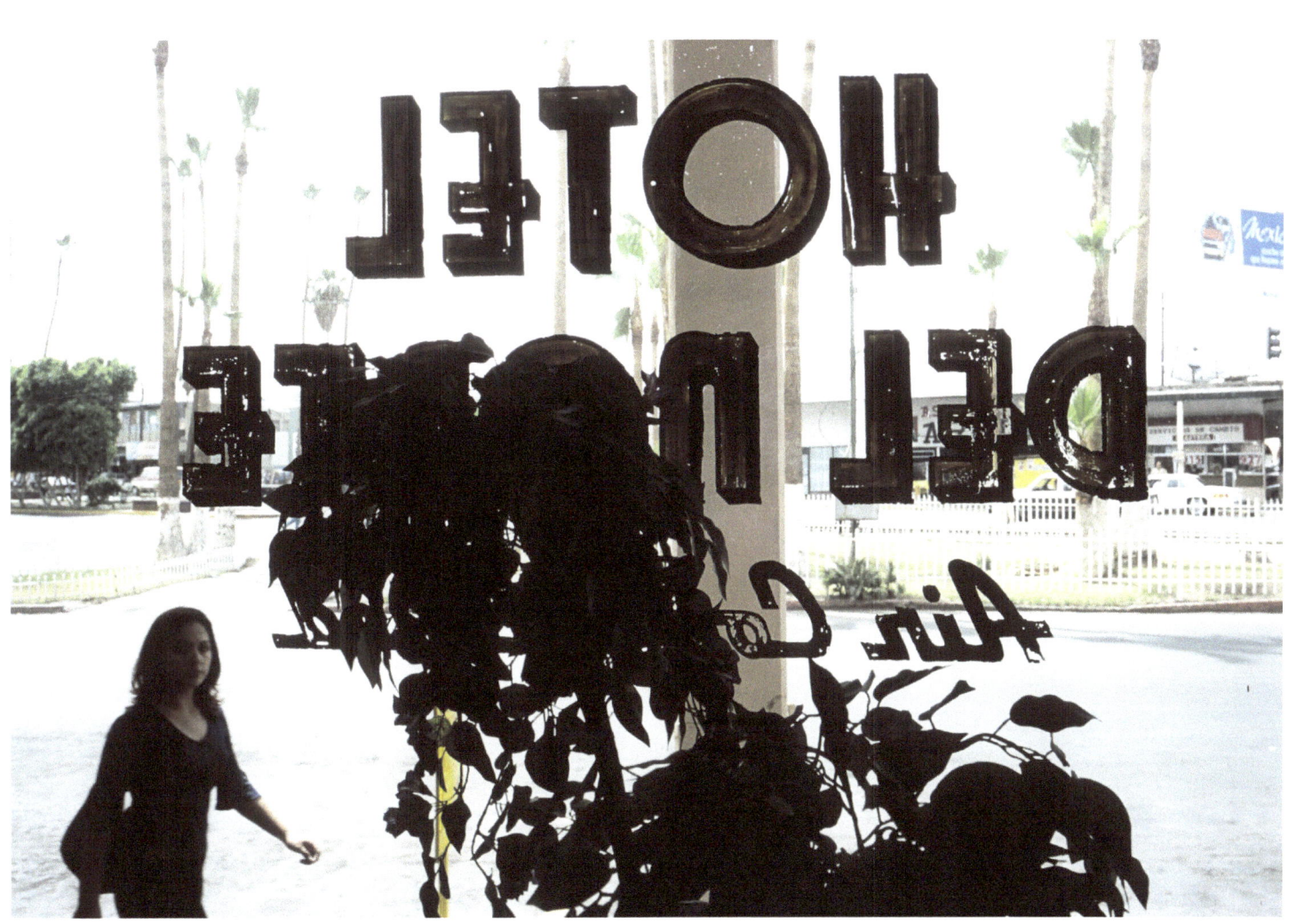

Mexicali, the hotel reception

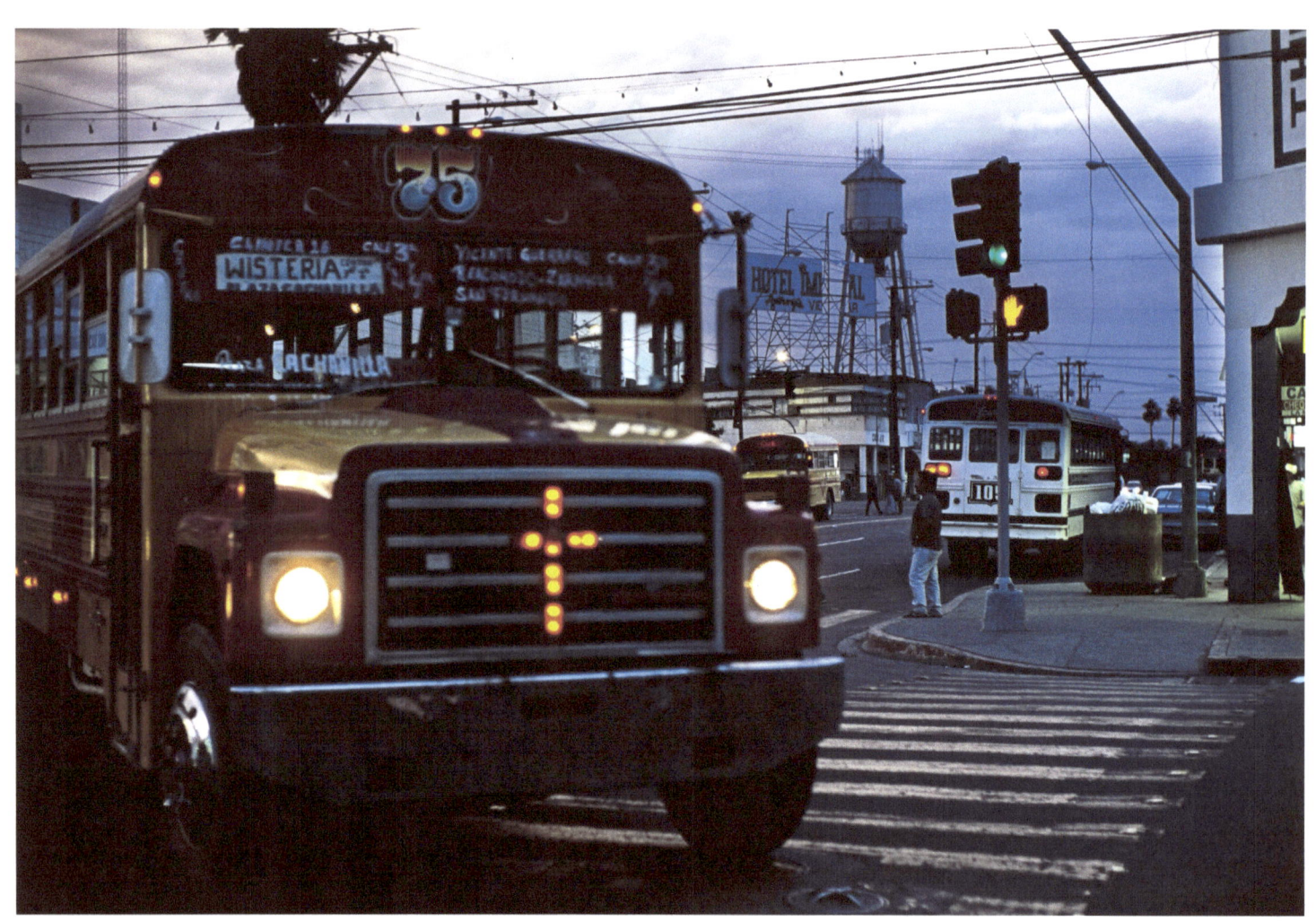

Mexicali, border city at night

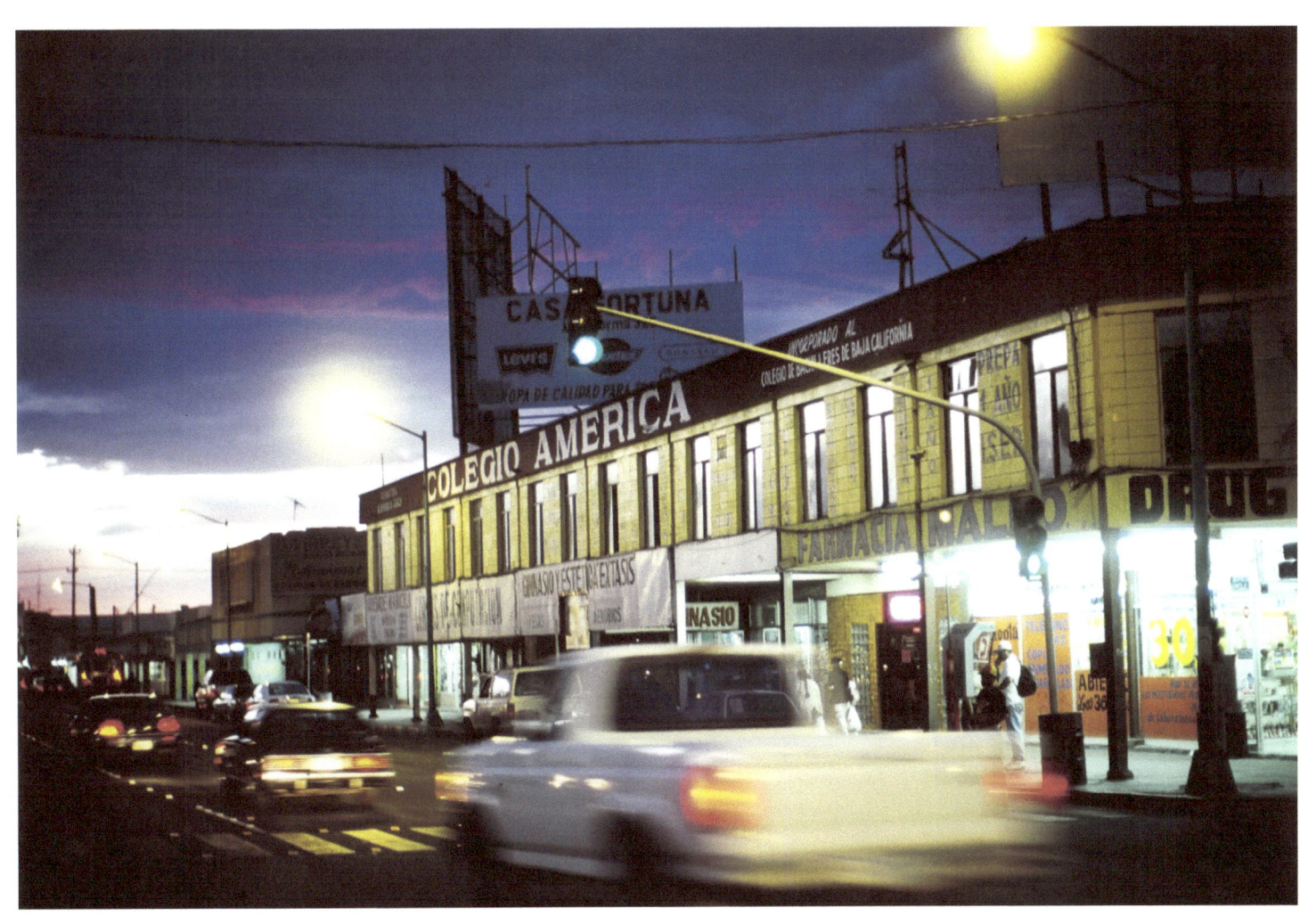

Mexicali, border city at night

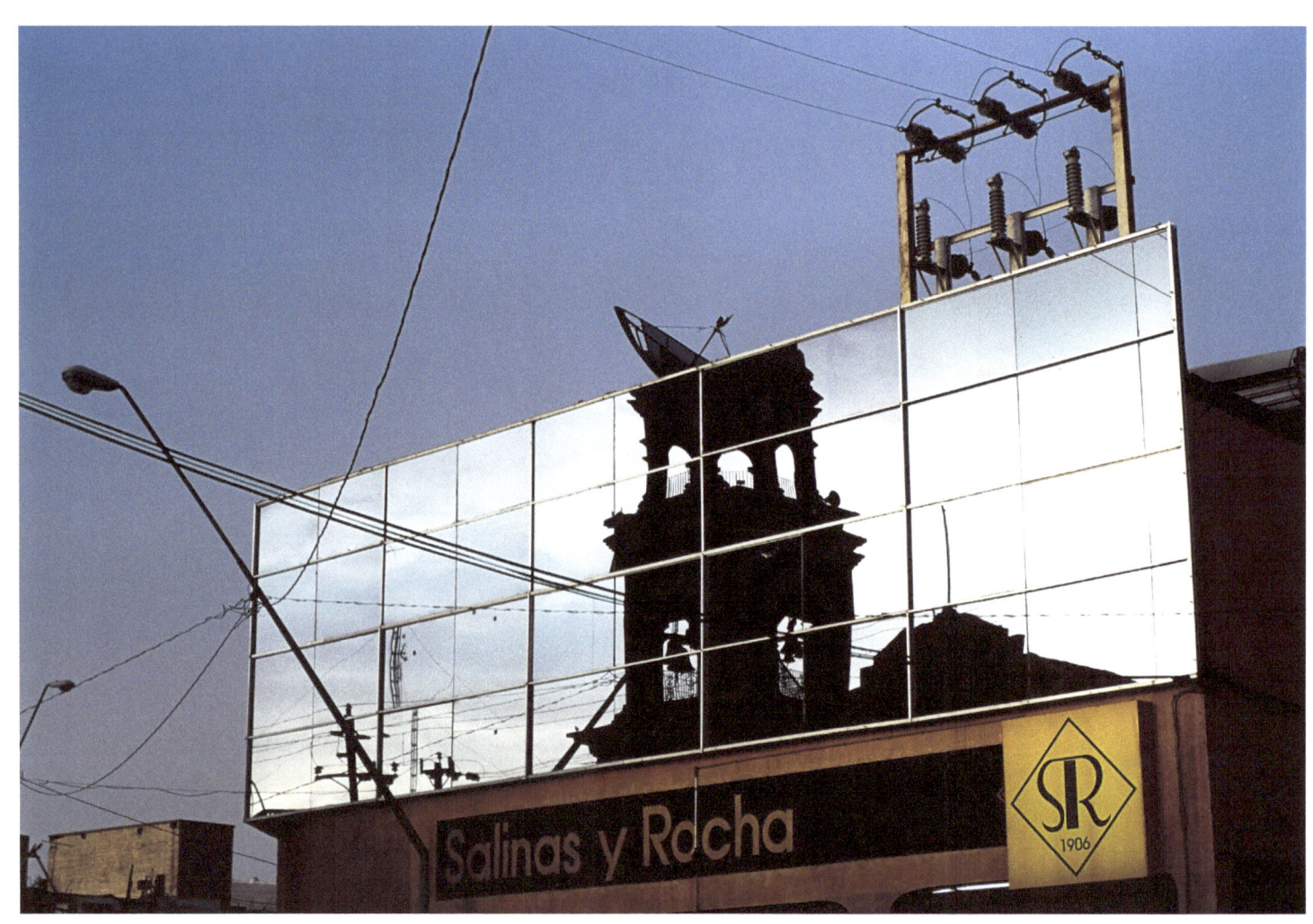

Mexicali, border city at night

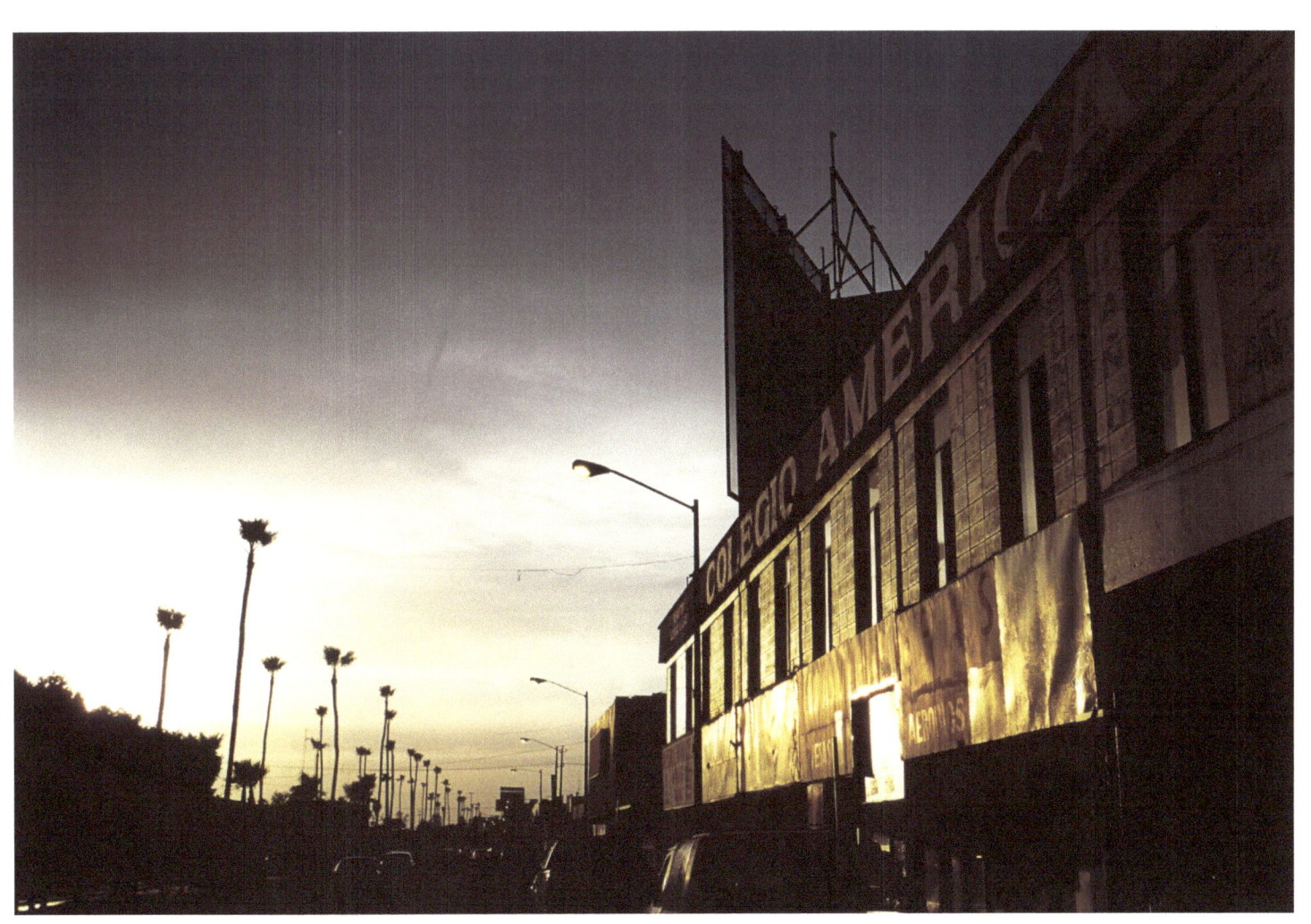
Mexicali, border city at night

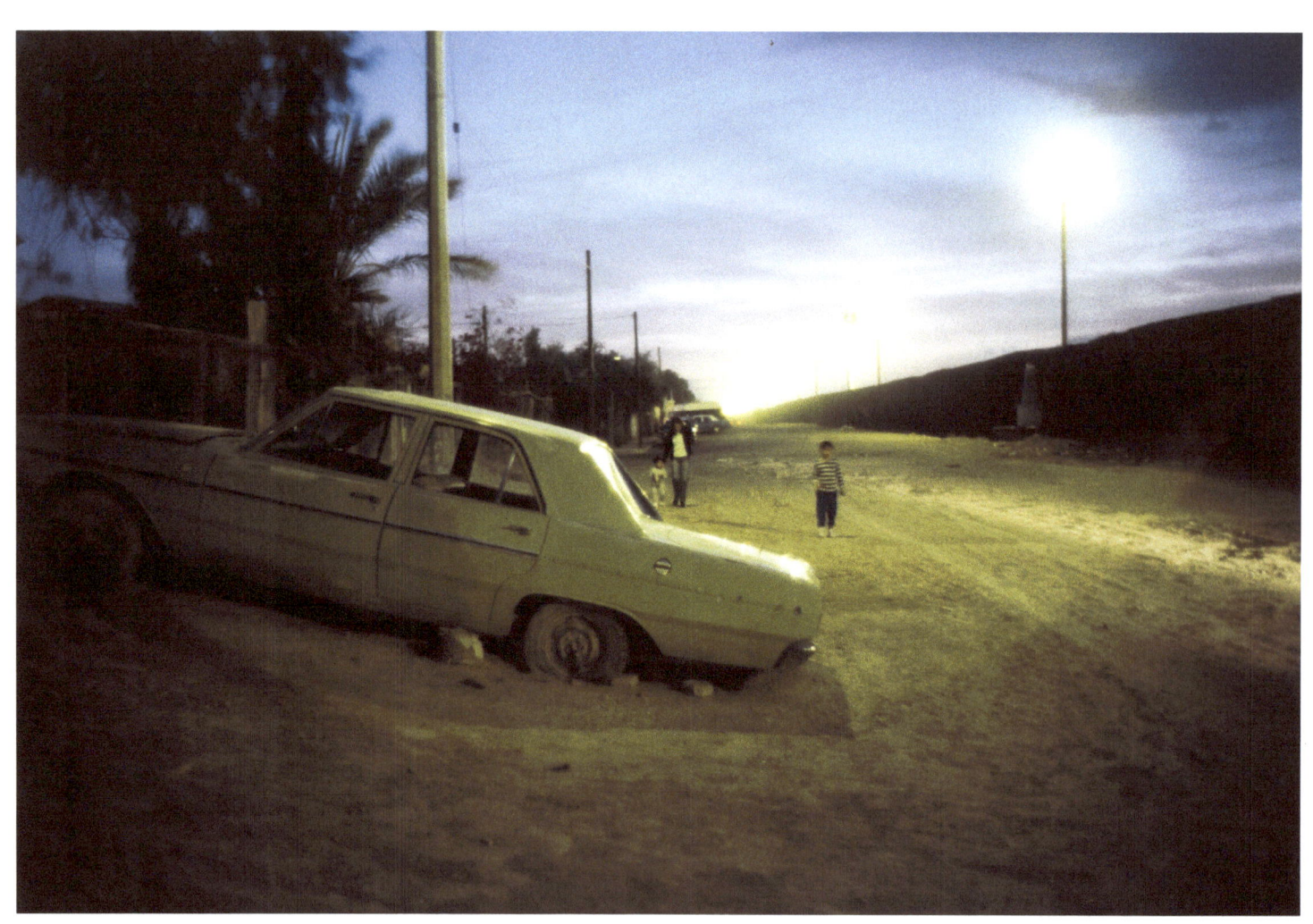
Mexicali, the Mexico-USA border wall

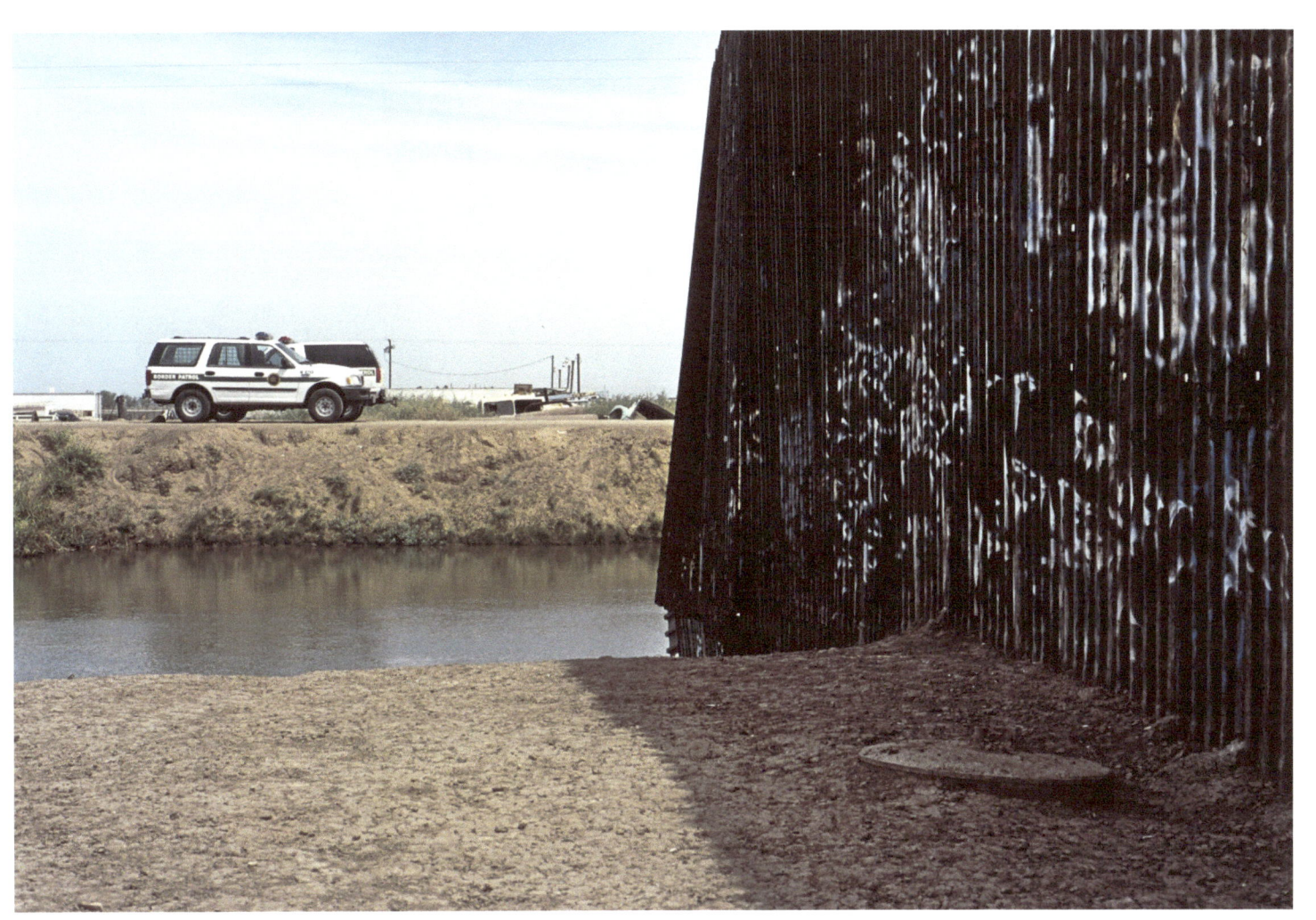

Mexicali, the Mexico-USA border wall

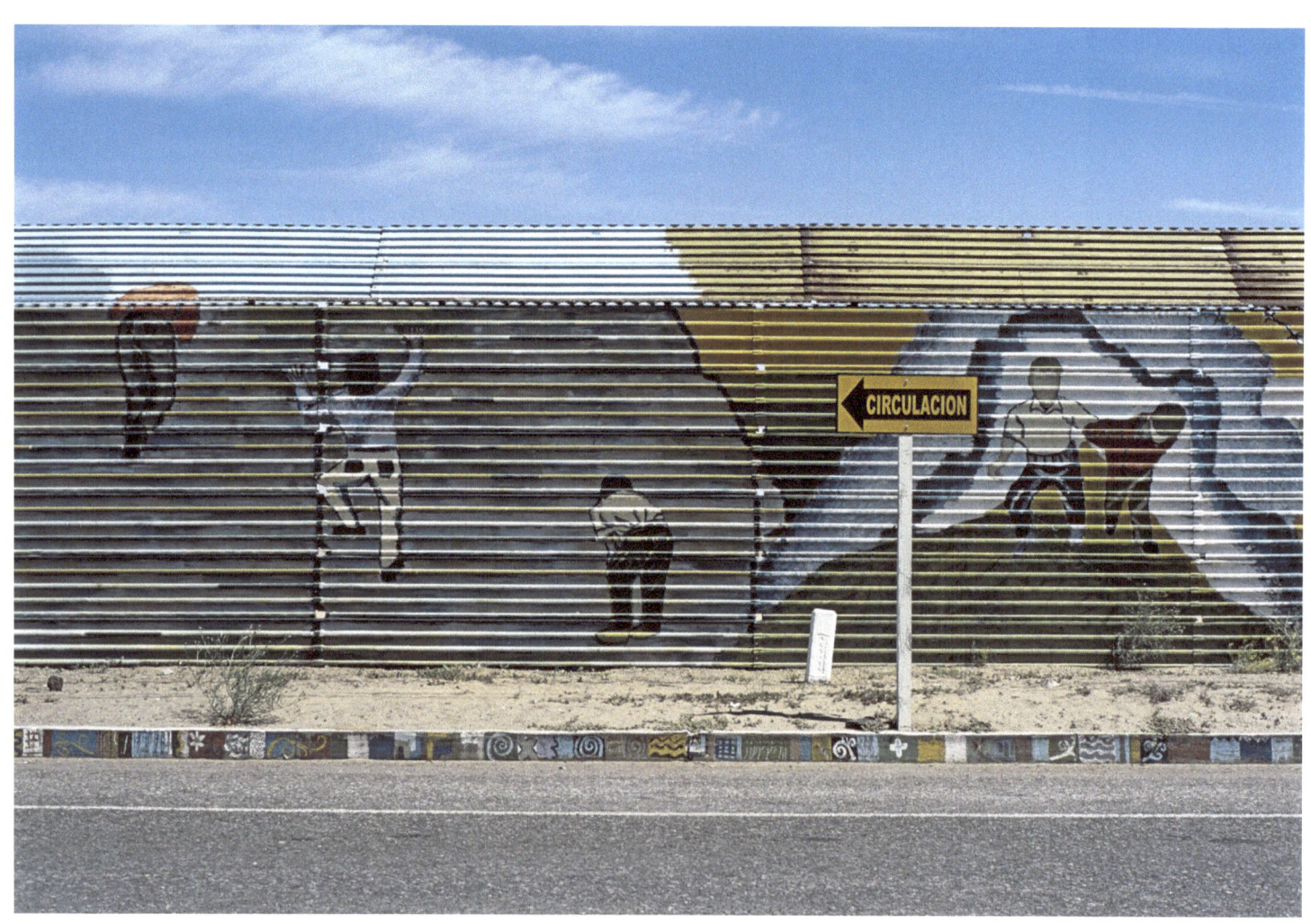

Mexicali, the Mexico-USA border wall

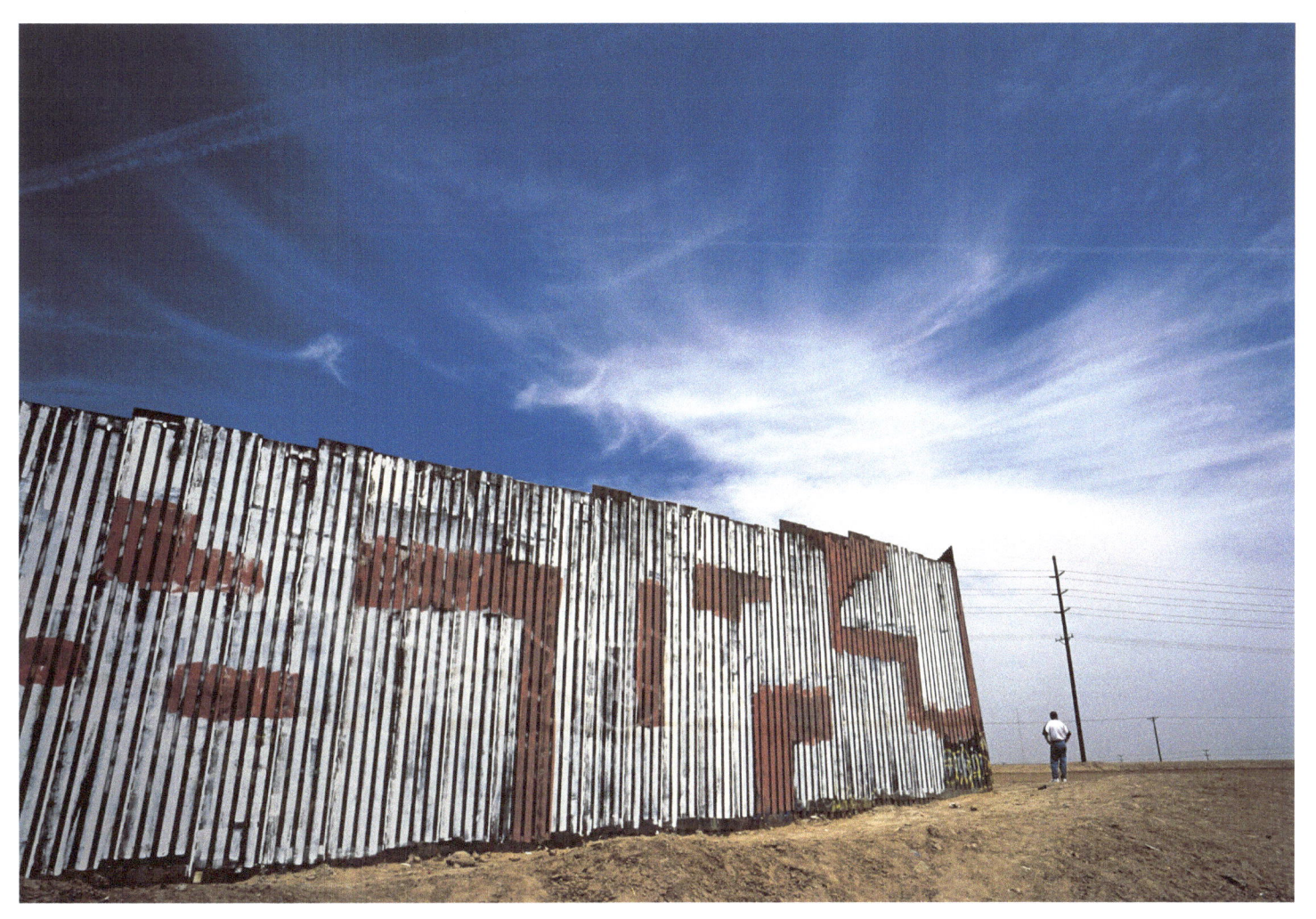

The Mexico-USA border wall: we have arrived...

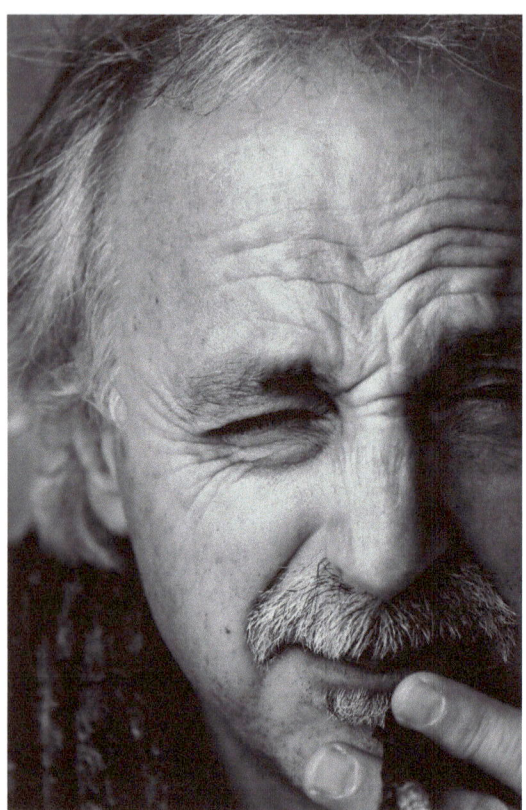

Andrea Pistolesi likes to call himself a traveler who takes photographs, rather than a photographer who travels.
He spends his time in Florence and Bangkok, from where he works for major international magazines.
He has published over a hundred photography books and held one-man shows around the world.
He has worked as a photographer for over thirty years.
A pioneer of digital technology (his book Back in Town, a collection of his early digital work, was published in 1998), he gives workshops and seminars every year.

All photos and texts ©2016 Andrea Pistolesi

No reproduction of images, texts and other content is permitted in any form and length without the written permission of the copyright owners.

All the images of this promotional photo book are covered by copyright and are available for licensing through the author archives, Getty Images®, and Hemis®.
Please contact info@pistolesiphoto.com for further, detailed information.

Published by PadPlaces
www.padplaces.com

ISBN 978-88-98437-62-7

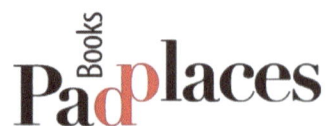

www.ingramcontent.com/pod-product-compliance
Lightning Source LLC
Chambersburg PA
CBHW051909210526
45473CB00006B/1962